The Evolution of C++

The USENIX Association, the UNIX and Advanced Computing Systems professional and technical organization, is a not-for-profit membership association of individuals and institutions with an interest in UNIX and UNIX-like systems, and, by extension, C++, X windows, and other programming tools. It is dedicated to

- fostering innovation and communicating research and technological developments,
- sharing ideas and experience, relevant to UNIX, UNIX-related and advanced computing systems, and
- providing a neutral forum for the exercise of critical thought and airing of technical issues.

USENIX publishes a journal (*Computing Systems*), Conference and Workshop Proceedings, and a Book Series.

The Evolution of C++: Language Design in the Marketplace of Ideas

Edited by Jim Waldo

A USENIX Association Book
The MIT Press
Cambridge, Massachusetts
London, England

First printing, 1993

This books was set in Palatino by Rob Kolstad and was printed and bound in the United States of America.

Distributed by the MIT Press, Cambridge, Massachusetts, and London, England

Library of Congress Cataloging-in-Publication Data

The Evolution of C++: Language Design in the Marketplace of Ideas/edited by Jim Waldo.
    p.   cm.
  Includes bibliographical references and index.
  "A Usenix Association book."
  ISBN 0-262-73107-X
  1. C++ (Computer program language) I. Waldo, Jim.
QA76.73.C15E96 1993
005.13'3--dc20   93-9588
                                                   CIP

Dedicated to the memory of Apollo Computer, prematurely object-oriented; and to Susan, Alan, Sarah, and Rebecca, who make it all worthwhile.

Contents

Preface

This book is meant to be something of a history of the evolution of the C++ language. Unlike other languages in common use, C++ is not the product of either a small group of researchers or some larger group charged with designing a language for a particular purpose. Instead, C++ has evolved in response to sets of discussions among the community of users of the language. These discussions, both formal and informal, have formed a marketplace of ideas about the language. Changes to the language have occurred because of the demands of that marketplace.

While these discussions have taken place in a variety of forums, the most significant have been the sort-of-annual C++ conferences sponsored by the USENIX Association. Starting with the Santa Fe C++ workshop in 1987 and continuing through the subsequent conferences, with debates amplified and extended in the pages of the Association's technical journal, *Computing Systems*, the USENIX Association has provided the premier forum for discussion and debate over the evolution, use, and abuse of C++.

When Mike O'Dell approached me with the idea of trying to collect some of the best of those works into a book, the task was both daunting and appealing. The number and quality of the candidates made the decision process difficult, and this difficulty was compounded by the range of subjects encompassed under the rubric of "C++". Works on compiler construction, language design, and library features compete with those on programming environments, operating system design, and the principles of object-oriented systems.

After reading and re-reading many of the candidate chapters, it became clear that there was no way to pick some small number of them as "the best." The selection would need to be based on some overall theme that would limit the large number of excellent choices. That decision made the subsequent choosing possible. It also means that the well of good papers on subjects related to C++ is far from dry. I hope that this will be the first of a series of books that will join together the efforts of the pioneers in C++.

The chapters selected are those I thought represented the more important trends in the evolution of C++. Whether these turn out to be the most interesting from a historical perspective remains to be seen. No doubt some works were left out that, over the next ten years, will be considered seminal in some way that cannot currently be foreseen. Others that have been included will be seen as flukes, showing some potentially interesting direction in which the language could have gone but never did.

This book is meant to show genuine history, with all its confusion and false starts. The chapters contained here are the primary sources for such a history, and as such are almost all presented in their original form. This should not be taken as an indication that the authors would now hold to all of the positions stated in these works. Given the clarity of hindsight, there could be a desire to change the contents. However, the aim of this book is to show what was said that caused the language to evolve, not what could have been said had the authors known what the evolution would be.

The Evolution of C++

Introduction

"May you live in interesting times." Traditional Chinese curse

The past seven years have been interesting times for users of the C++ language. Seven years ago, C++ was a promising variant of C for those of us who believed in the new, object-oriented approach to software. Since then C++ has become a mainstream programming language, one that many think will be the dominant system development language for the foreseeable future.

The growth in the interest in and the use of C++ has been mirrored by the rapid pace of change in the language itself. The language has expanded, semantics have been made more precise or, in some cases, subtly altered, and new features have been introduced at a rate that can barely be tracked by compiler writers.

The process of language change has been interesting in itself. While the language was confined to the AT&T research community, the decisions of what should and should not be a part of C++ were controlled by the small group, headed by Bjarne Stroustrup, that had as its research goal the development of the language. However, this concentration of decision making did not last beyond the emergence of the language from that lab.

Recently, of course, the shape of the language has been taken over by the ISO standards committee established for that purpose. In between the emergence of the language from the lab and the formation of the ISO committee the language evolved through a process of public debate. Some of this debate took place over electronic mail. Some of it took place through journals. But the majority of the debate took place at the USENIX C++ conferences.

These conferences, held roughly once a year, were (and continue to be) a gathering of programmers and researchers actively using the language. Each year, one or two topics seem to hold center stage, both within the formal program and in the discussion during breaks, at the receptions, and during the group dinners that always form at such conferences.

This book is an attempt to chronicle this process of designing a language through the open marketplace of ideas. The organization is meant to be by topic, but can also be seen as roughly chronological. In looking back, I find it surprising that these two organizations correspond so closely. The evolution of the language in fact took place via a series of sequentially ordered debates rather than through a set of parallel discussions.

Each section of the book is organized around one of the major debates concerning a feature to add to the language. The first section is the exception to this rule, and is an attempt to show the state of the debate back in the early days of C++.

All but one of the papers in this first section are from the Santa Fe workshop, or derive from papers given at that workshop. At that time, the future of the language looked straightforward and clean, and the optimism of the small group that gathered in Santa Fe to talk about this new, object-oriented system language was great.

That first gathering was an interesting collection of individuals and ideas. Most of the papers presented in Santa Fe concerned how one could go about implementing a C++ compiler or preprocessor on various machine architectures. Practice papers were few and far between.

The greatest number of such papers, not surprisingly, came from members of the Bell Labs community. In addition, Keith Gorlen presented a paper on the NIH class library, the first large-scale, well known use of C++ outside of the Bell organization. Mark Linton gave his first presentation of InterViews, a paper that is included here to show the beginnings of what is now a widely used library. Those who are familiar with the InterViews of today will appreciate how that library has evolved over the years.

The section begins with Bjarne Stroustrup's "The Evolution of C++: 1985 to 1989". This is an expanded and revised version of the paper by the same name that was given at Santa Fe. That paper, and this expansion, defined the move from the early versions of C++ (both 1.1 and 1.2) to 2.0. The article explains the notions of multiple inheritance, automatic generation of assignment and initialization functions, the ability to overload operators new and delete, and the ability to overload the "->" operator.

The features being discussed in this article were not at the time considered to be major implementation difficulties. The article states that "the features described are in use and the C++ implementation that supports them will become generally available within a few months". In fact, it was a number of years before any commercially available preprocessors or compilers were available that contained all of these features.

This article and the next, "Possible directions for C++", form a blueprint of the way the language was seen to be heading by its originator. While the previous article tried to show what C++ was going to be like in the near future, this article was meant to show were it could go after that.

Neither exception handling nor multiple inheritance are mentioned in this paper. These features were not considered possible future directions. Instead, Stroustrup assumed that multiple inheritance and exception handling would be part of the language. In fact, those features were scheduled to be available in generally available releases within the year. It was not until later, when the implementation of these features was seen to be non-trivial, that either topic engendered controversy.

Parameterized types are included with much the same syntax that is currently accepted (although as this is being written we are still waiting for compilers that implement this feature). In his discussion of adding a feature like parameterized types, Stroustrup sets out some principles that he argues should determine the minimum requirements that a feature should posses to be include in the language. Any such addition, he states, must be convenient for the programmer, efficient in the object code that is produced, and type safe.

A second possible addition to the language discussed by Stroustrup is a mechanism for exception handling. Everyone saw that such a mechanism was a requirement for C++ because of the need to call the destructors of objects that have been created between the time a disaster happens and some code to handle the disaster is found.

Unlike the parameterized types proposal, the discussion of exception handling feels far more preliminary. Indeed, the exact syntax and semantics of exception handling formed a major area of discussion in the years to come. Compared to the proposal for parameterized types, the exception handling proposal is sketchy and the list of open questions is longer. A set of issues are noted as settled, not because of abstract language design features but because the issues must be settled to allow the language to continue to be efficient and widely available.

Type identification is mentioned in sections about object I/O and persistence. In these sections, Stroustrup notes that the ability to reconstruct an object from data coming from some stream (either sent across a wire or coming from persistent store) requires that one know what kind of object it is that is to be reconstructed from the information. A way of actually determining this, currently the subject of much debate, is brushed off in the statement "a naming scheme must exist for both classes and individual objects. Such schemes and facilities for making them available to application programs are relatively easy to provide. ...."

Garbage collection is discussed at some length, but is rejected as being incapable of being implemented efficiently enough to fit into the design center of the language. The language, says Stroustrup, was never designed with garbage collection in mind. Because of these reasons garbage collection could not, according to Stroustrup, be added without unacceptable performance penalties.

Perhaps the most prescient section of the paper is the section labeled "Danger Areas." The two main pressures on C++ seen by Stroustrup were adding features to quickly, causing the language to become bloated and unusable; and adding features to the language too slowly, leading to the production of dialects of the language. Either of these, according to Stroustrup, create the danger of adding to C++ without keeping in sight the reasons for inventing the language. According to Stroustrup,

> ... a most important rule is not to damage the ability to write very efficient low-level C++ programs. ... The most obvious ways of damaging the basic efficiency of C++ would be to introduce new features that depend on either garbage collection or interpretation of dynamic type information in such a way that every program and every part of a program had to help carry the cost of the "advanced" features. ...

The most interesting part of the paper is not what features were seen as being needed, but rather the language design principles enunciated by Stroustrup. These principles constitute a statement of the original design center of the language, that is, what the language was meant to do stated as a set of requirements on the ways the language could be extended.

Mark Linton and Paul Calder's "The Design and Implementation of InterViews" shows the way early class libraries were constructed. Even at this early stage of the evolution of C++, real work was being done. This article gives a view of the early InterViews, currently one of the most widely used C++ class libraries. The article also shows the standard form of C++ practice articles at this time.

While Linton and Calder show how the use of an efficient, object-oriented language allowed the construction of the InterViews library, they conclude by making a series of suggestions concerning how C++ could be improved by the addition of certain features. In the case of this article, the requests were for garbage collection and multiple inheritance.

While the particular features requested would differ from author to author and paper to paper, this would be a pattern that is repeated again and again. C++, the authors would say, is a wonderful language because it allows us to do something that we couldn't have done before. However, with the addition of certain features, the language will be even better.

Rob Murray's paper, "Building Well-Behaved Type Relationships in C++", marks the end of the age of innocence for C++. The paper addresses a seemingly straightforward problem for library writers – when to write functions that convert objects of one type into objects of another type. The complexity of the relationships that could result from these sorts of conversions are reviewed in this paper, and anyone who thought that C++ was going to make the life of the programmer easier soon saw that this was clearly not going to be the case.

The second section, on multiple inheritance, is an attempt to encapsulate within a reasonable amount of space one of the hottest and certainly the longest running of the debates about the addition of a feature to C++.

Multiple inheritance was one of the features that was included in the list of additions that were already decided on for inclusion into the language when Stroustrup talked about the recent history of C++ at the Santa Fe conference. It was also one of the most mentioned of the features that was desired by library builders at that conference.

I'm not sure that anyone at that time realized just how complicated the task of adding multiple inheritance was going to be. When first discussed, it was expected that it would take a couple of months to produce a version of Cfront that supported multiple inheritance. In fact, by the time of the next conference, the feature was still only supported in Beta test compilers and preprocessors.

What had started out as a simple notion, that a class could have more than one parent class, turned complex in the ways it interacted with other parts of the language. If a class appeared as an ancestor of a class more than once, was it possible to distinguish the different occurrences? Sometimes it seemed that such a distinction was required, at other times it seemed that making such a distinction was incorrect. How were virtual functions to work in such a world? What was the notion of polymorphism?

In the end, all of these questions had to be addressed. The result was that the addition of multiple inheritance was far more complex than many of its early advocates had imagined.

One of those early advocates was Tom Cargill, who had presented a paper at the first conference that had argued for the inclusion of multiple inheritance in C++ ("Pi: A Case Study in Object-Oriented Programming"). However, once presented with the language as it evolved in response to such requests, Cargill decided that the price paid for multiple inheritance was not worth the benefits of the feature.

Cargill published a series of articles attacking multiple inheritance on two fronts. The first of these had to do with the complexity of the feature when it was finally added. The second attack was based on Cargill's claim that there was nothing that could be done with multiple inheritance that could not be done in C++ with only single inheritance.

Every time an example of the use of multiple inheritance was offered in the literature, Cargill would show how the example could be recast in a natural way without using the feature. As the number of published examples using multiple inheritance grew, Cargill's papers got longer. But every example met with the same fate; Cargill was able to show that the same functionality could be given without using multiple inheritance.

Finally, Peter Salus, editor of the USENIX technical journal *Computing Systems*, invited Cargill to write a "Controversy" piece for that publication, which is included here. This article summed up the points Cargill had been making in his previous articles. I was invited to write a counter article, which appeared the next month.

In my article, I attempted to show that Cargill's argument was more general than simply that no one had come up with a good example of multiple inheritance. In fact, I argued, Cargill was appealing to principles of programming language design that, while perhaps generally accepted, should be realized as the underpinnings of his view by those attempting to understand his argument.

I then tried to show that there are examples of multiple inheritance that could not be re-cast as single inheritance. The problem with the examples up to then, I argued, was that they attempted to get inheritance of implementation as well as inheritance of interface. Multiple inheritance, I claimed, was really only good for the latter, not the former.

Elana Granston and Vince Russo's "Signature-Based Polymorphism for C++" shows that there are alternatives to multiple inheritance that allow one the power of polymorphism based on interface. Granston and Russo show a way to allow objects to be matched based purely on their interfaces without any reference to their ancestry in the inheritance graph. By using this technique, many of the advantages of multiple inheritance can be obtained without the complexity that accompanied the introduction of that feature into the language.

Whether multiple inheritance is worth the price, or whether the gains of multiple inheritance could have been obtained in some more simple fashion, were really moot points when seen with the perspective of hindsight. Language features, once put in, are extremely difficult to remove. Removal of a feature means that code that was written assuming that feature will suddenly no longer work. Habits of thinking that count on the feature have to be changed. While interesting as history and entertaining at the time, the battle over multiple inheritance was lost before it began.

The 1990 USENIX C++ conference was dominated by the discussion of exception handling. Exception handling had been mentioned at the first conference, years before, as one of the possible extensions needed for the language. Three years later, the question was not whether it should be part of the language, but what the details of the syntax and semantics of exceptions should be.

The main contestants in this controversy were, on one side, Bjarne Stroustrup and Andrew Koenig, and on the other Michael Tiemann. Stroustrup and Koenig were the leaders of the effort to extend C++ within Bell Labs. Tiemann was the implementor of GNU C++, a compiler distributed as part of the Free Software Foundation's offerings. Given that the addition of exception handling would require direct support >from the compiler, it was fitting that the authors of what were then the best known C++ compilers would be the ones most directly involved in the debate.

The problem to be solved was a major one. Passing an exceptional condition up the stack to the place where that exception could be handled was seen as straightforward in C, since the creation of entities (and therefore the use of memory) was explicitly controlled by the programmer. In C++, however, entities could be created by constructors that are "magically" called, and handling an exception by jumping out of the scope containing those entities would mean that the destructors for those objects would never be called. These destructors, however, often free up significant amounts of memory (especially if objects contain references to other objects that are created in the containing objects constructor and deleted in the containing object's destructor, a common technique used by C++ programmers).

By the time of the debate represented by the Tiemann and Stroustrup articles, a number of fundamental questions had been answered. The need for some sort of exception handling mechanism had been accepted; the community of C++ users no longer felt that the problems could be solved in individual ways by individual developers. Earlier attempts at doing exception handling with a class library had been rejected as both too difficult to standardize and too inefficient; the community of users agreed that it would take some addition to the language itself.

The main question that formed the center of the debate was what exceptions were to be in the language. Clearly they were to be objects, but what kind of objects?

Michael Tiemann, in his article "Exception Handling Implementation for C++", answers the question by saying that exceptions should form a special kind of object within the language. The underlying entity encapsulated by such objects are continuations, that are themselves pairs of a return value and return address. This return address would be used to indicate the point within a program where control should resume at the end of a function. Thus an exception could generate a return to the exception handler registered for that exception.

In addition, Tiemann's scheme would allow arbitrary information to be added in to the exception objects, allowing extensions of the basic return value/return address form of a continuation. Tiemann then shows how his proposal could be added to the language in a way that keeps the language, with these extensions, highly efficient.

The mechanism proposed by Andrew Koenig and Bjarne Stroustrup in their paper "Exception Handling in C++ (revised)" relies on a far more general approach that makes fewer changes in the language. Exceptions are objects, on this scheme. When an exception occurs, an exception object is generated and passed up to the first exception handler that accepts objects of that type.

This is a more conservative approach than Tiemann's in that it required less change to the language. Koenig and Stroustrup do not introduce a new kind of entity into C++, and any kind of object could be an exception. Like Tiemann, Koenig and Stroustrup take care to show that their proposal can be implemented in a variety of ways.

One subtle difference between the two approaches has to do with the notion each has of keeping the C++ language efficient. Tiemann argues for his approach on the grounds that the implementation of that approach can be done in such a way that exception handling will be highly efficient.

Koenig and Stroustrup, on the other hand, argue for their approach not by showing that their approach to exceptions can be implemented efficiently, but by showing that the approach does not impose any cost on programs that do not use the mechanism. In fact, Koenig and Stroustrup explicitly state in their introduction that "A guiding principle is that exceptions are rare compared to function calls and that error handling code is rare compared to function definitions. ..." Because of this, they do not think that exceptions themselves need to be efficient.

In the end, the community of users was convinced by Koenig and Stroustrup. Exception handling in the current definition of C++ differs only slightly from the way it was proposed in their paper, with most of the differences centering around details of syntax.

Michael Tiemann's article from the second C++ conference, "Wrappers: Solving the RPC Problem in GNU C++" was one of the early attempts to extend C++ beyond its original environment of a single address space. The use of a function that would wrap all of the Remote Procedure Call (RPC) mechanisms for an entire class is, as pointed out, an approach taken by a number of the early distributed systems. Tiemann shows ways that this can be added to the language with compiler support. While the suggestion was ultimately rejected and the extensions that would have allowed wrappers were never made to the language, the paper did get a number of researchers thinking about the problem of distributed computing and C++.

Tiemann's notion of wrappers attempted to subsume an approach to distributed computing in a mechanism what would lend itself to other uses. The drawback to the approach is that it would require changes to both the syntax and semantics of the language. A different design tradeoff is shown in Graham Parrington's article, "Reliable Distributed Programming in C++: The Arjuna Approach."

The Arjuna system was built expressly for distributed computing rather than attempting to subsume distribution under a more general mechanism. The system also took as a foundation point that no changes would be made to the compiler.

The Arjuna system attempts to extend the uses of C++. As well as being the implementation language for the system, Arjuna uses C++ as an interface definition language that is used to generate code for remote procedure calls. While this is a natural use of the language in a distributed system, it is also not clear that it can be fully successful, as there are certain declarations that make sense in a non-distributed case that do not make sense in a distributed environment.

The fact that Arjuna was possible shows the power of C++. By extending the use of the language to distributed systems, Arjuna demonstrates the way the language can be used to do things that it had not originally been designed to do. The new use was not completely free of problems, but it could be done.

The approach also showed that a new use of the language could be accomplished without changing C++. While Parrington notes that there are features that, if added to the language, would have made the construction of Arjuna easier (such as garbage collection and multiple inheritance) the Arjuna system showed that C++ could be used for distributed computing without change.

Bruce Martin's "The Separation of Interface and Implementation in C++" closes out the section on distributed computing by moving the discussion into a different plane. Martin uses a distinction between inheriting an interface and inheriting an implementation of that interface to show how one could approach some of the problems of distributed computing that had been mentioned by Parrington.

While the distinction can be used in cases other than those involving distributed computing, it is in the programming of distributed systems that the distinction becomes vital. Unfortunately, C++ does not provide a way of distinguishing between the various forms of inheritance, making the clean separation required for distributed computing difficult at best. Even when one makes the distinction, the languages forces one to make it through conventions followed by the programmers of the system.

Current efforts in the realm of distributed computing, such as those taken by the Object Management Group's Common Object Request Broker Architecture (OMG CORBA) specification, are attempting to make the distinction between interface and implementation even more formal than advocated by Martin. The move appears to be towards separating the languages used for definition of the interface supported by an object and the language used to implement that interface. The CORBA specification includes an Interface Definition Language which, while it looks much like C++, differs from it in significant ways.

Most notably, the CORBA specification states that interfaces are defined using the interface definition language, and implementations of those interfaces are defined using other means. The CORBA approach has made the distinction between interface and implementation so strong that the two are not even expressed in the same language.

The final section contains early articles on what is shaping up to the be next major area of contention and extension in the language. From the very first, C++ was designed as a language that used type information only at the time a program was compiled (and linked). This meant that there was no way to find out the actual type of an object at runtime. You were assured by the compiler that the object you were holding was at least an instance of the type you had requested, but you had no way to tell if the object was of a type derived from the one that you had requested.

As with any limitation, this made it difficult to do some things that people wanted to do. The result, not surprisingly, was that those who really needed access to such information found a way to put it in. But these ways tended to be specific to the users and difficult to extend and combine. The request for a change in the language that would allow access to type information during runtime was the result.

One of the first articles to discuss what was needed to add runtime access to typing information is John Interrante and Mark Linton's "Runtime Access to Type Information." In this paper, the major authors of the InterViews class library discuss how they added tools that allowed them to determine the type of an object after the program had been compiled and linked.

Their solution was to create a class that held the information they needed (such as the name of the class and its ancestry) and a tool that would generate objects of this class for any type they defined. They then added a function to every class that would return one of these information-filled objects, that they called dossiers, when asked.

While the approach worked, it is not perfect. It required that the writer of a class have a member function that returned the dossier for that class. It required the use of a dossier construction tool, in effect adding yet another compilation pass to the building of an application. Worse yet, it did not aid programmers attempting to use libraries constructed by different groups – if those libraries had classes that clashed with respect to the identifiers in the dossiers, the only way to resolve those clashes required having access to the source code.

Not surprisingly, the authors of this first attempt concluded that a better approach would be to make a change in the language that would support the ability to find out the type of an object at runtime.

This theme was picked up the next year by Dmitry Lenkov, Michey Mehta, and Shankar Unni in their article "Type Identification in C++". In this article, the authors suggest that the language be extended to include a built-in type (analogous to int and float) called typeid, and that three operators be added to the language. One of the new operators, subtype, could be used to tell if a given type was a subtype of some other type. The second added operator, stype, would return the type identifier associated with the type that an object was known to be. A third operator, dtype, would return the type identifier associated with the type an object actually was.

The typeid proposed by Lenkov, et al., is much like the dossier class that Interrante and Linton had been added to the InterViews library. The base class defined more of the structure of a class and less identification information than was found in the dossier class, but this could be altered by the ability introduced in this paper of dynamically adding type information to the typeinfo object associated with a particular class. Also, while the dossier object was only created for classes, the proposed typeid object would be available for all types.

The major difference between the Linton and Interrante's dossier class and the proposals made by Lenkov, et al., was that the former was added as a part of the implementation of a library while the latter was proposed as an extension to the language. The implementation of the latter proposal would be in the compiler, and the access to such information would be guaranteed by the specification of the language. This was asked for by Interrante and Linton as a way of solving the problems of joining multiple libraries together, and of assuring that the way of gaining access to type information at runtime would be uniform from one author to another.

Unlike the controversy over multiple inheritance or exception handling (but like the questions raised concerning the use of C++ for distributed computing) the question of how (or, even, whether) to add runtime type information into C++ is far from answered. Proposals have been made to the ISO C++ committee, but currently none of those proposals have been added to the draft specifications. The 1993 USENIX C++ conference includes a session in which a new proposal for adding access to type information at runtime is being made by Lenkov and Stroustrup. However, this proposal is controversial, and it's future is far from assured.

From a historical perspective, it is ironic that Bjarne Stroustrup is the co-author of the current proposal to add access to runtime type information to the language. In his article from the proceedings of the First Workshop on future directions in C++, he uses access to runtime type information as an example of one of the features that should never be added to the language. Time changes opinions, and only time will tell if this feature is added to the language.

The debate about access to runtime type information will also be a debate that will be decided not by the abstract community of users, but by the ISO/ANSI committee that has the job of standardizing the C++ language. The other controversies were all over by the time the committee was established, and the solution was part of the base document for that group. The controversy over runtime access to type information, on the other hand, can be seen as the first to follow what may be the new path of discussion for C++. The topic was brought up before the technical community, but discussion and final resolution will take place as part of the standards process.

This change will, no doubt, affect the way C++ evolves. The evolution of a language, like the evolution of a biological species, is at least partly determined by the selection forces that surround that language. During the period covered by the articles in this book, the selection forces were informal and based on what certain users, who happened to write articles and correspond with other members of the community, thought was best for the language.

The community that controls the evolution of the language has changed >from this informal group selected by interest to the more formal standards body. The set of members of standards committees and the set of attendees of technical conferences overlap some, but the two populations are distinct. The formal nature of the standards process tends to put some braking pressure on changes in the language. There is no reason to think that the results of the change in evolutionary environment will be better or worse for the language. But things will be different.

In retrospect, the evolution of C++ as shown in this volume can be viewed as an evolution in the design center of the language. The design center has only been explicitly stated on rare occasions, but it is that design center that is appealed to as the arbiter of proposed change. The design center of C++ during this period changed as the community changed. It is these changes in what the language is meant to do and meant to be that structured the evolution of C++.

Part I
The Early Years

Chapter 1

The Evolution of C++: 1985 to 1989

Bjarne Stroustrup

Abstract

The C++ Programming Language[5] describes C++ as defined and implemented in August 1985. This paper describes the growth of the language since then and clarifies a few points in the definition.[1] It is emphasized that these language modifications are extensions; C++ has been and will remain a stable language suitable for long term software development. The main new features of C++ are: multiple inheritance, type-safe linkage, better resolution of overloaded functions, recursive definition of assignment and initialization, better facilities for user-defined memory management, abstract classes, `static` member functions, `const` member functions, `protected` members, overloading of operator `->`, and pointers to members. These features are provided in the 2.0 release of C++.

Introduction

As promised in *The C++ Programming Language*[5], C++ has been evolving to meet the needs of its users. This evolution has been guided by the experience of users of widely varying backgrounds working in a great range of application areas. The primary aim of the extensions has been to enhance C++ as a language for data abstraction and object-oriented programming[7] in general and to enhance it as a tool for writing high-quality libraries of user-defined types in particular. By a high-quality library I mean a library that provides a concept to a user in the form of one or more classes that are convenient, safe, and efficient to use. In this context, *safe* means that a class provides a specific type-secure interface between the users of the library and its providers; *efficient* means that use of the class does not impose large overhead in run-time or space on the user compared with hand written C code.

Portability of at least some C++ implementations is a key design goal. Consequently, extensions that would add significantly to the porting time or to the demands on resources for a C++ compiler have been avoided. This ideal of language evolution can be contrasted with plausible alternative directions such as making programming convenient

- at the expense of efficiency or structure;
- for novices at the expense of generality;

---

[1]This paper is a revised and extended version of a paper with a similar title presented at the USENIX C++ Workshop in Santa Fe, New Mexico, November 1987.

- in a specific application area by adding special purpose features to the language;
- by adding language features to increase integration into a specific C++ environment.

For some ideas of where these ideas of language evolution might lead C++ see [7, 8, 10].

A programming language is only one part of a programmer's world. Naturally, work is being done in many other fields (such as tools, environments, libraries, education and design methods) to make C++ programming more pleasant and effective. This paper, however, deals strictly with language and language implementation issues. Furthermore, this paper discusses only features that are generally available. Speculative or experimental features, such as exception handling and parameterized types, are not presented here.

Overview

This paper is a brief overview of new language features; it is not a manual[2] or a tutorial. The reader is assumed to be familiar with the language as described in *The C++ Programming Language* and to have sufficient experience with C++ to recognize many of the problems that the features described here are designed to solve or alleviate. Most of the extensions take the form of removing restrictions on what can be expressed in C++.

First some extensions to C++'s mechanisms for controlling access to class members are presented. Like all extensions described here, they reflect experience with the mechanisms they extend and the increased demands posed by the use of C++ in relatively large and complicated projects, see the section named 'Access Control'.

C++ software is increasingly constructed by combining semi-independent components (modules, classes, libraries, etc.) and much of the effort involved in writing C++ goes into the design and implementation of such components. To help these activities, the rules for overloading function names and the rules for linking separately compiled code have been refined and documented in the sections named 'Overloading Resolution' and Type-Safe Linkage.

Classes are designed to represent general or application specific concepts. Originally, C++ provided only single inheritance, that is, a class could have at most one direct base class, so that the directly representable relations between classes had to be a tree structure. This is sufficient in a large majority of cases. However, there are important concepts for which relations cannot be naturally expressed as a tree, but where a directed acyclic graph is suitable. As a consequence, C++ has been extended to support multiple inheritance, that is, a class can have several immediate base classes, directly. The rules for ambiguity resolution and for initialization of base classes and members have been refined to cope with this extension and are discussed in the 'Multiple Inheritance', 'Base and Member Initialization', and 'Abstract Classes' sections.

The concept of a class member has been generalized. Most important, the introduction of const member functions allows the rules for const class objects to be enforced are discussed in the 'static Member Functions',

---

[2] A revised C++ manual is under review and will appear in the future.

'const Member Functions', 'Initialization of static Members', and 'Pointers to Members' sections.

The mechanisms for user-defined memory management have been refined and extended to the point where the old and inelegant "assignment to this" mechanism has become redundant are explained in the 'User-Defined Free Store Management' section.

The rules for assignment and initialization of class objects have been made more general and uniform to require less work from the programmer are laid out in the 'Assignment and Initialization' section.

Some minor extensions are presented in the 'Operator ->', 'Operator ,', and 'Initialization of static' sections.

The last section ('Resolutions') does not describe language extensions but presents the resolution of some details of the C++ language definition.

In addition to the extensions mentioned here, many details of the definition of C++ have been modified for greater compatibility with the proposed ANSI C standard[13].

Access Control

The rules and syntax for controlling access to class members have been made more flexible.

protected *Members*

The simple private/public model of data hiding served C++ well where C++ was used essentially as a data abstraction language and for a large class of problems where inheritance was used for object-oriented programming. However, when derived classes are used there are two kinds of users of a class: derived classes and "the general public." The members and friends that implement the operations on the class operate on the class objects on behalf of these users. The private/public mechanism allows the programmer to distinguish clearly between the implementors and the general public, but does not provide a way of catering specifically to derived classes.[3] This often caused the data hiding mechanisms to be ignored:

```
class X {    // One bad way:
    // ... public:
    int a;   // ''a'' should have been private
             // don't use it unless you are
             // a member of a derived class
    // ...
};
```

Another symptom of this problem was overuse of friend declarations:

```
class X {          // Another bad way:
friend class D1;   // make derived classes friends
friend class D2;   // to give access to private member ''a''
    // ...
friend class Dn;   // ...
    int a;
public:
    // ...
};
```

---

[3]An interesting discussion of access and encapsulation problems in languages with inheritance mechanisms can be found in [4].

The solution adopted was `protected` members. A `protected` member is accessible to members and friends of a derived class as if it were `public`, but inaccessible to "the general public" just like `private` members. For example:

```
class X {
// private by default:
    int priv;
protected:
    int prot;
public:
    int publ;
};
class Y : public X {
    void mf();
};
Y::mf()
{
    priv = 1;    // error: priv is private
    prot = 2;    // OK: prot is protected and mf() is
                 //     a member of Y
    publ = 3;    // OK: publ is public
}
void f(Y* p)
{
    p->priv = 1; // error: priv is private
    p->prot = 2; // error: prot is protected and f() is not
                 //     a friend or a member of X or Y
    p->publ = 3; // OK: publ is public
}
```

A more realistic example of the use of `protected` can be found in the 'Multiple Inheritance' section.

A `friend` function has the same access to `protected` members as a member function.

A subtle point is that accessibility of protected members depends on the static type of the pointer used in the access. A member or a friend of a derived class has access only to protected members of objects that are known to be of its derived type. For example:

```
class Z : public Y {
    // ...
};
void Y::mf()
{
    prot = 2;    // OK: prot is protected and mf() is a member

    X a;
    a.prot = 3;  // error: prot is protected and a is not a Y

    X* p = this;
    p->prot = 3; // error: prot is protected
                 //         and p is not a pointer to Y

    Z b;
    b.prot = 4;  // OK: prot is protected
                 //     and mf() is a member and a Z is a Y
}
```

A protected member of a class `base` is a protected member of a class derived from `base` if the derivation is public and private otherwise.

Access Control Syntax

The following example confuses most beginners and even experts get bitten sometimes:

```
class X {
    // ...
public:
    int f();
};

class Y : X { /* ... */ };

int g(Y* p)
{
    // ...
    return p->f();   // error!
};
```

Here X is by default declared to be a `private` base class of Y. This means that Y is not a subtype of X so the call `p->f()` is illegal because Y does not have a public function `f()`. Private base classes are quite an important concept, but to avoid confusion it is recommended that they be declared `private` explicitly:

```
class Y : private X { /* ... */ };
```

Several `public`, `private`, and `protected` sections are allowed in a class declaration:

```
class X {
public:
    int i1;
private:
    int i2;
public:
    int i3;
};
```

These sections can appear in any order. This implies that the public interface of a class may appear textually before the private "implementation details":

```
class S {
public:
    f();
    int i1;
    // ...
private:
    g();
    int i2;
    // ...
};
```

Adjusting Access

When a class base is used as a private base class all of its members are considered private members of the derived class. The syntax

base-class-name : : member-name

can be used to restore access of a member to what it was in the base:

```
class base {
public:
    int publ;
protected:
    int prot;
private:
    int priv;
};
class derived : private base {
protected:
    base::prot;      // protected in derived
public:
    base::publ;      // public in derived
};
```

This mechanism cannot be used to grant access that was not already granted by the base class:

```
class derived2 : public base {
public:
    base::priv;      // error: base::priv is private
};
```

This mechanism can be used only to restore access to what it was in the base class:

```
class derived3 : private base {
protected:
    base::publ;      // error: base::publ was public
};
```

This mechanism cannot be used to remove access already granted:

```
class derived4 : public base {
private:
    base::publ;      // error: base::publ is public
};
```

We considered allowing the last two forms and experimented with them, but found that they caused total confusion among users about the access control rules and the rules for private and public derivation. Similar considerations led to the decision not to introduce the (otherwise perfectly reasonable) concept of protected base classes.

Details

A friend function has the same access to base class members as a member function. For example:

```
class base {
protected:
    int prot;
public:
    int pub;
};
class derived : private base {
public:
    friend int fr(derived *p) { return p->prot; }
    int mem() { return prot; }
};
```

In particular, a friend function can perform the conversion of a pointer to a derived class to its private base class:

```
class derived2 : private base {
public:
    friend base* fr2(derived2 *p) { return p; }
    base* mem() { return this; }
};
base* f(derived2* p)
{
    return p;    // error: cannot convert;
                 // base is a private base class of derived
}
```

However, friendship is *not* transitive. For example:

```
class X {
friend class Y;
private:
    int a;
};
class Y {
    friend int fr3(Y *p)
        { return p->a; }  // error: fr3() is not a friend of X
    int mem(Y* p)
        { return p->a; }  // OK: mem() is a friend of X
};
```

Overloading Resolution

C++'s overloading mechanism was revised to allow resolution of types formerly "too similar" and to gain independence of declaration order. The resulting scheme is more expressive and catches more ambiguity errors. Consider:

```
double abs(double);
float abs(float);
```

To cope with single precision floating point arithmetic it must be possible to declare both of these functions; now it is. The effect of any call of abs() given the declarations above is the same if the order of declarations was reversed:

```
float abs(float);
double abs(double);
```

Here is a slightly simplified explanation of the new rules. Note that with the exception of a few cases where the the older rules allowed order dependence the new rules are compatible and old programs produce identical results under the new rules. For the last two years or so C++ implementations have issued warnings for the now "outlawed" order dependent resolutions.

C++ distinguishes five kinds of "matches":

1. Match using no or only unavoidable conversions (for example, array name to pointer, function name to pointer to function, and T to const T).
2. Match using integral promotions (as defined in the proposed ANSI C standard; that is, char to int, short to int and their unsigned counterparts) and float to double.
3. Match using standard conversions (for example, int to double, derived* to base*, unsigned int to int).
4. Match using user defined conversions (both constructors and conversion operators).
5. Match using the ellipsis ... in a function declaration.

Consider functions of a single argument. The idea is always to choose the "best" match, that is the one highest on the list above. If there are two best matches the call is ambiguous and thus a compile time error. For example:

```
float abs(float);
double abs(double);
int abs(int);
unsigned abs(unsigned);
char abs(char);

abs(1);        // abs(int);
abs(1U);       // abs(unsigned);
abs(1.0);      // abs(double);
abs(1.0F);     // abs(float);
abs('a');      // abs(char);
abs(1L);       // error: ambiguous, abs(int) or abs(double)
```

Here, the calls exploit the ANSI C notation for unsigned and float literals and of the C++ rule that a character constant is of type char.[4] The call with the long argument 1L is ambiguous since abs(int) and abs(double) would be equally good matches (match with standard conversion).

Hierarchies established by public class derivations are taken into account in function matching and where a standard conversion is needed the conversion to the "most derived" class is chosen. A void* argument is chosen only if no other pointer argument matches. For example:

```
class B { /* ... */ };
class BB : public B { /* ... */ };
class BBB : public BB { /* ... */ };

f(B*);
f(BB*);
f(void*);

void g(BBB* pbbb, int* pi)
{
    f(pbbb);  // f(BB*);
    f(pi);    // f(void*);
}
```

This ambiguity resolution rule matches the rule for virtual function calls where the member from the most derived class is chosen.

If two otherwise equally good matches differ in terms of const, the const specifier is taken into account in function matching for pointer and reference arguments. For example:

```
char* strtok(char*, const char*);
const char* strtok(const char*, const char*);

void g(char* vc, const char* vcc)
{
    char* p1 = strtok(vc,"a");        // strtok(char*, char*);
    const char* p2 = strtok(vcc,"a"); // strtok(const char*, char*);
    char* p3 = strtok(vcc,"a");       // error
}
```

---

[4]Surprisingly, giving character constants type char does not cause incompatibilities with C where they have type int. Except for the pathological example sizeof('a'), every construct that can be expressed in both C and C++ gives the same result. The reason for the surprising compatibility is that even though character constants have type int in C, the rules for determining the values of such constants involves the standard conversion from char to int.

In the third case, strtok(const char*, const char*) is chosen because vcc is a const char*. This leads to an attempt to initialize the char* p3 with the const char* result.

For calls involving more than one argument a function is chosen provided it has a better match than every other function for at least one argument and at least as good a match as every other function for every argument. For example:

```
class complex { /* ... */ complex(double); };

f(int,double);
f(double,int);
f(complex,int);
f(int ...);
f(complex ...);

complex z = 1;

f(1, 2.0);    // f(int,double);
f(1.0, 2);    // f(double,int);
f(z, 1.2);    // f(complex,int);
f(z, 1, 3);   // f(complex ...);
f(2.0, z);    // f(int ...);
f(1, 1);      // error: ambiguous, f(int,double) and f(double,int)
```

The unfortunate narrowing from double to int in the third and the second to last cases causes warnings. Such narrowings are allowed to preserve compatibility with C. In this particular case the narrowing is harmless, but in many cases double to int conversions are value destroying and they should never be used thoughtlessly.

As ever, at most one user-defined and one built-in conversion may be applied to a single argument.

Type-Safe Linkage

Originally, C++ allowed a name to be used for more than one name ("to be overloaded") only after an explicit overload declaration. For example:

```
overload max;             // 'overload' now obsolete
int max(int,int);
double max(double,double);
```

It used to be considered too dangerous simply to use a name for two functions without previous declaration of intent. For example:

```
int abs(int);
double abs(double);       // used to be an error
```

This fear of overloading had two sources:

1. concern that undetected ambiguities could occur
2. concern that a program could not be properly linked unless the programmer explicitly declared where overloading was to take place.

The former fear proved largely groundless and the few problems found in actual use have been taken care of by the new order-independent overloading resolution rules. The latter fear proved to have a basis in a general problem with C separate compilation rules that had nothing to do with overloading.

On the other hand, the redundant overload declarations themselves became an increasingly serious problem. Since they had to precede (or be part of) the declarations they were to enable, it was not possible to merge pieces of software using the same function name for different functions unless both pieces had declared the function overloaded. This is not usually the case. In particular, the name one wants to overload is often the name of a C standard library function declared in a C header. For example, one might have standard headers like this:

```
/* Header for C standard math library, math.h: */
    double sqrt(double);
    /* ... */
```

```
// header for C++ standard complex arithmetic library, complex.h:
    overload sqrt;
    complex sqrt(complex);
    // ...
```

and try to use them like this:

```
#include <math.h>
#include <complex.h>
```

This causes a compile time error when the overload for sqrt() is seen after the first declaration of sqrt(). Rearranging declarations, putting constraints on the use of header files, and sprinkling overload declarations everywhere "just in case" can alleviate this kind of problem, but we found the use of such tricks unmanageable in all but the simplest cases. Abolishing overload declarations and getting rid of the overload keyword in the process is a much better idea.

Doing things this way does pose an implementation problem, though. When a single name is used for several functions, one must be able to tell the linker which calls are to be linked to which function definitions. Ordinary linkers are not equipped to handle several functions with the same name. However, they can be tricked into handling overloaded names by encoding type information into the names seen by the linker. The names for these two functions

```
double sqrt(double);
complex sqrt(complex);
```

become

```
sqrt__Fd
sqrt__F7complex
```

in the compiler output to the linker. The user and the compiler see the C++ source text where the type information serves to disambiguate and the linker sees the names that have been disambiguated by adding a textual representation of the type information. Naturally, one might have a linker that understood about type information, but it is not necessary and such linkers are certainly not common.

Using this encoding or any equivalent scheme solves a long standing problem with C linkage. Inconsistent function declarations in separately compiled code fragments are now caught. For example

```
// file1.c:
extern name* lookup(table* tbl, const char* name);
// ...
void some_fct(char* s)
{
    name* n = lookup(gtbl,s);
}
```

looks plausible and the compiler can find no fault with it. However, if the definition of lookup() turns out to be

```
// file2.c:
int lookup(const char* name)
{
    // ...
}
```

the linker now has enough information to catch the error.

Finally, we have to face the problem of linking to code fragments written in other languages that do not know the C++ type system or use the C++ type encoding scheme. One could imagine all compilers for all languages on a system agreeing on a type system and a linkage scheme such that linkage of code fragments written in different languages would be safe. However, since this will not typically be the case we need a way of calling functions written in a language that does not use a type-safe linkage scheme and a way to write C++ functions that obey the different (and typically unsafe) linkage rules for other languages. This is done by explicitly specifying the name of the desired linkage convention in a declaration:

```
extern "C" double sqrt(double);
```

or by enclosing whole groups of declarations in a linkage directive:

```
extern "C" {
#include <math.h>
}
```

By applying the second form of linkage directive to standard header files one can avoid littering the user code with linkage directives. This type-safe linkage mechanism is discussed in detail in [9].

Multiple Inheritance

Consider writing a simulation of a network of computers. Each node in the network is represented by an object of class Switch, each user or computer by an object of class Terminal, and each communication line by an object of class Line. One way to monitor the simulation (or a real network of the same structure) would be to display the state of objects of various classes on a screen. Each object to be displayed is represented as an object of class Displayed. Objects of class Displayed are under control of a display manager that ensures regular update of a screen and/or data base. The classes Terminal and Switch are derived from a class Task that provides the basic facilities for co-routine style behavior. Objects of class Task are under control of a task manager (scheduler) that manages the real processor(s).

Ideally Task and Displayed are classes from a standard library. If you want to display a terminal, class Terminal must be derived from class Displayed. Class Terminal, however, is already derived from class Task. In a single inheritance language, such as Simula67, we have only two ways of solving this problem: deriving Task from Displayed or deriving Displayed from Task. Neither is ideal since they both create a dependency between the library versions of two fundamental and independent concepts. Ideally, one would want to be able to say that a Terminal is a Task *and* a Displayed; that a Line is a Displayed *but not* a Task; and that a Switch is a Task *but not* a Displayed.

The ability to express this class hierarchy, that is, to derive a class from more than one base class, is usually referred to as *multiple inheritance*. Other examples involve the representation of various kinds of windows in a window system[12] and the representation of various kinds of processors and compilers for a multi-machine, multi-environment debugger[1].

In general, multiple inheritance allows a user to combine concepts represented as classes into a composite concept represented as a derived class. C++ allows this to be done in a general, type-safe, compact, and efficient manner. The basic scheme allows independent concepts to be combined and ambiguities to be detected at compile time. An extension of the base class concept, called *virtual base classes*, allows dependencies between classes in an inheritance DAG (Directed Acyclic Graph) to be expressed.

Ambiguity Detection
Ambiguous uses are detected at compile time:

```
class A { public: f(); /* ... */ };
class B { public: f(); /* ... */ };
class C : public A, public B { };

void g() {
    C* p;
    p->f(); // error: ambiguous
}
```

Note that it is not an error to combine classes containing the same member names in an inheritance DAG. The error occurs only when a name is used in an ambiguous way – and only then does the compiler have to reject the program. This is important since most potential ambiguities in a program never appear as actual ambiguities. Considering a potential ambiguity an error would be far too restrictive.[5]

Typically one would resolve the ambiguity by adding a function:

```
class C : public A, public B {
public:
    f()
    {
            // C's own stuff
            A::f();
            B::f();
    }
    // ...
};
```

This example shows the usefulness of naming members of a base class explicitly with the name of the base class. In the restricted case of single inheritance, this way is marginally less elegant than the approach taken by Smalltalk and other languages (simply referring to "my super class" instead of using an explicit name). However, the C++ approach extends cleanly to multiple inheritance.

In this context it might be worth noting that Y::f means "the f from class Y or one of Y's base classes" and not simply "the f declared in class Y." For example:

---

[5]The strategy for dealing with ambiguities in inheritance DAGs is essentially the same as the strategy for dealing with ambiguities in expression evaluation involving overloaded operators and user-defined coercions. Note that the access control mechanism does not affect the ambiguity control mechanism. Had B::f() been private the call p->f() would still be ambiguous.

```
class X { public: int f(); };
class Y : public X { };
class Z : public Y { public: f(); };

int Z::f() { return Y::f(); }    // calls the X::f()
```

Multiple Inclusion

A class can appear more than once in an inheritance DAG:

```
class A : public L { /* ... */ };
class B : public L { /* ... */ };
class C : public A, public B { /* ... */ };
```

In this case, an object of class C has two sub-objects of class L, namely A::L and B::L. This is often useful, as in the case of an implementation of lists requiring each element on a list to contain a link element. If in the example above L is a link class then a C can be on both the list of As and the list of Bs at the same time.

Virtual functions work as expected; that is the version from the most derived class is used:

```
class A { public: virtual f(); /* ... */ };
class B { public: virtual g(); /* ... */ };
class C : public A, public B { public: f(); g(); /* ... */ };

void ff()
{
    C obj;
    A* pa = &obj;
    B* pb = &obj;

    pa->f();        // calls C::f
    pb->g();        // calls C::g
}
```

This way of combining classes is ideal for representing the union of independent or nearly independent concepts. However, in some interesting cases, such as the window example, a more explicit way of expressing sharing and dependency is needed.

Virtual Base Classes

Virtual base classes provide a mechanism for sharing between sub-objects in an inheritance DAG and for expressing dependencies among such sub-objects:

```
class A : public virtual W { /* ... */ };
class B : public virtual W { /* ... */ };
class C : public A, public B, public virtual W { /* ... */ };
```

In this case there is only one object of class W in class C.

A virtual base class is considered an immediate virtual base class of every class directly or indirectly derived from it. Therefore, the explicit specification of W as a base of C is redundant. Class C could equivalently be declared like this:

```
class C : public A, public B { /* ... */ };
```

I prefer to mention the virtual base explicitly, though, since the presence of a virtual base typically affects the way member functions are programmed (see below).

Constructing the tables for virtual function calls can get quite complicated when virtual base classes are used. However, virtual functions work as usual by choosing the version from the most derived class in a call:

```
class W {
    // ...
public:
    virtual void f();
    virtual void g();
    virtual void h();
    virtual void k();
    // ...
};
class AW : public virtual W
    { /* ... */ public: void g(); /* ... */ };
class BW : public virtual W
    { /* ... */ public: void f(); /* ... */ };
class CW : public AW, public BW, public virtual W {
    // ...
public:
    void h();
    // ...
};
CW* pcw = new CW;

pcw->f();              // invokes BW::f()
pcw->g();              // invokes AW::g()
pcw->h();              // invokes CW::h()
((AW*)pcw)->f();       // invokes BW::f() !!!
```

The reason that BW::f() is invoked in the last example is that the only f() in an object of class CW is the one found in the (shared) sub-object W, and that one has been overridden by BW::f().

Ambiguities are easily detected at the point where CW's table of virtual functions is constructed. The rule for detecting ambiguities in a class DAG is that all re-definitions of a virtual function from a virtual base class must occur on a single path through the DAG. The example above can be drawn like this:

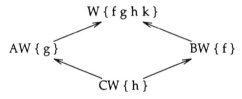

Note that a call "up" through one path of the DAG to a virtual function may result in the call of a function (re-defined) in another path (as happened in the call ((AW*)pcw)->f() in the example above). In this example, an ambiguity would occur if a function f() was added to AW. This ambiguity might be resolved by adding a function f() to CW.

Programming with virtual bases is trickier than programming with non-virtual bases. The problem is to avoid multiple calls of a function in a virtual class when that is not desired. Here is a possible style:

```
class W {
    // ...
protected:
    _f() { my stuff }
    // ...
public:
    f() { _f(); }
    // ...
};
```

Each class provides a protected function doing "its own stuff", _f(), for use by derived classes and a public function f() as the interface for use by the "general public."

```
class A : public virtual W {
    // ...
protected:
    _f() { my stuff }
    // ...
public:
    f() { _f(); W::_f(); }
    // ...
};
```

A derived class f() does its "own stuff" by calling _f() and its base classes' "own stuff" by calling their _f()s.

```
class B : public virtual W  {
    // ...
protected:
    _f() { my stuff }
    // ...
public:
    f() { _f(); W::_f(); }
    // ...
};
```

In particular, this style enables a class that is (indirectly) derived twice from a class W to call W::f() once only:

```
class C : public A, public B, public virtual W {
    // ...
protected:
    _f() { my stuff }
    // ...
public:
    f() { _f(); A::_f(); B::_f(); W::_f(); }
    // ...
};
```

Method combination schemes, such as the ones found in Lisp systems with multiple inheritance, were considered as a way of reducing the amount of code a programmer needed to write in cases like the one above. However, none of these schemes appeared to be sufficiently simple, general, and efficient enough to warrant the complexity it would add to C++.

Time and Space Efficiency

As described in [6], a virtual function call is about as efficient as a normal function call – even in the case of multiple inheritance. The added cost is 5 to 6 memory references per call. This compares with the 3 to 4 extra memory references incurred by a virtual function call in a C++ compiler providing only single inheritance. The multiple inheritance scheme currently used causes an increase of about 50% in the size of the tables used to implement the virtual functions compared with the older single inheritance implementation. To offset that, the multiple inheritance implementation optimizes away quite a few spurious tables generated by the older single-inheritance implementations so that the memory requirement of a program using virtual functions actually decreases in most cases.

It would have been nice if there had been absolutely no added cost for the multiple inheritance scheme when only single inheritance is used. Such schemes exist, but involve the use of tricks that cannot be done by a C++ compiler generating C.

Base and Member Initialization

The syntax for initializing base classes and members has been extended to cope with multiple inheritance and the order of initialization has been more precisely defined. Leaving the initialization order unspecified in the original definition of C++ gave an unnecessary degree of freedom to language implementors at the expense of the users. In most cases, the order of initialization of members doesn't matter and in most cases where it does matter, the order dependency is an indication of bad design. In a few cases, however, the programmer absolutely needs control of the order of initialization. For example, consider transmitting objects between machines. An object must be reconstructed by a receiver in exactly the reverse order in which it was decomposed for transmission by a sender. This cannot be guaranteed for objects communicated between programs compiled by compilers from different suppliers unless the language specifies the order of construction.

Consider:

```
class A { public: A(int); A(); /* ... */ };
class B { public: B(int); B(); /* ... */ };

class C : public A, public B {
    const a;
    int& b;
public:
    C(int&);
};
```

In a constructor the sub-objects representing base classes can be referred to by their class names:

```
C::C(int& rr) : A(1), B(2), a(3), b(rr) { /* ... */ }
```

The initialization takes place in the order of declaration in the class with base classes initialized before members,[6] so the initialization order for class C is A, B, a, b. This order is independent of the order of explicit initializers so

```
C::C(int& rr) : b(rr), B(2), a(3), A(1) { /* ... */ }
```

also initializes in the declaration order A, B, a, b.

The reason for ignoring the order of initializers is to preserve the usual FIFO ordering of constructor and destructor calls. Allowing two constructors to use different orders of initialization of bases and members would constrain implementations to use more dynamic and more expensive strategies.

Using the base class name explicitly clarifies even the case of single inheritance without member initialization:

```
class vector {
    // ...
public:
    vector(int);
    // ...
};
```

---

[6]Virtual base classes force a modification to this rule; see below.

```
class vec : public vector {
    // ...
public:
    vec(int,int);
    // ...
};
```

It is reasonably clear even to novices what is going on here:

```
vec::vec(int low, int high) : vector(high-low-1) { /* ... */ }
```

On the other hand, this version:

```
vec::vec(int low, int high) : (high-low-1) { /* ... */ }
```

has caused much confusion over the years. The old-style base class initializer is of course still accepted. It can be used only in the single inheritance case since it is ambiguous otherwise.

A virtual base is constructed before any of its derived classes. Virtual bases are constructed before any non-virtual bases and in the order they appear on a depth-first left-to-right traversal of the inheritance DAG. This rule applies recursively for virtual bases of virtual bases.

A virtual base is initialized by the "most derived" class of which it is a base. For example:

```
class V { public: V(); V(int); /* ... */ };
class A : public virtual V { public: A(); A(int); /* ... */ };
class B : public virtual V { public: B(); B(int); /* ... */ };
class C : public A, public B { public: C(); C(int); /* ... */ };

A::A(int i) : V(i) { /* ... */ }
B::B(int i) { /* ... */ }
C::C(int i) { /* ... */ }

    V v(1); // use V(int)
    A a(2); // use V(int)
    B b(3); // use V()
    C c(4); // use V()
```

The order of destructor calls is defined to be the reverse order of appearance in the class declaration (members before bases). There is no way for the programmer to control this order – except by the declaration order. A virtual base is destroyed after all of its derived classes.

It might be worth mentioning that virtual destructors are (and always have been) allowed:

```
struct B { /* ... */ virtual ~B(); };

struct D : B { ~D(); };

void g() {
    B* p = new D;
    delete p;        // D::~D() is called
}
```

The word `virtual` was chosen for virtual base classes because of some rather vague conceptual similarities to virtual functions and to avoid introducing yet another keyword.

Abstract Classes

One of the purposes of static type checking is to detect mistakes and inconsistencies before a program is run. It was noted that a significant class of detectable errors was escaping C++'s checking. To add insult to injury, the language actually forced programmers to write extra code and generate larger programs to make this happen.

Consider the classic "shape" example. Here, we must first declare a class shape to represent the general concept of a shape. This class needs two virtual functions rotate() and draw(). Naturally, there can be no objects of class shape, only objects of specific shapes. Unfortunately, C++ did not provide a way of expressing this simple notion.

The C++ rules specify that virtual functions, such as rotate() and draw(), must be defined in the class in which they are first declared. The reason for this requirement is to ensure that traditional linkers can be used to link C++ programs and to ensure that it is not possible to call a virtual function that has not been defined. So the programmer writes something like this:

```
class shape {
    point center;
    color col;
    // ...
public:
    where() { return center; }
    move(point p) { center=p; draw(); }
    virtual void rotate(int) { error("cannot rotate"); abort(); }
    virtual void draw() { error("cannot draw"); abort(); }
    // ...
};
```

This ensures that innocent errors such as forgetting to define a draw() function for a class derived from shape and silly errors such as creating a "plain" shape and attempting to use it cause run time errors. Even when such errors are not made, memory can easily get cluttered with unnecessary virtual tables for classes such as shape and with functions that are never called, such as draw() and rotate(). The overhead for this can be noticeable.

The solution is simply to allow the user to say that a virtual function does not have a definition; that is, it is a "pure virtual function." This is done by an initializer =0:

```
class shape {
    point center;
    color col;
    // ...
public:
    where() { return center; }
    move(point p) { center=point; draw(); }
    virtual void rotate(int) = 0;   // pure virtual function
    virtual void draw() = 0;        // pure virtual function
    // ...
};
```

A class with one or more pure virtual functions is an abstract class. An abstract class can only be used as a base for another class. In particular, it is not possible to create objects of an abstract class. A class derived from an abstract class must either define the pure virtual functions from its base or again declare them to be pure virtual functions.

The notion of pure virtual functions was chosen over the idea of explicitly declaring a class to be abstract because the selective definition of functions is much more flexible.

Static Member Functions

A static data member of a class is a member for which there is only one copy rather than one per object and which can be accessed without referring to any particular object of the class it is a member of. The reason for using static members is to reduce the number of global names, to make obvious which static objects logically belong to which class, and to be able to apply access control to their names. This is a boon for library providers since it avoids polluting the global name space and thereby allow easier writing of library code and safer use of multiple libraries.

These reasons apply for functions as well as for objects. In fact, *most* of the names a library provider wants local are function names. It was also observed that nonportable code, such as

```
((X*)0)->f();
```

was used to simulate static member functions. This trick is a time bomb because sooner or later someone will make an `f()` that is used this way `virtual` and the call will fail horribly because there is no X object at address zero. Even where `f()` is not virtual such calls will fail under some implementations of dynamic linking,

A static member function is a member so that its name is in the class scope and the usual access control rules apply. A static member function is not associated with any particular object and need not be called using the special member function syntax. For example:

```
class X {
    int mem;
    static int smem;
public:
    static void f(int,X*);
};

void g()
{
    X obj;
    f(1,&obj);       // error (unless there really is
                     // a global function f())
    X::f(1,&obj);    // fine
    obj.f(1,&obj);   // also fine
}
```

Since a static member function isn't called for a particular object it has no `this` pointer and cannot access non-static members without explicitly specifying an object. For example:

```
void X::f(int i, X* p)
{
    mem = i;       // error: which mem?
    p->mem = i;    // fine
    smem++;        // fine: only one smem
}
```

const *Member Functions*

Consider this example:

```
class s {
    int aa;
public:
    void mutate() { aa++; }
    int value() { return aa; }
};
void g()
{
    s o1;
    const s o2;
    o1.mutate();
    o2.mutate();
    int i = o1.value() + o2.value();
}
```

It seems clear that the call o2.mutate() ought to fail since o2 is a const.

The reason this rule until now has not been enforced is simply that there was no way of distinguishing a member function that may be invoked on a const object from one that may not. In general, the compiler cannot deduce which functions will change the value of an object. For example, had mutate() been defined in a separately compiled source file the compiler would not have been able to detect the problem at compile time.

The solution to this has two parts. First const is enforced so that "ordinary" member functions cannot be called for a const object. Then we introduce the notion of a const member function, that is, a member function that may be called for all objects including const objects. For example:

```
class X {
    int aa;
public:
    void mutate() { aa++; }
    int value() const { return aa; }
};
```

Now X::value() is guaranteed not to change the value of an object and can be used on a const object whereas X::mutate() can only be called for non-const objects:

```
int g()
{
    X o1;
    const X o2;
    o1.mutate();          // fine
    o2.mutate();          // error
    return o1.value() + o2.value(); // fine
}
```

In a const member function of X the this pointer points to a const X. This ensures that non-devious attempts to modify the value of an object through a const member will be caught:

```
class X {
    int a;
    void cheat() const { a++; } // error
};
```

Note that the use of const as a suffix to () is consistent with the use of const as a suffix to *.

It is occasionally useful to have objects that appear as constants to users but do in fact change their state. Such classes can be written using explicit casts:

```
class XX {
    int a;
    int calls_of_f;
    int f() const { ((XX*)this)->calls_of_f++; return a; }
    // ...
};
```

Since this can be quite deceptive and is error-prone in some contexts it is often better to represent the variable part of such an object as a separate object:

```
class XX {
    int a;
    int& calls_of_f;
    int f() const { calls_of_f++; return a; }
    // ...
    XX() : calls_of_f(*new int) { /* ... */ }
    ~XX() { delete &calls_of_f; /* ... */ }
    // ...
};
```

Initialization of static Members

A static data member of a class must be defined somewhere. The static declaration in the class declaration is only a declaration and does not set aside storage or provide an initializer.

This is a change from the original C++ definition of static members, which relied on implicit definition of static members and on implicit initialization of such members to 0. Unfortunately, this style of initialization cannot be used for objects of all types. In particular, objects of classes with constructors cannot be initialized this way. Furthermore, this style of initialization relied on linker features that are not universally available. Fortunately, in the implementations where this used to work it will continue to work for some time, but conversion to the stricter style described here is strongly recommended.

Here is an example:

```
class X {
    static int i;
    int j;
    X(int);
    int read();
};
class Y {
    static X a;
    int b;
    Y(int);
    int read();
};
```

Now X::i and Y::a have been declared and can be referred to, but somewhere definitions must be provided. The natural place for such definitions is with the definitions of the class member functions. For example:

```
// file X.c:
X::X(int jj) { j = jj; }
int X::read() { return j; }
int X::i = 3;

// file Y.c:
Y::Y(int bb) { b = bb; }
int Y::read() { return b; }
X Y::a = 7;
```

Pointers to Members

As mentioned in [5], it was an obvious deficiency that there was no way of expressing the concept of a pointer to a member of a class in C++. This lead to the need to "cheat" the type system in cases, such as error handling, where pointers to functions are traditionally used. Consider this example:

```
struct S {
    int mf(char*);
};
```

The structure S is declared to be a (trivial) type for which the member function mf is declared. Given a variable of type S the function mf can be called:

```
S a;
int i = a.mf("hello");
```

The question is *"What is the type of mf?"*

The equivalent type of a non-member function

```
int f(char*);
```

is

```
int (char*)
```

and a pointer to such a function is of type

```
int (*)(char*)
```

Such pointers to "normal" functions are declared and used like this:

```
int f(char*);               // declare function
int (*pf)(char*) = &f;      // declare and init pointer to function
int i = (*pf)("hello");     // call function through pointer
```

A similar syntax is introduced for pointers to members of a specific class. In a definition mf appears as

```
int S::mf(char*)
```

The type of S::mf is

```
int S:: (char*)
```

that is, "member of S that is a function that takes a char* argument and returns an int." A pointer to such a function is of type

```
int (S::*)(char*)
```

That is, the notation for pointer to member of class S is S::*. We can now write:

```
    // declare and initialize pointer to member function
int (S::*pmf)(char*) = &S::mf;

S a;
    // call function through pointer for the object ''a''
int i = (a.*pmf)("hello");
```

The syntax isn't exactly pretty, but neither is the C syntax it is modeled on.

A pointer to member function can also be called given a pointer to an object:

```
S* p;
    // call function through pointer for the object ''*p'':
int i = (p->*pmf)("hello");
```

In this case, we might have to handle virtual functions:

```
struct B {
    virtual f();
};
```

```
struct D : B {
     f();
};
int ff(B* pb, int (B::*pbf)())
{
     return (pb->*pbf)();
};
void gg()
{
     D dd;
     int i = ff(&dd, &B::f);
}
```

This causes a call of D::f(). Naturally, the implementation involves a lookup in dd's table of virtual functions exactly as a call to a virtual function that is identified by name rather than by a pointer. The overhead compared to a "normal function call" is the usual about 5 memory references (dependent on the machine architecture).

It is also possible to declare and use pointers to members that are not functions:

```
struct S {
     int mem;
};
int S::* psm = &S::mem;
void f(S* ps)
{
     ps->*psm = 2;
}
void g()
{
     S a;
     f(&a);
}
```

This is a complicated way of assigning 2 to a.mem.

Pointers to members are described in greater detail in [11].

User-Defined Free Store Management

C++ provides the operators new and delete to allocate memory on the free store and to release store allocated this way for reuse. Occasionally a user needs a finer-grained control of allocation and deallocation. The first section below shows "the bad old way" of doing this and the following sections show how the usual scope and overloaded function resolution mechanisms can be exploited to achieve similar effects more elegantly. This means that assignment to this is an anachronism and will be removed from the implementations of C++ after a decent interval. This will allow the type of this in a member function of class X to be changed to X *const.

Assignment to this

If a user wanted to take over allocation of objects of a class X the only way used to be to assign to this on each path through every constructor for X. Similarly, the user could take control of deallocation by assigning to this in a destructor. This is a very powerful and general mechanism. It is also non-obvious, error prone, repetitive, too subtle when derived classes are used, and essentially unmanageable when multiple inheritance is used. For example:

```
class X {
    int on_free_store;
    // ...
public:
    X();
    X(int i);
    ~X();
    // ...
}
```

Every constructor needs code to determine when to use the user-defined allocation strategy:

```
X::X() {
    if (this == 0) {           // 'new' used
        this = myalloc(sizeof(X));
        on_free_store = 1;
    }
    else {               // static, automatic, or member of aggregate
        this = this; // forget this assignment at your peril
        on_free_store = 0;
    }
    // initialize
}
```

The assignments to this are "magic" in that they suppress the usual compiler generated allocation code.

Similarly, the destructor needs code to determine when to use the user-defined de-allocation strategy and must use an assignment to this to indicate that it has taken control over deallocation:

```
X::~X() {
    // cleanup
    if (on_free_store) {
        myfree(this);
        this = 0;        // forget this assignment at your peril
    }
}
```

This user-defined allocation and de-allocation strategy isn't inherited by derived classes in the usual way.

The fundamental problem with the "assign to this" approach to user-controlled memory management is that initialization and memory management code are intertwined in an ad hoc manner. In particular, this implies that the language cannot provide any help with these critical activities.

Class-Specific Free Store Management

The alternative is to overload the allocation function operator new() and the deallocation function operator delete() for a class X:

```
class X {
    // ...
public:
    void* operator new(size_t sz) { return myalloc(sz); }
    void operator delete(X* p) { myfree(p); }

    X() { /* initialize */ }
    X(int i) { /* initialize */ }

    ~X() { /* cleanup */ }

    // ...
};
```

The type `size_t` is an implementation defined integral type used to hold object sizes.[7] It is the type of the result of `sizeof`.

Now `X::operator new()` will be used instead of the global `operator new()` for objects of class `X`. Note that this does not affect other uses of operator new within the scope of `X`:

```
void* X::operator new(size_t s)
{
    void* p = new char[s];   // global operator new as usual
    //...
    return p;
}
void X::operator delete(X* p)
{
    //...
    delete (void*) p;        // global operator delete as usual
}
```

When the new operator is used to create an object of class `X`, operator new() is found by a lookup starting in `X`'s scope so that `X::operator new()` is preferred over a global `::operator new()`.

Inheritance of `operator new()`

The usual rules for inheritance apply:

```
class Y : public X        // objects of class Y are also allocated
{                         // using X::operator new
    // ...
};
```

This is the reason `X::operator new()` needs an argument specifying the amount of store to be allocated; `sizeof(Y)` is typically different from `sizeof(X)`. Naturally, a class that is never a base class need not use the size argument:

```
void* Z::operator new(size_t) { return next_free_Z(); }
```

This optimization should not be used unless the programmer is perfectly sure that `Z` is never used as a base class because if it is disaster will happen.

An `operator new()`, be it local or global, is used only for free store allocation so

---

[7]`operator new()` used to require a `long`; `size_t` was adopted to bring C++ allocation mechanisms into line with ANSI C.

```
X a1;                     // allocated statically
void f()
{
    X a;                  // allocated on the stack
    X v[10];              // allocated on the stack
}
```

does not involve any operator new(). Instead, store is allocated statically and on the stack.

X::operator new() is only used for individual objects of class X (and objects of classes derived from class X that do not have their own operator new()) so

```
X* p = new X[10];
```

does not involve X::operator new() because X[10] is an array.

Like the global operator new(), X::operator new() returns a void*. This indicates that it returns uninitialized memory. It is the job of the compiler to ensure that the memory returned by this function is converted to the proper type and – if necessary – initialized using the appropriate constructor. This is exactly what happens for the global operator new().

X::operator new() and X::operator delete() are static member functions. In particular, they have no this pointer. This reflects the fact that X::operator new() is called before constructors so that initialization has not yet happened and X::operator delete() is called after the destructor so that the memory no longer holds a valid object of class X.

Overloading operator new()
Like other functions, operator new() can be overloaded. Every operator new() must return a void* and take a size_t as its first argument. For example:

```
void* operator new(size_t sz);   // the usual allocator

void* operator new(size_t sz, heap* h)   // allocate from heap 'h'
{
    return h->allocate(sz);
}

void* operator new(size_t, void* p)   // place object at 'p'
{
    return p;
}
```

The size argument is implicitly provided when operator new is used. Subsequent arguments must be explicitly provided by the user. The notation used to supply these additional arguments is an argument list placed immediately after the new operator itself.

```
static char buf [sizeof(X)];    // static buffer

class heap {
    // ...
};

heap h1;
```

```
f() {
    X* p1 = new X;          // use the default allocator
                            // operator new(size_t sz):
                            // operator new(sizeof(X))

    X* p3 = new(&h1) X;     // use h1's allocator
                            // operator new(size_t sz, heap* h):
                            // operator new(sizeof(X),&h1)

    X* p2 = new(buf) X;     // explicit allocation in 'buf'
                            // operator new(size_t, void* p):
                            // operator new(sizeof(X),buf)
}
```

Note that the explicit arguments go after the new operator but before the type. Arguments after the type goes to the constructor as ever. For example:

```
class Y {
    void* operator new(size_t, const char*);
    Y(const char*);
};

Y* p = new("string for the allocator")
                Y("string for the constructor");
```

Controlling Deallocation

Where many different operator new() functions are used one might imagine that one would need many different and matching operator delete() functions. This would, however, be quite inconvenient and often unmanageable. The fundamental difference between creation and deletion of objects is that at the point of creation the programmer knows just about everything worth knowing about the object whereas at the point of deletion the programmer holds only a pointer to the object. This pointer may not even give the exact type of the object, but only a base class type. It will therefore typically be unreasonable to require the programmer writing a delete to choose among several variants.[8]

Consider a class with two allocation functions and a single deallocation function that chooses the proper way of deallocating based on information left in the object by the allocators:

```
class X {
    enum { somehow, other_way } which_allocator;

    void* operator new(size_t sz)
    {       void* p = allocate_somehow();
            ((X*)p)->which_allocator = somehow;
            return p;
    }

    void* operator new(size_t sz , int i)
    {       void* p = allocate_some_other_way();
            ((X*)p)->which_allocator = other_way;
            return p;
    }

    void operator delete(void*);
    // ...
};
```

---

[8]The requirement that a programmer must distinguish between delete p for an individual object and delete[n] p for an array is an unfortunate hack and is mitigated only by the fact that there is nothing that forces a programmer to use such arrays.

Here operator delete() can look at the information left behind in the object by the operator new() used and deallocate appropriately:

```
void X::operator delete(void* p)
{
    switch (((X*)p)->which_allocator) {
    case somehow:
        deallocate_somehow();
        break;
    case other_way:
        deallocate_some_other_way();
        break;
    default:
        /* something is funny */
    }
}
```

Since operator new() and operator delete() are static member functions they need to cast their "object pointers" to use member names. Furthermore, these functions will be invoked only by explicit use of operators new and delete. This implies that X::which_allocator is not initialized for automatic objects so in that case it may have an arbitrary value. In particular, the default case in X::operator delete() might occur if someone tried to delete an automatic (on the stack) object.

Where (as will often be the case) the rest of the member functions of X have no need for examining the information stored by allocators for use by the deallocator this information can be placed in storage outside the object proper ("in the container itself") thus decreasing the memory requirement for automatic and static objects of class X. This is exactly the kind of game played by "ordinary" allocators such as the C malloc() for managing free store.

The example of the use of assignment to this above contains code that depends on knowing whether the object was allocated by new or not. Given local allocators and deallocators, it is usually neither wise nor necessary to do so. However, in a hurry or under serious compatibility constraints, one might use a technique like this:

```
class X {
    static X* last_X;
    int on_free_store;
    // ...

    X();

    void* operator new(long s)
    {
        return last_X = allocate_somehow();
    }
    // ...
};
X::X()
{
    if (this == last_X) { // on free store
        on_free_store = 1;
    }
    else {  // static or automatic or member of aggregate
            on_free_store = 0;
    }
    // ...
}
```

Note that there is no simple and implementation independent way of determining that an object is allocated on the stack. There never was.

Placement of Objects

For ordinary functions it is possible to specifically call a non-member version of the function by prefixing a call with the scope resolution operator `::`. For example,

```
::open(filename,"rw");
```

calls the global `open()`. Prefixing a use of the new operator with `::` has the same effect for `operator new()`; that is,

```
X* p = ::new X;
```

uses a global `operator new()` even if a local `X::operator new()` has been defined. This is useful for placing objects at specific addresses (to cope with memory mapped I/O, etc.) and for implementing container classes that manage storage for the objects they maintain. Using `::` ensures that local allocation functions are not used and the argument(s) specified for new allows selection among several global `operator new()` functions. For example:

```
// place object at address p:
void* operator new(size_t, void* p) { return p; }

char buf [sizeof(X)];    // static buffer

f()
{
    X* p = ::new(buf) X;   // explicit allocation in 'buf'
    p = ::new((void*)0777) X;     // place an X at address 0777
}
```

Naturally, for most classes the `::` will be redundant since most classes do not define their own allocators. The notation `:: delete` can be used similarly to ensure use of a global deallocator.

Memory Exhaustion

Occasionally, an allocator fails to find memory that it can return to its caller. If the allocator must return in this case, it should return the value 0. A constructor will return immediately upon finding itself called with `this==0` and the complete new expression will yield the value 0. In the absence of more elegant error handling schemes, this enables critical software to defend itself against allocation problems. For example:

```
void f()
{
    X* p = new X;
    if (p == 0) { /* handle allocation error */ }
    // use p
}
```

The use of a new_handler[5] can make most such checks unnecessary.

Explicit Calls of Destructors

Where an object is explicitly "placed" at a specific address or in some other way allocated so that no standard deallocator can be used, there might still be a need to destroy the object. This can be done by an explicit call of the destructor:

```
p->X::~X();
```

The fully qualified form of the destructor's name must be used to avoid potential parsing ambiguities. This requirement also alerts the user that something unusual is going on. After the call of the destructor, p no longer points to a valid object of class X.

Size Argument to operator delete()

Like X::operator new(), X::operator delete() can be overloaded, but since there is no mechanism for the user to supply arguments to a deallocation function this overloading simply presents the programmer with a way of using the information available in the compiler. X::operator delete() can have two forms (only):

```
class X {
    void operator delete(void* p);
    void operator delete(void* p, size_t sz);
    // ...
};
```

If the second form is present it will be preferred by the compiler and the second argument will be the size of the object to the best of the compiler's knowledge. This allows a base class to provide memory management services for derived classes:

```
class X {
    void* operator new(size_t sz);
    void operator delete(void* p, size_t sz);

    virtual ~X();
    // ...
};
```

The use of a virtual destructor is crucial for getting the size right in cases where a user deletes an object of a derived class through a pointer to the base class:

```
class Y : public X {
    // ...
    ~Y();
};

X* p = new Y;
delete p;
```

Assignment and Initialization

C++ originally had assignment and initialization default defined as bitwise copy of an object. This caused problems when an object of a class with assignment was used as a member of a class that did not have assignment defined:

```
class X {
    // ...
public:
    X& operator=(const X&);
    // ...
};
class Y {
    X a;
    // ...
};
```

```
void f()
{
    Y y1, y2;
    // ...
    y1 = y2;
}
```

Assuming that assignment was not defined for Y, y2.a is copied into y1.a with a bitwise copy. This invariably turns out to be an error and the programmer has to add an assignment operator to class Y:

```
class Y {
    X a;
    // ...
    const Y& operator=(const Y& arg)
    {
        a = arg.a;
        // ...
    }
};
```

In order to cope with this problem in general, assignment in C++ is now defined as memberwise assignment of non-static members and base class objects.[9] Naturally, this rule applies recursively until a member of a built-in type is found. This implies that for a class X, X(const X&) and const X& X::operator=(const X&) will be supplied where necessary by the compiler, as has always been the case for X::X() and X::~X(). In principle every class X has X::X(), X::X(const X&), and X::operator=(const X&) defined. In particular, defining a constructor X::X(T) where T isn't a variant of X& does not affect the fact that X::X(const X&) is defined. Similarly, defining X::operator=(T) where T isn't a variant of X& does not affect the fact that X::operator=(const X&) is defined.

To avoid nasty inconsistencies between the predefined operator=() functions and user defined operator=() functions, operator=() must be a member function. Global assignment functions such as ::operator=(X&, const X&) are anachronisms and will be disallowed after a decent interval.

Note that since access controls are correctly applied to both implicit and explicit copy operations we actually have a way of prohibiting assignment of objects of a given class X:

```
class X {
    // Objects of class X cannot be copied
    // except by members of X
    void operator=(X&);
    X(X&);
    // ...
public:
    X(int);
    // ...
};
void f() {
    X a(1);
    X b = a;        // error: X::X(X&) private
    b = a;          // error: X::operator=(X&) private
}
```

---

[9]One could argue that the original definition of C++ was inconsistent in requiring bitwise copy of objects of class Y, yet guaranteeing that X::operator=() would be applied for copying objects of a class X. In this case both guarantees cannot be fulfilled.

The automatic creation of `X::X(const X&)` and `X::operator=(const X&)` has interesting implications on the legality of some assignment operations. Note that if `X` is a public base class of `Y` then a `Y` object is a legal argument for a function that requires an `X&`. For example:

```
class X { public: int aa; };
class Y : public X { public: int bb; };
void f() {
    X xx;
    Y yy;
    xx = yy;        // ok: a Y is an X
                    //     xx=yy; means xx.operator=((X&)yy);
                    //     and is optimized to xx.aa = yy.aa
}
```

Defining assignment as memberwise assignment implies that `operator=()` isn't inherited in the ordinary manner. Instead, the appropriate assignment operator is – if necessary – generated for each class. This implies that the "opposite" assignment of an object of a base class to a variable of a derived class is illegal as ever:

```
void f() {
    X xx;
    Y yy;
    yy = xx;        // error: an X is not a Y
}
```

The extension of the assignment semantics to allow assignment of an object of a derived class to a variable of a public base class had been repeatedly requested by users. The direct connection to the recursive memberwise assignment semantics became clear only through work on the two apparently independent problems.

Operator `->`

Until now `->` has been one of the few operators a programmer couldn't define. This made it hard to create classes of objects intended to behave like "smart pointers." When overloading, `->` is considered a unary operator (of its left hand operand) and `->` is reapplied to the result of executing `operator->()`. Hence the return type of an `operator->()` function must be a pointer to a class or an object of a class for which `operator->()` is defined. For example:

```
struct Y { int m; };

class X {
    Y* p;
    // ...
    Y* operator->() {
        if (p == 0) {
            // initialize p
        }
        else {
            // check p
        }
        return p;
    }
    // ...
};
```

Here, class `X` is defined so that objects of type `X` act as pointers to objects of class `Y`, except that some suitable computation is performed on each access.

```
void f(X x, X& xr, X* xp)
{
    x->m;    // x.p->m
    xr->m;   // xr.p->m
    xp->m;   // error: X does not have a member m
}
```

Like operator=(), operator[](), and operator()(), operator->()
must be a member function (unlike operator+(), operator-(), opera-
tor<(), etc., that are often most useful as friend functions).

The dot operator still cannot be overloaded.

For ordinary pointers, use of -> is synonymous with some uses of unary *
and [ ]. For example, for

```
Y* p;
```

it holds that:

```
p->m == (*p).m == p[0].m
```

As usual, no such guarantee is provided for user-defined operators. The
equivalence can be provided where desired:

```
class X {
    Y* p;
public:
    Y* operator->() { return p; }
    Y& operator*() { return *p; }
    Y& operator[](int i) { return p[i]; }
};
```

If you provide more than one of these operators it might be wise to provide
the equivalence exactly as it is wise to ensure that x+=1 has the same effect as
x=x+1 for a simple variable x of some class if +=, =, and + are provided.

The overloading of -> is important to a class of interesting programs, just
like overloading [ ], and not just a minor curiosity. The reason is that *indirection* is a key concept and that overloading -> provides a clean, direct, and
efficient way of representing it in a program. Another way of looking at
operator -> is to consider it a way of providing C++ with a limited, but very
useful, form of *delegation[2]*.

Operator ,

Until now the comma operator , has been one of the few operators a programmer couldn't define. This restriction did not appear to have any purpose so it
has been removed. The most obvious use of an overloaded comma operator is
list building:

```
class X { /* ... */ };

class Xlist {
    // ...
public:
    Xlist();
    Xlist(const X&);
    friend Xlist operator,(const X&, const X&);
};
void f()
{
    X a,b,c;
    Xlist xl = (a,b,c);       // meaning operator,(operator,(a,b),c)
}
```

If you have a bit of trouble deciding which commas mean what in this example you have found the reason overloading of comma was originally left out.

Initialization of static Objects

In C, a static object can only be initialized using a slightly extended form of constant expressions. In C++, it has always been possible to use completely general expressions for the initialization of static class objects. This feature has now been extended to static objects of all types. For example:

```
#include <math.h>
double sqrt2 = sqrt(2);
main()
{
    if (sqrt(2)!=sqrt2) abort();
}
```

Such dynamic initialization is done in declaration order within a file and before the first use of any object or function defined in the file. No order is defined for initialization of objects in different source files except that all static initialization takes place before any dynamic initialization.

Resolutions

This section does not describe additions to C++ but gives answers to questions that have been asked often and do not appear to have clear enough answers in the reference manual[5]. These resolutions involve slight changes compared to earlier rules. This was done to bring C++ closer to the ANSI C draft.

Function Argument Syntax

Like the C syntax, the C++ syntax for specifying types allows the type int to be implicit in some cases. This opens the possibility of ambiguities. In argument declarations, C++ chooses the longest type possible when there appears to be a choice:

```
typedef long I;
f1(const I);    // f1() takes an unnamed 'const long' argument
f2(const i);    // f2() takes a 'const int' argument (called 'i')
```

This rule applies to the const and volatile specifiers, but not to unsigned, short, long, or signed:

```
f3(unsigned int I); // ok
f4(unsigned I);     // ok: equivalent to f4(unsigned int I);
```

A type cannot contain two basic type specifiers; these are legal:

```
f5(char I) { I++; }
f6(I I) { I++; }
```

Declaration and Expression Syntax

There is an ambiguity in the C++ grammar involving *expression-statements* and *declarations*: An *expression-statement* with a "function style" explicit type conversion as its leftmost sub-expression can be indistinguishable from a *declaration* where the first *declarator* starts with a (. For example:

```
    T(a);              // declaration or type conversion of 'a'
```
In those cases the *statement* is a *declaration*.

To disambiguate, the whole *statement* may have to be examined to determine if it is an *expression-statement* or a *declaration*. This disambiguates many examples. For example, assume T is the name of some type:

```
    T(a)->m = 7;       // expression-statement
    T(a)++;            // expression-statement
    T(a,5)<<c;         // expression-statement
    T(*d)(double(3));  // expression-statement

    T(*e)(int);        // declaration
    T(f)[];            // declaration
    T(g) = { 1, 2 };   // declaration
```

The remaining cases are *declarations*. For example:

```
    T(a);         // declaration
    T(*b)();      // declaration
    T(c)=7;       // declaration
    T(d),e,f=3;   // declaration
    T(g)(h,2);    // declaration
```

The disambiguation is purely syntactic; that is, the meaning of the names, beyond whether they are names of types or not, is not used in the disambiguation.

This resolution has two virtues compared to alternatives: It is simple to explain and completely compatible with C. The main snag is that it is not well adapted to simple minded parsers, such as YACC, because the lookahead required to decide what is an *expression-statement* and what is a *declaration* in a statement context is not limited.

However, note that a simple lexical lookahead can help a parser disambiguate most cases. Consider analysing a *statement*; the troublesome cases look like this

```
    T ( d-or-e )  tail
```

Here, *d-or-e* must be a *declarator*, an *expression*, or both for the statement to be legal. This implies that *tail* must be a semicolon, something that can follow a parenthesized *declarator* or something that can follow a parenthesized *expression*. That is, an *initializer*, const, volatile, (or [or a postfix or infix operator.

A user can explicitly disambiguate cases that appear obscure. For example:

```
void f()
{
    auto int(*p)();    // explicitly declaration
    (void) int(*p)();  // explicitly expression-statement
    0,int(*p)();       // explicitly expression-statement
    (int(*p)());       // explicitly expression-statement
    int(*p)();         // resolved to declaration
}
```

Enumerators

An enumeration is a type. Each enumeration is distinct from all other types. The set of possible values for an enumeration is its set of enumerators. The type of an enumerator is its enumeration. For example:

```
enum wine { red, white, rose, bubbly };
enum beer { ale, bitter, lager, stout };
```

defines two types, each with a distinct set of 4 values.

```
wine w = red;
beer b = bitter;

w = b;      // error, type mismatch: beer assigned to wine
w = stout;  // error, type mismatch: beer assigned to wine
w = 2;      // error, type mismatch: int assigned to wine
```

Each enumerator has an integer value and can be used wherever an integer is required; in such cases the integer value is used:

```
int i = rose; // the value of 'rose' (that is 2) is used
i = b;        // the value of 'b' is assigned to 'i'
```

This interpretation is stricter than what has been used in C++ until now and stricter than most C dialects. The reason for choosing it was ANSI C's requirement that enumerations be distinct types. Given that, the details follow from C++'s emphasis on type checking and the requirements of consistency to allow overloading, etc. For example:

```
int f(int);
int f(wine);

void g()
{
    f(i);       // f(int)
    f(w);       // f(wine)

    f(1);       // f(int)
    f(white);   // f(wine)

    f(b);       // f(int), standard conversion
                //         from beer to int used
}
```

C++'s checking of enumerations is stricter than ANSI C's, in that assignments of integers to enumerations are disallowed. As ever, explicit type conversion can be used:

```
w = wine(257);   /* caveat emptor */
```

An enumerator is entered in the scope in which the enumeration is defined. In this context, a class is considered a scope and the usual access control rules apply. For example:

```
class X {
    enum { x, y, z };
    // ...
public:
    enum { a, b, c };

    f(int i = a) { g(i+x); ... }
    // ...
}
void h() {
    int i = a; // error: 'X::a' is not in scope
    i = X::a;  // ok
    i = X::x;  // error: 'X::x' is private
}
```

The const *Specifier*

Use of the const specifier on a non-local object implies that linkage is *internal* by default (static); that is, the object declared is local to the file in wich it occurs. To give it external linkage it must be explicitly declared extern.

Similarly, inline implies that linkage is *internal* by default.

External linkage can be obtained by explicit declaration:

```
extern const double g;
const double g = 9.81;

extern inline f(int);
inline f(int i) { return i+c; }
```

Function Types

It is possible to define function types that can be used exactly like other types, except that variables of function types cannot be defined – only variables of pointer to function types:

```
typedef int F(char*);    // function taking a char* argument
                         // and returning an int
F* pf;                   // pointer to such function
F f;                     // error: no variables of function
                         //   type allowed
```

Function types can be useful in friend declarations. Here is an example from the C++ task system:

```
class task : public scheduler {
friend SIG_FUNC_TYP sig_func; // the type of a function must
                              //    be specified in a friend
                              //    function declaration
    // ...
}
```

The reason to use a `typedef` in the friend declaration `sig_func` and not simply to write the type directly is that the type of `signal()` is system dependent:

```
// BSD signal.h:
typedef void SIG_FUNC_TYP(int, int, sigcontext*);

// 9th edition signal.h:
typedef void SIG_FUNC_TYP(int);
```

Using the `typedef` allows the system dependencies to be localized where they belong: in the header files defining the system interface.

Lvalues

Note that the default definition of assignment of an X as a call of

```
    X& operator=(const X&)
```

makes assignment of Xs produce an lvalue. For uniformity, this rule has been extended to assignments of built-in types. By implication, +=, -=, *=, etc., now also produce lvalues. So – again by implication – does prefix ++ and -- (but not the postfix versions of these operators).

In addition, the comma and ?: can also produce lvalues. The result of a comma operation is an lvalue if its second operand is. The result of a ?: operator is an lvalue provided both its second and third operands are and provided they have exactly the same type.

Multiple Name Spaces

C provides a separate name space for structure tags whereas C++ places type names in the same name space as other names. This gives important notational conveniences to the C++ programmer but severe headaches to people managing header files in mixed C/C++ environments. For example:

```
struct stat {
    // ...
};
extern "C" int stat(const char*, struct stat *);
```

was not legal C++ though early implementations accepted it as a compatibility
hack. The experience has been that trying to impose the '"pure C++" single
name space solution (thus outlawing examples such as the one above) has
caused too much confusion and too much inconvenience to too many users.
Consequently, a slightly cleaned up version of the C/C++ compatibility hack
has now become part of C++. This follows the overall principle that where
there is a choice between inconveniencing compiler writers and annoying
users, the compiler writers should be inconvenienced.[10] It appears that the
compromise provided by the rules presented below enables all accepted uses
of multiple name spaces in C while preserving the notational convenience of
C++ in all cases where C compatibility isn't an essential issue. In particular,
every legal C++ program remains legal. The restrictions on the use of constructors and typedef names in connection with the use of multiple name
spaces are imposed to prevent some nasty cases of hard to detect ambiguities
that would cause trouble for the composition of C++ header files.

A typedef can declare a name to refer to the same type more than once. For
example:

```
typedef struct s { /* ... */ } s;
typedef s s;
```

A name s can be declared as a type (struct, class, union, enum) *and* as a
non-type (function, object, value, etc.) in a single scope. In this case, the name
s refers to the non-type and struct s (or whatever) can be used to refer to
the type. The order of declaration does not matter. This rule takes effect only
after both declarations of s have been seen. For example:

```
struct stat { /* ... */ };
stat a;
void stat(stat* p);
struct stat b;   // struct is needed to avoid the function name
stat(0);         // function call

int f(int);
f(1);
struct f { /* ... */ };
struct f a;      // struct is needed to avoid the function name
```

A name cannot simultaneously refer to two types:

```
struct s { /* ... */ };
typedef int s;  // error
```

The name of a class with a constructor cannot also simultaneously refer to
something else:

```
struct s { s(); /* ... */ };
int s();        // error

struct t* p;
int t();        // ok
int i = t();
struct t { t(); /* ... */ }      // error
i = t();
```

---

[10]sorry Jens, Mike, Mike, Mike, Phil, Walter, et al.

If a non-type name s hides a type name s, `struct s` can be used to refer to the type name. For example:

```
struct s { /* ... */ };
f(int s) { struct s a; s++; }
```

Note: If a type name hides a non-type name the usual scope rules apply:

```
int s;
f()
{
    struct s { /* ... */ }; // new 's' refers to the type
                            // and the global int is hidden
    s a;
}
```

Use of the `::` scope resolution operator implies that its argument is a non-type name. For example:

```
int s;
f()
{
    struct s { /* ... */ };
    s a;
    ::s = 1;
}
```

Function Declaration Syntax

To ease use of common C++ and ANSI C header files, void may be used to indicate that a function takes no arguments:

```
extern int f(void);            // same as ''extern int f();''
```

Conclusions

C++ is holding up nicely under the strain of large scale use in a diverse range of application areas. The extensions added so far have been have all been relatively easy to integrate into the C++ type system. The C syntax, especially the C declarator syntax, has consistently caused much greater problems than the C semantics; it remains barely manageable. The stringent requirements of compatibility and maintenance of the usual run-time and space efficiencies did not constrain the design of the new features noticeably. Except for the introduction of the keywords `catch`, `private`, `protected`, `signed`, `template`, and `volatile` the extensions described here are upward compatible. Users will find, however, that type-safe linkage, improved enforcement of const, and improved handling of ambiguities will force modification of some programs by detecting previously uncaught errors.

Acknowledgements

Most of the credit for these extensions goes to the literally hundreds of C++ users who provided me with bugs, mistakes, suggestions, and most importantly with sample problems.

Phil Brown, Tom Cargill, Jim Coplien, Steve Dewhurst, Keith Gorlen, Laura Eaves, Bob Kelley, Brian Kernighan, Andy Koenig, Archie Lachner, Stan Lippman, Larry Mayka, Doug McIlroy, Pat Philip, Dave Prosser, Peggy Quinn, Roger Scott, Jerry Schwarz, Jonathan Shopiro, and Kathy Stark supplied many valuable suggestions and questions.

The C++ multiple inheritance mechanism was partially inspired by the work of Stein Krogdahl from the University of Oslo[3].

References

[1] Tom Cargill: *PI: A Case Study in Object-Oriented Programming*. OOPSLA'86 Proceedings, pp 350-360, September 1986.

[2] Gul, Agha: *An Overview of Actor languages*. SIGPLAN Notices, pp 58-67, October 1986.

[3] Krogdahl, Stein: *An Efficient Implementation of Simula Classes with Multiple Prefixing*. Research Report No. 83 June 1984, University of Oslo, Institute of Informatics.

[4] Snyder, Alan: *Encapsulation and Inheritance in Object-Oriented Programming Languages*. SIG-PLAN Notices, November 1986, pp 38-45.

[5] Stroustrup, Bjarne: *The C++ Programming Language*. Addison-Wesley, 1986.

[6] Stroustrup, Bjarne: *Multiple Inheritance for C++* Proc. EUUG Spring'87 Conference. Helsinki. Also to appear in a future issue of Computing Systems.

[7] Stroustrup, Bjarne: *What is "Object-Oriented Programming"?* Proc. 1st European Conference on Object-Oriented Programming. Paris, 1987. Springer Verlag Lecture Notes in Computer Science, Vol 276, pp 51-70. Also in IEEE Software. May 1988.

[8] Stroustrup, Bjarne: *Possible Directions for C++* Proc. USENIX C++ workshop. Santa Fe, November 1987.

[9] Stroustrup, Bjarne: *Type-safe Linkage for C++* Proc. USENIX C++ conference. Denver, October 1988. Also in Computing Systems vol 1 no 4 Fall 1988.

[10] Stroustrup, Bjarne: *Parameterized Types for C++* Proc. USENIX C++ conference. Denver, October 1988. Also in Computing Systems vol 2 no 1 Spring 1989 and Journal of Object-Oriented Programming, January 1989.

[11] Stan Lippman and Bjarne Stroustrup: *Pointers to Members in C++* Proc. USENIX C++ conference. Denver, October 1988.

[12] Daniel Weinreb and David Moon: *Lisp Machine Manual*. Symbolics, Inc. 1981.

[13] Draft Proposed American National Standard X3J11/88/090 dated December 7, 1988.

Chapter 2

Possible Directions for C++

Bjarne Stroustrup

Abstract

C++ has shown itself an effective tool for programming in an extremely wide range of application areas. This paper examines the strengths and weaknesses of C++ and its associated tools in order to see what developments might yield significant further advantages to C++ users. The main topics for discussion are libraries, container classes, parameterized types, exception handling, incremental compilation, incremental linking and loading, object I/O, persistent objects, automatic storage management, and design methods.

Introduction

A programming language is only a small part of a programmer's world, but a very important part. The tools, techniques, libraries, and culture that surround a language, constituting what is often referred to as the programming environment, are of crucial importance.

No major program is ever written in the programming language as described in its basic language manual; libraries of all sorts are used and often determine the structure of the program. The naive user cannot even distinguish between a language and its basic support libraries; the experienced user often attaches so much importance to the available libraries that the language itself is considered of secondary importance.

Similarly, the compilation (or interpretation) environment determines the approach to program development, debugging, and testing. This again can shift the focus of attention away from the basic language.

However, a language is typically a crucial factor in the design of tools such as compilers and debuggers and in the design of libraries. This paper focuses on C++ as a base for building and using libraries and as a raw material for designers of programming support tools. The programming environment is considered from the point of view of how it can support such library building and how it can support the styles of programming that occur when large numbers of high-quality libraries are available.

My notion of high quality involves the idea of a definite structure of a program that can be documented and the idea that a library must be affordable. In C++, the structure is supported by a strong static type system with a flexible and general notion of encapsulation and interfaces. The concern for

From *Proceedings and Additional Papers*, USENIX C++ Workshop, pp. 399-416, Santa Fe, New Mexico, 1987.

affordability becomes an efficiency requirement: it doesn't matter how elegant a library is if it is too expensive to use.

C++ is taken to be the language as exists today (October 1987) with multiple inheritance, recursive memberwise assignment semantics, protected members, pointers to members, etc. For details of the evolution of C++ from the publication of *The C++ Programming Language*[10] to now see [12].

Naturally, the areas for improvement of C++ and its related tools and techniques considered here do not constitute an exhaustive list of areas in which one might do useful C++ related work. For example, the absence of a discussion of debuggers does not imply that nobody needs a C++ debugger. Furthermore, a mention of a solution or a technique here does not imply that that technique is the only solution to the problem it was designed to solve.

Libraries

The standard libraries shipped with a C++ translator are:

- streams for uniform, flexible, type-safe I/O;
- tasks for simulation and other applications requiring light-weight processes;
- complex numbers and basic complex functions;
- a set of macros for "faking" parameterized types;
- parameterized vector and stack classes.

In addition, many specialized libraries are available in local environments. Several obvious candidates for the standard library are in wide use within AT&T. For example:

- strings with a full set of operations;
- maps; that is, associative arrays;
- lists of various sorts;
- counted Pointers for automatic storage management of specific objects.

Most C++ users simply use the standard and not so standard C and Fortran libraries found on UNIX, VMS, MS-DOS, OS/2, or whatever operating system they use. This is a very important source of libraries since it grants the C++ programmer access to millions of lines of tested code.

The basic strength of C++ for library building is its facilities for defining efficient and type-safe classes where a single underlying type exists for a problem area. Examples are characters for string manipulation and pattern matching, floating point numbers for many kinds of numerical work, and bits, bytes, and pointers for many kinds of systems work. The basic weakness of C++ for library building is its lack of special features to support classes for which no such single underlying type exists. The best examples of such classes are container classes, such as sets, vectors, lists, and associative arrays.

Container Classes

The standard libraries that come with languages such as Smalltalk[2] and the object-oriented Lisp dialects[1, 13] show one possible direction of development. This style, relying mostly or even exclusively on dynamic type checking, can be used in C++ as demonstrated by Keith Gorlen's OOPS library[4]. This leads to flexible and general libraries suitable for open-ended program development. Such libraries have proven useful for exploratory and prototype development but high run-time cost has made such libraries uneconomical in applications with heavy computational components. There have also been problems in ensuring correctness of programs in large multi-person projects due to the lack of statically specified and verifiable interfaces.

An alternative style of library building can be found in the "generic" or "parameterized" types in Clu[6] and Ada[3]. Here, strong static typing is maintained with the obvious result of increasing efficiency while providing a more definite and solid program structure. To achieve run-time efficiency comparable with that of built-in types the basic operations on instances of such parameterized classes must (on most machine architectures) be implemented without function call overhead. Jonathan Shopiro's list classes[7] and Andy Koenig's associative array classes[5] demonstrate that this style can be used in C++. However, this style of libraries is not as flexible as the Smalltalk and Lisp libraries and not as supportive of the open-ended style of programming as one might like.

The Smalltalk-style of containers has the important benefit of providing a single common concept of a container from which all specific containers are derived. This allows a user to write code that does not have to deal with details of any particular container. For example, it is trivial to write a function that accepts any kind of container.

This is harder to achieve in the Clu-style where there is not necessarily a single concept of a container, just individual containers such as sets and sorted lists. The advantage of this approach is that the overhead of operations can be minimal; less than a function call for the simplest operations. Using the Smalltalk-style makes every operation on a container a method invocation. In C, of course, one would use special "hand coded" containers with minimal overhead. For the standard containers to be genuinely useful it must be possible to approximate the efficiency (in time and space) of the C approach where it matters.

The ability to write functions that depend only on a general concept of a container rather than on properties on individual containers is fundamental to the design of general utility functions and classes. If the Clu-style is adopted it must be augmented by a unifying container class concept.

A very attractive solution is to combine the two approaches by utilizing a set of basic and standard parameterized classes to provide efficiency and a definite static structure. These parameterized classes can then be instantiated for base types to provide the code sharing and polymorphism necessary for large open-ended systems. C++'s virtual functions are ideal for this in that they provide a way for a base class to present a strongly typed interface to a variety of derived classes.

The key feature needed in C++ to support this style of programming is parameterized types. Currently, in C++ one must rely on macros to "fake" parameterized types, but that approach does not work well except on a small scale.[1]

---

[1]Use of macros interposes a level of translation between the programmer and the programming support tools. This often renders such tools ineffective, as when the compiler reports errors at the

Parameterized Types

Assuming that C++ did have a proper set of features supporting parameterized types we could write:

```
#include <Vector.h>    // standard vector class
#include <Shape.h>     // standard geometric shape class

main()
{
    Vector<int> ivec(200);     // vector of 200 integers
    Vector<Shape*> svec(10);   // vector of 10 Shape pointers

    svec[0] = new Rectangle( ... );
    svec[1] = new Circle( ... );
    ...
    do_something(svec);
    ...
}
void do_something(Vector<Shape*>& v)
{
    for (int i = 0; i<v.size(); i++) {
        ...
        v[i]->draw();        // draw v[i] according to its type
        ...
    }
}
```

The Vector class might be declared like this:

```
class Vector<class T> {
    T* v;
    int sz;
public:
    Vector(int);
    ~Vector() { delete v; }

    T& operator[](int i);
    int size() { return sz; }
    ...
};
```

Why bother with container classes such as Vector? After all, if I want a vector of shapes I can write one in C++ in a couple of minutes. Here are some reasons for using a parameterized class rather than hand crafted classes:

- The more interesting container classes take much more than a couple of minutes to write.
- It is tedious and error-prone to re-write such classes for each element type.
- Programmers will soon learn to recognize and use standard container classes – hence programs will become more readable (to the experienced programmer if not to the complete novice).

---

point of use rather at the point of declaration for a macro. It also renders communication between different tools cumbersome, as when identifiers are unavailable to a symbolic debugger because they were expanded by the macro processor. Furthermore, the C preprocessor, cpp, used with C++ isn't elegant when it comes to multi-line macros and using it to "fake" parameterized types often presses both it and other tools to the limit. For example, it is not uncommon to find tools that cannot handle the 3000 character output lines you occasionally get from cpp when using these techniques.

· Standard container classes are more likely to be correct and more likely to have been optimized in some way – hence *both* program development and run-time performance will improve.

These benefits will only manifest themselves provided the use of such classes is both convenient and efficient enough. The macro approach is efficient enough, but not convenient. The Smalltalk-like use of dynamic typing to define standard container classes is convenient, but isn't efficient enough for many applications. Neither approach provides a proper type-safe foundation for the design of large systems. A proper mechanism for parameterized types is needed for that. Such a mechanism can and must be understood, relied on, and exploited by all major tools in the programming environment.

Type parameterization is most crucial for container classes because such classes can provide the glue used to bind systems together, but there are many other uses; probably the most obvious and important is that type parameterization will allow arithmetic functions to be parameterized over their basic number type so that programmers can (finally) get a uniform way of dealing with integers, single precision floating point numbers, double precision floating point numbers, etc.

Exception Handling

In any language it is difficult to cope with errors that are detected in one context but cannot be properly understood and handled except in some other context. For example, a compiler often detects a type or syntax error while analyzing an expression but can only recover by returning to the routines handling the statement level. Similarly, a system output routine may encounter an unusual state of its device and need to return to a higher level routine that has sufficient information to decide what to do about it. In both cases a normal return through the sequence of calls that led to the point of error is tedious and error prone since the "normal state" of the computation cannot be assumed and there is typically no good value to pass back as the return value. Coping with this for a particular kind of "error" is tedious, but feasible. Coping with all such cases leads to an explosion in code size and complexity. Not coping with such cases leads to disasters.

In higher level languages, some form of "exception handling" mechanism is often provided as part of the programming language. In C, one usually relies on `setjmp()` and `longjmp()` to cope with the nastier examples of such errors. Because of destructors the C solution is insufficient and C++ will eventually be forced to develop an exception handling mechanism. Consider a class X for which a destructor is defined:

```
void f()
    X a;
    g();
    // here we know how to handle disasters
}
g()
{
    X b;
    h();
}
```

```
h()
{
    X c;
    // here a disaster happens
}
```

The problem is that if f() knows how to recover from the problem found in h(), how does the control get back into f() in such a way that the destructors for c and b are called correctly?[2]

Here is what a solution might look like:

```
void f()
    X a;
    try {  // exception handler defined for statements in this
           // scope and all statements reached from calls made
           // in this scope
        g();
    }
    except {
           // here we know how to handle exceptions
           // we only get here if an exception was raised
    }
}
g()
{
    X b;
    h();
}
h()
{
    X c;
    if (something_strange_happened) except!  // raise exception
}
```

When the exception is raised the stack is unraveled and destructors called until a scope is reached in which an exception handler is defined. In this case, X::~X() is called for c and b before the exception handling code in f() is called.

There are many issues to consider when designing a mechanism for doing this in the context of C++. For example:

- Can there be many different exceptions?
- If so, how are they named?
- What is a good syntax?

However, some of the more important design issues are settled by the nature of C++:

- It is not possible for an exception handler to request that the program continue at the point where the exception was raised (destructors may have been called so that the context has been destroyed).
- The exception handling mechanism must function properly even when C++ functions call non-C++ functions and when non-C++ functions call C++ functions.

---

[2]If they needn't be called, the setjmp() approach is sufficient. Getting c destroyed properly can be handled easily by the compiler; the difficult case is b.

- The major run-time cost of the exception handling mechanism should be incurred when an exception is raised (and *not* at every function call or at every point where an exception handler is established).
- The implementation should be very simple to port (or else the exception handling mechanism might become a bottleneck for increased C++ use).

The alternative to having such an exception handling mechanism is to avoid the use of classes with destructors in contexts where "exceptions" may occur and use longjmp() to handle the exceptions. This approach isn't feasible in an environment where standard libraries are heavily used because a user typically will not know whether destructors are used in a particular call chain.

An exception handling mechanism would also be used as the standard mechanism by which library routines signal errors to their users. The (current) alternative is to rely on a variety of ad hoc methods.[3]

Special-Purpose Languages

Special-purpose languages can be an important source for ideas for library designers. Over the years, many languages have been designed to cope with specific problems either as special-purpose languages or as languages with "unusual" facilities supporting a specific application area. For example, consider the following languages as special-purpose languages (deliberately ignoring their general-purpose features):

Fortran	arithmetic
Snobol	pattern matching
APL	vector manipulation
Simula	simulation
Smalltalk	interactive user interfaces
Lisp	list manipulation
Awk	ASCII file manipulation
Prolog	logic programming
Ada	concurrency

The scope for "borrowing" features from such languages into C++ in the form of libraries rather than in the form of language extensions is large. For example, the simulation facility from Simula was relatively cleanly incorporated into C++ in the form of the task library and that library has recently been extended to cope with real-time for robot control[8]. The key here is C++'s ability to link to non-C++ code. In case of the task library, a few assembler instructions are used to manipulate machine registers to accomplish the basic co-routine context switch that cannot be implemented in C++ proper. For more delicate surgery, say for implementing a vector type using special vector operations available in a vector processor, **asms** in inline functions can be used to achieve non-C++ operations without the overhead of a function call.

---

[3]It could be argued that an exception handling mechanism is therefore essential for the design of large high-quality libraries, but I don't want to push that argument too far.

The alternative to borrowing key ideas as C++ libraries is either to make special-purpose language extensions or to use a special-purpose language instead of C++. The problem with the first alternative is language size and complexity; the problem with the second alternative is that it requires communication between the special-purpose language and a general-purpose language to implement a complete system. Such communication is notoriously hard to achieve except where one can afford to go through some language independent medium such as a UNIX pipe. Where it is easy to achieve such communication, as with closely related languages such as C++ and C, there isn't a problem in the first place.

Library building is no panacea, but to avoid language fragmentation one should consider the library building approach very seriously before undertaking a project to extend the language by modifying a compiler or by providing yet another preprocessor. The likelihood is that any such extension will drastically reduce its users' ability to take advantage of alternative C++ compilers and/or other tools built in environments where the extension isn't in use. Furthermore, any two independently designed extensions are unlikely to be compatible or to possess facilities for convenient and type-safe interaction between the two extensions.

Environment Support

An environment can support the programmer in two ways: by supporting the activity of programming (providing tools for designing, specifying, implementing, and debugging programs) and by providing a congenial environment for the final program to execute in (standard utility libraries, operating system interfaces, etc.).

For C++ at least, there will always be several different development and execution environments and there will be radical differences between such environments. It would be unrealistic to expect a common execution environment for, say, an Intel 80286 and a Cray XMP, and equally unrealistic to expect a common program development environment for an individual researcher and for a team of 200 programmers engaged in large scale development. It is also clear, however, that many techniques can be used to enhance both kinds of environments and that one must strive to exploit commonality wherever it makes sense. For example, incremental linking of classes can be used both to decrease the time needed for the debug cycle during program development and to enable incremental build-up of a user-interface in an interactive application. The system-dependent aspects of incremental linking can also be localized so that a common style of incremental linking of classes can be available on a large range of systems.

Assume C++ were extended with parameterized types and exception handling. This would make design of libraries easier. What support could be provided in the programming environment to make programming more convenient? Consider the steps in a traditional C or C++ compilation.

1. Run the preprocessor to incorporate the header files into the source.
2. Compile.
3. Link and search libraries for pre-compiled standard functions and data.

For C, the major part of the text processed (say 90%) is in the .c file that is often thought of as "the program." In C++, the header files are often larger than the .c file, and with a systematic use of libraries most of the source code (say 80%) will be in the header files defining classes, etc. Furthermore, in C most of the code in a final program typically comes from the user's (or users') .c files and relatively little (say 20%) is added from the library search. The libraries searched are typically small. This too will change. I expect most small C++ programs will search large libraries and that most (say 80%) of the final program will be found in some library or other.

The effect of all this is that whereas with C the speed of the compiler proper when processing .c files is the dominant factor in a compilation, with C++ processing headers, linking, and library lookup will dominate.

Incremental Compilation

An important observation about the scenario outlined above is that between successive compilations a user only changes a small fraction of the files. Typically only a minor change to one or more .c files is done. This implies that if the cost of re-compilation can be made proportional to the size of the change, rather than the traditional "proportional to the size of the files in which the change occurred plus the size of header files included by those files", then compilation of C++ programs using large libraries would become faster than traditional C compilations. A back of the envelope calculation suggests that a 20 times improvement in apparent compiler speed is feasible. I conclude that we need incremental compilation and some form of incremental loading to complement it.[4]

Incremental compilation clearly requires that "the compiler" can determine what the increment is. In other words, there must exist a program that determines what has changed between two compilations and how much must be compiled because of this change (a C++ dependency analyzer). There are several ways of ensuring the correct use of such a set of compilation tools. Using an editor that understands both is a common technique, but there is nothing in the concept of incremental compilation that requires an integrated environment with a dedicated editor/browser, debugger, etc.

The C equivalent to this is simply cc and make. The problem with make for C++ programs (as it is for C programs) is that make doesn't understand C, let alone C++. Therefore make decides on what to re-compile based only on the file structure used to store the program and not the structure of the program itself. These decisions are typically far too conservative; that is, make often decides to re-compile files that are unaffected by a change.

One problem that will have to be looked into is that like C, C++ does not have a very strong notion of a "module" that helps a "smart" C++ environment to maintain a correspondence between program fragments and the way they are stored.

---

[4]Using an interpreter during program development is an alternative. Such an interpreter would have to handle full context-dependent strong static type checking and would have to handle a mixture of compiled and interpreted code to be useful. I conjecture that the distinction between an interpreter and an incremental compiler isn't very significant in this context.

One extreme approach to this problem is to maintain the C convention of .c and .h files with no constraints on what kind of information is stored where. The opposite approach is to keep a program in a "program data base" of more or less compiled fragments. The storage of such fragments is organized exclusively by the program structure and the form in which they are kept is determined by the current state of the incremental compilation and linking. The fragments are annotated with with "useful information" such as dependency graphs, cross references, and time stamps.

It should be observed that keeping a "precompiled data base of classes" doesn't by itself provide rapid compilations. Typically, a "compiled form" of a class will be *larger* that its source language form and experience with Simula shows that it can easily take something like 85% of the time needed to compile a class declaration simply to read a precompiled version of the class and integrate its information into the compilers tables. Pre-compiling header files may be essential for providing rapid dependency analysis, but it is likely that additional techniques will have to be employed to achieve compile speed. This might involve merging many headers into "standard environments" that can be stored in a form where they can be read back into the compiler without expensive unraveling of linked structures and adjustment of pointer values.

The C preprocessor will probably become a problem when designing a "smart" C++ environment. The key weakness of cpp in this context is that a .h file has no semantic meaning in C or in C++.

I conjecture that there will soon be several "smart" C++ environments. In my opinion, the single most important design criterion for such programming environments should be that each and every one of them should be capable to read in a C++ program on the "standard and dumb" form of .h and .c files as described in *The C++ Programming Language* and be able to emit a version of every program developed in the environment in this form. This is essential to maintain portability of C++ programs across environments.

Similarly, one must not *in general* assume an integrated system of the kind where the program development environment and the program execution environment are indistinguishable. It must be possible to "break out" a "final program" for use in a specific execution environment. It should also be observed that typically a C++ programmer cannot assume that there is a programmer of any sort (let alone a C++ programmer) available when the program is executed in its intended environment. This implies that to the end-user an invocation of a smart debugging environment and an ignominious core dump are completely equivalent.

Incremental Linking and Loading

Incremental linking and loading are desirable for systems that are designed to allow a user to extend a running system. For example, in a CAD/CAM system it can be useful to allow a user to define a new kind of component and add it to a layout currently on the screen. Using traditional compile, load, and go techniques it is difficult to add the new component class to the layout program without having to re-create the "current layout" from scratch after re-compilation of the layout program. At best, there would be a noticeable disruption of service. A very similar example is a "user interface manager" that controls a user's interaction with application programs. Here, it can be useful to allow the user to add a new style of interaction but it would be most disruptive to stop, re-compile, and re-start the user interface manager to do so.

The key problem with incremental linking is to provide a way of adding a new class to a running program. To add a new class two problems have to be faced. It must be possible to define an interface to a yet-to-be-defined class and it must be possible to invoke operations on objects of the new class from the original program. The latter, incremental linking of functions, is a solved problem in most C environments. The former problem has a surprisingly clean and elegant solution in C++.

Traditionally, systems supporting incremental loading of classes have relied on some form of interpretation. A user can try any operation on such an object and it examines the request to decide if it can be accepted. If so, everything is fine and the operation is performed; if not, a run-time error ("method not found") occurs. In other words, static type-checking is impossible in such systems. This is unacceptable in many environments and clashes directly with the view that every object in a C++ program must be of a specific type so that the set of acceptable operations and argument types is known at compile time.

The virtual function mechanism of C++ allows objects to be manipulated in a type-safe manner without knowing their exact type. This mechanism can be exploited to support type-safe incremental linking.[5] If the new class is derived from an already existing class with virtual member functions, the interface of the base class can be used to type-check calls to member functions of the derived class; the virtual function mechanism provides the binding between old code and the new.

Here is an example of a way the virtual function concept might be used to achieve this kind of incremental loading of classes. All one needs to do is to supply a base class with a function new_object() that takes a string argument designating a new derived class. For example:

```
class shape {    // some base class
    ...
public:
    shape* new_object(const char *);
    ...
    virtual void rotate(int);   // functions defining an interface
    virtual void draw();        // for all classes derived
    ...                         // from shape
};
```

The new_object() function creates objects of classes that are undefined at the time when the program starts executing. For example:

```
shape* select(istream& input)
{
    shape* p;
    char class_name[MAX];
    // read name of shape class from 'input' into 'class_name'
    ...
    return p->new_object(class_name);
}
```

The class named by class_name must be a class derived from class shape. A object returned by select() can be used exactly like any other shape:

---

[5]The technique for type-safe incremental linking described here is due to Jonathan Shopiro.

```
void some_function(int n)
{
    shape* p = select(cin)
    for (int i = 1; i<n; i++) {
        p->draw();
        p->rotate(180/n);
    }
    ...
}
```

All calls to the new object have been statically type checked and the overheads are exactly the same (i.e., very low) as the overhead on operations on objects of classes known when the program was originally compiled. Clearly, this differs from the usual "shape example" of virtual functions *only* in that the derived class might be defined *after* the program started executing.

When shape::new_object() is called, a class of the specified name must have been defined as derived from shape. Alternatively, shape::new_object() might prompt the user to write one. The functions for this derived class must then be compiled (if they were not already compiled) and the functions are linked to the running program using whatever technique for incremental linking and loading is available.

It is crucial that new_object() can find a constructor for the new class in the object file. A call of that constructor is used to create the new object (of the new class). This relieves new_object() of the responsibility of knowing the layout of objects of the new class, the size of such objects, the virtual functions re-defined by the new class, etc. To avoid loading a class twice, new_object() maintains a table of known class names. Since the compiler didn't know about classes linked into the program in this way at the time when the program was originally written there cannot be static or automatic variables of such classes – except in parts of the program written and linked in later yet. Several (overloaded) versions of new_object() can be provided for a base class to give the effect of several constructors. Naturally, new_object() functions would employ standard library functions to do most of their work.

Complete re-compilation is only necessary when a new class with a hitherto undefined calling interface needs to be added. This method combines flexibility with efficiency and type safety in a very appealing manner.

Object I/O

Some problems are traditionally handled by providing "utility routines" with detailed information about the structure of all objects in a system. Examples of such utility programs are debuggers that allow a programmer to inspect the representation of objects in the program being debugged, routines that print objects, routines that write objects to and from disc, and routines that transmit and receive objects over a communication line.

Such routines traditionally rely on "maps" describing the layout of objects. Such maps are produced by "the system" specifically to allow objects to be inspected at run-time. For C++, such a map would describe a class in such a way that the names, types, and relative position of every member of a class object would be known at compile time. In addition, information about the class hierarchy and maybe about friends would be needed. Naturally, a C++ compiler could produce such maps. However, it might be better to do without such maps as far as possible. In essence, any use of such a map represents a violation of the encapsulation of objects and is at odds with idea of a system as a set of self contained objects each with a single well-defined checked interface. In other words, to a routine using such a map every object is just global data – and a major design aim of C++ is to get away from programming styles relying on anarchic use of run-time global data. The use of such maps should be avoided where reasonable alternatives exist.

The alternative to using such maps is to provide classes with member functions that provide operations necessary to compose inspection, I/O, communication, etc., without introducing functions treating objects as mere data.

Consider the problem of producing a copy of an object of a class X in a form that can be transmitted over a wire and reconstituted at the other end:

```
class X {
    int a;
    char* b;
    Y c;
public:
    ...
}
```

Fundamentally, the problem breaks down into two parts: to transmit the members and to transmit the information that these members were part of an X. There are various techniques for expressing the latter and also various techniques for coping with the nasty details such as linked structures. These can be applied independently of the approach taken to transmit the members, so this set of problems can be ignored here.

Clearly, any approach that respects the encapsulation properties of class X must involve the introduction of a member function to transmit the members. For example:

```
class X {
    int a;
    char* b;
    Y c;
public:
    xmit(ostream& s);    // encode members
                         // and write them to output stream ''s''
    ...
}
```

Basically, xmit() can be written by applying xmit() to each of the members:

```
X::xmit(ostream& s)
{
    // write transmission header
    xmit(s,a);
    xmit(s,b,ZERO_TERMINATED);  // xmit b as zero terminated str
    c.xmit();
    // write transmission trailer
}
```

This way object output is defined as memberwise and recursive. Naturally, this depends on each of the members having an xmit() operation. Keith Gorlen's OOPS library is an example of this technique in the context of C++.

Writing such a set of xmit() functions is easy, so easy in fact that it can become tedious. Given a set of xmit() routines for the built-in types (taking care of C problems such as the inability to distinguish a pointer from a vector in general) the compiler or a similar tool can write the xmit() functions in cases where the user hasn't specified one and where the default rules for constructing an xmit() function apply.

A tool that generates member functions in this way and a tool that generates an object map with a function that takes advantage of it are largely equivalent. The difference only appears if object maps become an integral part of a system used by large numbers of application level programs. Object maps and mechanisms for automatically generating large numbers of functions are both mechanisms for applying global operations to a system and should be used sparingly.

Persistent Objects

A mechanism that allows an object to be stored and restored can be used to implement a notion of persistent objects. In addition to the basic I/O operations a naming scheme must exist for both classes and individual objects. Such schemes and facilities for making them available to application programs are relatively easy to provide.

Consider writing an object of class X out from one program and reading it into another. The object I/O is handled using the techniques described above. In the case of a persistent object, the object is read in by a constructor, the "permanent copy" is if necessary updated appropriately from the copy in temporary store, and the final update of the permanent copy is guaranteed by X's destructor.

This leaves only one problem: What if the program that is trying to read in the object doesn't know class X? This problem can be handled using the technique   for incremental linking and loading described above provided X is derived from a known class B. In that case, the program simply looks up X in some directory of classes, requests loading of class X using something like new_object(), and continues reading in the object using a constructor for X.

Automatic Storage Management

C++ inherited from C a view of objects where an object can be of one of several storage classes, each with its own rules for allocation and de-allocation. This provides important efficiencies in both time and space but can be a burden on the programmer.

The management of static and automatic objects in C++ is automatic in the sense that storage is managed without intervention from the programmer and that constructors and destructors are called appropriately. The same applies to objects that are members of aggregates. Objects allocated on the free store must be explicitly de-allocated before the space can be re-used. The manual aspects of this are a source of complexity in programs and a common source of nasty bugs in C programs. On the other hand, the overheads of a perfectly general free storage allocator and de-allocator are typically quite noticeable for programs relying on it.

In C++, a large fraction of objects on the free store is typically managed as "secondary data structures" of other objects. That is, they are allocated by a constructor for some other object and de-allocated by the destructor of that object. The management of such "secondary objects" is so simple that it does not affect the complexity of a program noticeably. This reduces the complexity of handling objects on the free store considerably – naturally, the number of errors goes down too. Furthermore, where class specific allocators and de-allocators are employed the overheads of free store use drops to insignificance.

The problem of managing storage "automatically" is now reduced to minimizing the effort of the programmer in handling the remaining set of "primary objects". This, however, can still be a problem when writing general purpose libraries where the storage class of objects handed to utility functions are not generally known. For example, a user inserts a pointer to an object into a container. Who is responsible for de-allocating the object (and ensuring that its destructor is called):

- The user?
- The container?
- The system?

In general, the user cannot do the de-allocation since the user does not know if the container has stored a pointer to the object somewhere. If the container has done that and the user deletes the object chaos will erupt. Similarly, the container cannot delete the object because it does not know what the user might be doing with that object.

The system, provided there is a system, can look at all of memory and delete the object only when it becomes unreferenced. This garbage collection approach is expensive,[6] does not take advantage of the structure of C++'s memory as organized by the storage classes, and is hampered by the fact that C++ wasn't designed with garbage collection in mind.

The actual cost of garbage collection is notoriously hard to estimate. The notion of "managed store" pervasively affects both the design of language features and the implementation strategies of languages designed with garbage collection in mind. Similarly, the notion of storage classes pervasively affects C++ and the implementation strategies for C++. For example, it is not possible to estimate the cost of garbage collection simply by comparing a run of a program in a small memory (where the garbage collector is activated) with a run of the same program on the same input in a memory large enough to ensure that the garbage collector isn't activated.

---

[6]This discussion of garbage collection assumes that C++ is used on a fairly traditional machine. C++ was designed for such traditional architectures. The fundamental assumption is that relatively simple, relatively traditional architectures will remain more cost effective than more complicated architectures which support higher-level concepts such as garbage collection directly.

The volume of production of traditional "general purpose" machines is likely to far outstrip the production of more specialized architectures for the foreseeable future. This assures a heavy investment in keeping such traditional hardware efficient. Simpler architectures typically also have a lower design time thus ensuring that a traditional architecture will on average be ahead in manufacturing technology.

Should a situation arise where this fundamental assumption does not hold the question of garbage collection for C++ will be re-evaluated. This situation can of course arise locally, making garbage collected C++ feasible on a particular range of machines. In this case, portability issues become interesting.

Languages designed for garbage collection (e.g., Lisp and Clu) access an object of a non-primitive type through a fixed sized handle. C++ allocates and accesses all objects directly. Compared with a language designed to minimize allocation costs and memory accesses, such as C or C++, "garbage collection languages" spend cycles simply accessing objects, allocating objects, and maintaining information for garbage collection should it become necessary.[7] This implies a less compact representation of objects in memory; that is, in most cases a garbage collection language will require more memory to represent the same set of objects than does C++.

To complicate matters further, it is (obviously?) difficult to measure the cost of *not* using garbage collection, since the code related to memory management will be scattered throughout the system and the design of the system is typically done so as to minimize the effort needed to manage store.

Naturally, run-time and memory isn't all one needs look at when estimating cost. Ideally, the cost of using or not using garbage collection should be considered in terms of design time, debugging effort, maintenance effort, portability, run-time, store usage, complexity of supporting hardware, complexity of program development, complexity of run-time support software, complexity of compilers, etc.

It seems unlikely that simply applying the garbage collection techniques perfected for languages designed with garbage collection in mind to C++ would make C++ into a good garbage collected language. It might be done, but I suspect that since the fundamental design choices for C++ were made assuming the absence of garbage collection, a C++ garbage collector would be less efficient than, say, a good Lisp or Clu garbage collector. Worse, I suspect that a garbage collected C++ would fail to deliver the low-level performance people have come to expect from C++.

A more appropriate course of action seems to be to continue the C and C++ approach to increase the programmers set of choices for allocating objects with something that could be seen as a "garbage collected" storage class. This would simply allow some objects to be used with the convenience of *automatic* (stack) storage, but with unrestricted life times like objects on the C++ *free store* (dynamic storage). Unfortunately, this is not simple and especially not simple given the obvious requirement that the use of such "managed" objects should not be expensive compared with other C++ objects or compared with the use of objects in a garbage collected language. To make matters worse, the extra complexity to the user *must* be minimal to make the scheme attractive and it would also be nice if the scheme did not require modification to the compilers.

Surprisingly enough, such schemes appear to be feasible. There are at least two possible approaches. A storage manager can use constructors, destructors, etc. to keep track of

---

[7]There is unfortunately very little hard information available. The comparisons of "efficient" garbage collected languages such as compiled Common Lisp and "efficient" non garbage collected languages such as C seem to point to a factor of 3 to 5 difference. Sloppy use of garbage collection can easily lead to factors of 10 to 50, but sloppy choice of algorithms or sloppy use of C-style free store can also lead to drastic increases of costs. In both cases, the nastiest aspect of such overheads is that the programmer typically doesn't know if they are fundamental or simply the result of lack of understanding or bad engineering. It is often easier for the programmer simply to assume the former than to try to discover if there really is a problem.

- all "managed objects", or
- all pointers to managed objects.

Jonathan Shopiro's "counted pointer" classes[9] take the latter approach. A counted pointer is an object that acts like a pointer. Counted pointers for an object are "counted" and when the last counted pointer to an object is destroyed the object is freed. Overloading of operators usually denoting indirection such as unary * and -> is essential for this approach.

The following program makes and manipulates sequences of integers. A `ListCell_CP` is a counted pointer to a list cell:

```
main( )
{
    ListCell_CP p = makeSeq(10);               // p = (0 1 2 .. 9)

    ListCell_CP temp = select(&*p,isPrime);    // temp = (1 3 5 7)
    cout << "\nPrimes: " << *temp << "\n";

    p = select(&*p,isOdd);                      // p = (1 3 5 7 9)
    cout << "\nOdds: " << *p << "\n";

    temp = upTo(10,isPrime);                    // temp = (1 3 5 7)
    cout << "\nPrimes: " << *temp << "\n";
    cout << "\nOdds: " << *upTo(10,isOdd) << "\n";
                                                // print (1 3 5 7 9)
}
```

Naturally, several libraries were included to compile and run this program. The main point about it is the absence of end-user-specified memory management code. Note for example, the assignment to p in the statement that selects odd numbers from p. All memory is reclaimed – and if possibly re-used – automatically. In particular, all memory is reclaimed before the completion of the program. No modifications to the compiler were required to achieve this. The output was:

```
Primes: 1 3 5 7
Odds: 1 3 5 7 9
Primes: 1 3 5 7
Odds: 1 3 5 7 9
```

For some applications an extremely crude and effective approach to memory management is possible: never delete anything. This technique can lead to spectacular improvements for programs that simply doesn't need as much memory as is available on the machine. C++'s compact representation of data and direct access to data makes it well suited to this. Naturally, systems intended for runs of uncertain duration or uncertain memory requirements cannot use this approach; neither can general purpose library functions and classes.

Design Methods

It is not always clear how best to take advantage of a language such as C++. Significant improvements in productivity and code quality have consistently been achieved using C++ as "a better C" with a bit of data abstraction thrown in where it is clearly useful. However, further and noticeably larger improvements have been achieved by taking advantage of class hierarchies in the design process. This is often called object-oriented design and this is where the greatest benefits of using C++ have been found. For my views of what "object-oriented programming" and "data abstraction" are see [11].

Two levels of problems face us here. Firstly, most of the experience relating to object-oriented design is either not written down or only written down in a form that makes it inaccessible to novices. Hence, education is a major concern; the bottleneck is the low number of genuinely experienced people and the fact that they are typically frantically busy.

After solving the problem of getting experience in object-oriented design put on paper and in other ways made accessible we must face a harder problem. There exists (to my knowledge) no specific "object-oriented design method", with associated conventions, notations, standardized terminology, standardized procedures, and (ideally) tools. Such methods are needed to allow *large* numbers of designers and programmers to cooperate. Using a standard non-object-oriented design method simply doesn't deliver the results that have been shown to be attainable from C++.

Design methods that have the concepts of class, hierarchy, inheritance, and statically typed interface as integral parts are badly needed. The requirement that a design method should cope with all of these concepts implies that a designer must keep in mind that C++ isn't

- Smalltalk
- Lisp
- Ada
- (just) C

etc. Conversely, those languages are not C++ and a C++ programmer switching to one of those for a project should not uncritically try to impose C++ notions on them. It is a well known problem that someone's first program in a new language often simply is a program in the programmer's previous language written using the new language's syntax. A very similar trap exists for designers.

Naturally, a design method must be chosen and applied with care. Projects with different aims, different organizations, different magnitudes of problems, and different skills of the people involved require differences in design method and in the style of its use. There is no – and there can be no – simple set of rigid rules and conventions that turns novices into first rate programmers and designers. Only education and experience can do that. On the other hand, a set of rigid rules and conventions can completely cripple perfectly capable programmers and designers.

There is no substitute for experience, taste, and insight when designing a complex system; a design method should enhance these attributes of a designer by reducing trivia, mistakes, and oversights. Typically, a design method is no substitute for experiment either.

Sometimes it will be necessary to adjust the organizational structure to make best use of a design method. For example, it may often be necessary to make adjustments to ensure that the sharing of libraries and the creation of libraries that can be shared are genuinely encouraged. Similarly, a change of the unit of job assignment and in the unit of ownership of code (that is, responsibility for maintenance) may be needed when moving from a traditional design method to a C++ object-oriented style of design.

Danger Areas

There are two major dangers that must be faced when considering the evolution of C++:[8]

- Extend the language fast to please users. This could cause rampant featurism and lead to increases in:

  o compiler sizes and compilation times;
  o the time needed to learn C++;
  o the time needed to port a C++ implementation;
  o run-time and size of C++ programs.

- Freezing the language specification at the current stage and accepting new features, libraries, and tools extremely slowly to ensure stability.

  o Language fragmentation; every supplier would add a few "essential features;"
  o Rampant featurism as suppliers compete to produce better C++ supersets;
  o Loss of portability of programs between different C++ implementations.

Avoiding all of these problems simultaneously isn't easy. A most important rule is not to damage the ability to write very efficient low-level C++ programs. A bit of this kind of code is essential to almost every large application and almost all interesting libraries have a few key operations where efficiency is essential to make the use of the library an acceptable alternative to "hand optimized" code. The most obvious ways of damaging the basic efficiency of C++ would be to introduce new features that depended on either garbage collection or interpretation of dynamic type information in such a way that every program and every part of a program had to help carry the cost of the "advanced" features. This would cause C++ libraries to become less affordable and produce even greater demands for specialized language extensions. This again would cause C++ to become harder to port and probably lead to a greater number of dialects.

It is essential to maintain link compatibility with C program fragments and important to make calls to and from routines written in other languages as simple and efficient as possible.

Conclusions

C++ can be developed into a better language for library design and use. This probably means adding a parameterized type mechanism and an exception handling mechanism. C++ should be extended primarily as a tool for building libraries and not by adding features for coping with specialized applications.

---

[8]Assuming, of course, that the most obvious source of incompatibilities, an imprecise or incomplete language specification, is taken care of. The C++ reference manual[10] isn't sufficient as an implementor's guide. To complement that a commentary for implementors is being developed together with a C++ verification suite. The work of the ANSI C committee is also of great help.

Such applications should be supported through libraries. Efficiency of C++ primitives (compared to C primitives) must be maintained.

C++ programming environments with incremental compilation and incremental linking and loading would be of great use to programmers, but care must be taken to ensure that program source can be cost-effectively transferred between different such environments. The C++ mechanisms for specifying statically typed interfaces and its encapsulation mechanisms shouldn't be undermined by the introduction of dynamic type information except as a last resort.

We need design methods that allow a designer to take advantage of the data abstraction and object-oriented features of C++.

Acknowledgements

This paper owes most to people who have been pushing the limits of C++ in new application areas and tried out techniques that will only become feasible on a large scale as the C++ language and its associated tools matures further; notably, Keith Gorlen, Andy Koenig, and Jonathan Shopiro. Much has also been learned from discussions with Tom Cargill, Jim Coplien, Brian Kernighan, Doug McIlroy, and with C++ users acquainted with the Smalltalk and Lisp integrated environments.

This paper extrapolates from techniques already used and tools already being considered or built for C++. This implies that just about every problem mentioned here is actively being addressed somewhere.

Thanks to Andy Koenig for inviting me to give a talk with the given title "What will C++ look like two years from now?" that eventually became this paper.

Postscript

This is *not* a paper I enjoyed writing. It describes things that *might be*, not things that *are*; *possibilities*, not *experiences*. It seemed a useful paper to write, though, because each of the possibilities described will be explored many times in many contexts and if each is considered only in isolation a terrible mess will result.

Each individual part described is reasonably straightforward to design and given a bit of experimentation and common sense it can be gotten "reasonably right." Combinations do not appear to be so. Combine any two parts together, say, parameterized types and exception handling or persistence and incremental linking, and the possibilities for making serious mistakes increase dramatically and the feasibility of conducting reasonably sized experiments decreases.

I consider no part of this paper self evident or even just un-controversial. For each part of a C++ system, there are several alternatives to the design outlined here – and many ways of turning that vague design into a real tool. I hope this paper can be the starting point for many discussions and designs. It should remind designers of individual parts of a C++ system about the potential of a complete system, warn about the potential complexity of such a system, and point out that theirs isn't going to be the only such C++ system.

References

[1] DeMichiel, Linda G. and Gabriel, Richard P.: *The Common Lisp Object System: An Overview.* Proc. ECOOP '87. Lecture Notes in Computer Science, Springer Verlag. Vol 276. June 1987.

[2] Goldberg, A. and Robson, D.: *Smalltalk-80: The Language and its Implementation.* Addison-Wesley 1983.

[3] Ichbiah, J. D., et al.: *Rationale for the Design of the Ada Programming Language.* SIGPLAN Notices, June 1979.

[4] Gorlen, Keith: *An Object-Oriented Class Library for C++ Programs.* Software – Practice and Experience, December, 1987.

[5] Koenig, Andrew: *Associative Arrays in C++.* AT&T Bell Labs Internal Report.

[6] Liskov, Barbara, et al.: *Clu Reference Manual.* MIT/LCS/TR-225, October 1979.

[7] Shopiro, Jonathan: *Lists and Strings for C++.* AT&T Bell Labs Internal Report.

[8] Shopiro, Jonathan: *Extending the C++ Task System for Real-Time Applications.* Proc. USENIX C++ Workshop, Santa Fe, November 1987.

[9] Shopiro, Jonathan: *Counted Pointers – An Automatic Storage Management System for C++.* To be written.

[10] Stroustrup, Bjarne: *The C++ Programming Language.* Addison-Wesley, 1986.

[11] Stroustrup, Bjarne: *What is "Object-Oriented Programming"?.* Proc. 1st European Conference on Object-Oriented Programming. Paris, 1987. Springer Verlag Lecture Notes in Computer Science, Vol 276, pp 51-70.

[12] Stroustrup, Bjarne: *The Evolution of C++: 1985-1987.* Proc. USENIX C++ workshop. Santa Fe, November 1987.

[13] Weinreb, D. and Moon, D.: *Lisp Machine Manual.* Symbolics, Inc. 1981.

Chapter 3

The Design and Implementation of InterViews

Mark A. Linton and Paul R. Calder

Abstract

We have implemented an object-oriented user interface package, called InterViews, that provides **box** and **glue** classes that are used to compose a user interface from a set of interactive objects. The base class for interactive objects, called an **interactor**, and base class for composite objects, called a **scene**, define the protocol for combining several interactive behaviors. The InterViews library also provides common objects such as text, structured graphics objects, scroll bars, menus, and buttons.

InterViews is written in C++ and runs on top of the X window system. We are currently using InterViews to build an experimental programming environment.

Introduction

User interfaces are difficult to implement because of diverse user needs and preferences. Tools for programming a user interface are often too restrictive to build a variety of interfaces or too low-level to offer enough help to the programmer.

InterViews (*Inter*active *Views*) is a library of C++[5] classes that provides a set of powerful and flexible tools for constructing user interfaces. The design of InterViews was driven by two desires: (1) to provide a framework for implementing user interfaces without constraining the styles we could build, and (2) to make it convenient to build a user interface from smaller components.

Like Smalltalk MVC[1] and MacApp[4], the InterViews approach is to separate interactive behavior from abstract behavior. An interactive object, called a **view**, defines the user interface to an abstract object, called the **subject**. The separation of subject and view permits the use of different views of the same subject to customize interactive style. The user can dynamically customize this behavior using a **metaview**, a view of another view's internal state. For example, a text view may interpret keystrokes as commands using an internal mapping. A text metaview might display this mapping and let a user modify it interactively.

The base class, **interactor**, defines the behavior of all interactive objects. All views are interactors, but not all interactors need be views; for example, it

From *Proceedings and Additional Papers*, USENIX C++ Workshop, pp. 256-267, Santa Fe, New Mexico, 1987.
Research supported by the SUNDEC project through a gift from Digital Equipment Corporation.

is more of a nuisance than a help to have a subject associated with a simple pop-up menu.

To build user interfaces from reusable components requires the ability to define an interactive object that is independent of its surrounding context. In particular, interactors must be flexible enough to handle variations in window size. The **scene** class defines the basic operations for managing a group of component interactors. One scene subclass, **box**, implements side-by-side composition of interactors using a simplified version of TEX[2] boxes and glue. Boxes arrange interactors to fit within a given area; glue specifies variable-sized space between interactors that is stretched or shrunk for a box of a given size. This model enables interactors to be composed within a box without specifying detailed layout information.

We have implemented InterViews on top of the X window system[3]. A small set of primitive classes completely encapsulate graphics and window operations. The remaining library classes and applications do not contain any

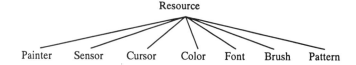

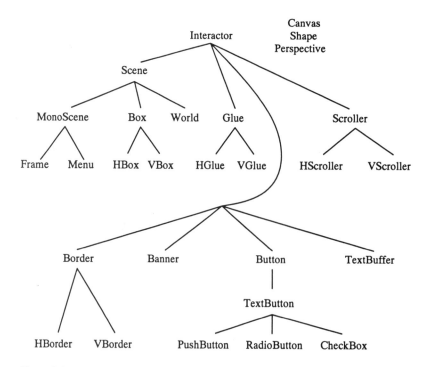

Figure 3.1
Class Organization

X calls; they call operations defined on the primitives. This approach makes it possible to port InterViews quickly to other window systems.

Class Organization

Several factors influenced the structure of the InterViews class hierarchy. Our overall goal was simplicity: to make the classes easy to understand, straightforward to implement, and convenient to extend.

In order from most important to least important, the factors were:

- Shallow Nesting. Classes are a good partitioning mechanism, but there are drawbacks associated with a large number of classes. Our experience with an earlier library was that a large class hierarchy overwhelms programmers, especially when there are many levels of subclasses. The earlier library had many small classes nested 12 deep. Users of the library had trouble grasping all the different classes and all the inherited behavior. InterViews currently has one class that is nested 5 deep; most classes are at level 2 or 3. Throughout the evolution of InterViews we have generally attempted to add an operation to some existing class rather than to add a new class.
- Many-to-Many Relationships. One reason for introducing new classes is to enable some state to be shared among several objects. For example, several interactors should be able to use the same graphics state; therefore, graphics state is a separate class. Similarly, several graphics states should be able to refer to the same font, so font is a separate class.
- Common Usage. It is often preferable to design for a specific common case than for the general case. For example, InterViews does not define a unifying class for all kinds of menus. Instead, it provides one particular style, namely pop-up menus. The advantage is that a user need not understand a complicated menu model to use pop-up menus. The disadvantage is that there is no support for other kinds of menus, though they are straightforward to implement.

Figure 3.1 shows a subset of the InterViews classes. The top set of classes are all subclasses of **resource** because they are shared objects. Resources contain a reference count that can be manually incremented. When a resource is destroyed, the reference count is decremented but the resource is not deallocated unless the count is zero.

Interactors

All user interface objects are derived from the interactor class. Every interactor has an associated **shape** that it uses to define the desired display area characteristics, including natural size, shrinkability, and stretchability. An interactor's parent scene uses the shape when it allocates display space for the interactor. The actual display area is assigned to the **canvas** associated with the interactor. Because the current implementation runs on top of X, canvases are always rectangular and may overlap.

When an interactor's canvas is set or changed in size, the interactor's `Resize` operation is called. If the interactor is a scene, it in turn assigns the canvases of its component interactors. The one exception is the root scene for a workstation display, called a **world**. A world's canvas is set to the entire screen when a program starts up. When an interactor is inserted into a world, its canvas is allocated immediately.

After a scene calls an interactor's `Resize` operation, it calls the interactor's `Draw` operation. The interactor should draw all of itself, including any components. When part of a canvas should be redrawn, perhaps because it had been obscured but is now visible, the interactor's `Redraw` operation is called with the coordinates of the affected area. In this case, the interactor should not redraw affected subcomponents; their `Redraw` operations will be called independently.

An interactor can perform output to its canvas using a **painter**. A painter provides drawing operations and manages graphics state such as foreground and background colors, font, and fill pattern. Each drawing operation is passed the target canvas. Canvas coordinates address pixels by default; however, coordinate values can be expressed in inches or centimeters by multiplying by the predefined global values "inch" or "cm". Also, painters can perform arbitrary coordinate transformations composed of translations, rotations, and scalings.

Associated with every interactor is a **cursor** that describes the visual representation of the pointing device (mouse) on the screen. When the mouse is over a visible part of the interactor's canvas, it is displayed as defined by the interactor's cursor.

An interactor can receive input events one of two ways:

1. It can read the next event on the (global) input queue.
2. An event can be passed from another interactor using the `Handle` procedure.

A **sensor** defines interest in certain kinds of events. Interactors interested in input events have a sensor that defines their current input interest. Each event is targeted to a particular interactor. The target is guaranteed to be interested in an event, but the reader may choose to process or ignore the event itself.

A purely event-driven organization, such as in MacApp, can be produced by using the following C++ loop:

```
for (;;) {
    Read(e);
    e.target->Handle(e);
}
```

A more traditional control flow, which is not possible in pure event-driven systems, can be produced by reading events as part of interactor operations. For example, it may be desirable when a button is pressed in a pop-up menu to ignore events for targets other than menu items. In this case, having the menu interactor read events directly results in more straightforward code than in an event-driven implementation.

Because most interactors perform some output and are interested in some input events, every interactor has a sensor called "input" and a painter called "output". The initial values for input and output are defined when the interactor is created. Thus, the event interest and graphics state for most interactors is defined dynamically. Interactors can, of course, define additional sensors and painters.

Scenes often pass input and output to their component interactors, effectively sharing the state among several interactors. Because the state may be shared, it is inconvenient to make one particular interactor responsible for destroying the sensor and painter. The sensor and painter classes are therefore subclasses of resource. The interactor constructor explicitly increments the reference counts of input and output and the destructor decrements them. The object will only be deallocated when its count reaches zero.

Because we sometimes want to destroy an interactor without knowing which subclass it belongs to, we implement the concept of a "virtual destructor". Interactor subclasses do not define their own destructor; instead they define a Delete operation that is called by the base class destructor.

Scenes

All interactors that contain one or more component interactors are derived from the scene class. A common case is an interactor that is implemented in terms of another interactor. For example, a menu is implemented by a box containing the menu items. A menu does not share the behavior of a box in the sense of a subclass; it simply uses the box to compose the items. This distinction is important, and it helps simplify the class hierarchy.

The scene subclass **monoscene** contains a single component interactor. A monoscene normally gives all of its display area to the interactor. One subclass of monoscene, **frame**, allocates all of its display space except for an outline around the interactor.

The most common scenes that contain several interactors are boxes. Two subclasses of box, **hbox** and **vbox**, arrange component interactors side-by-side horizontally and vertically, respectively. The box Resize operation shrinks or stretches each interactor according to the specification provided in the interactor's shape. A box tries to allocate each component interactor its natural size, then distributes any excess or shortfall in the available space according to the proportion of the total stretchability or shrinkability contributed by each component.

Glue is an interactor subclass that is used as a component in boxes. It has two subclasses, **hglue** and **vglue**, that are used to define horizontal and vertical space, respectively. A glue interactor therefore only shrinks or stretches along one axis, the same axis as that along which the box arranges components.

Thus, using boxes and glue we can define a presentation more flexibly. The layout can take on a variety of shapes and sizes without modification to the component interactors. More importantly, the interactors can appear in different layouts without being changed. By defining the natural sizes of components in a box, we can specify a default size for the box. By defining the relative stretchability and shrinkability of components, we can control the way in which they will be composed into the available space to maintain a pleasing or functional layout.

The World

Every program using InterViews must create a world object. This object represents the root scene of the display. The constructor opens a connection to the window server. In the X environment, is also specifies a display name. If the name is nil, then the value of the DISPLAY environment variable is used.

The world object also provides an interface to the X defaults file and the standard X geometry specification syntax.

Scrollers

Scroller is an interactor subclass that displays a scroll bar. The **hscroller** and **vscroller** subclasses support horizontal and vertical scrolling, respectively. A scroller is a view of the **perspective** associated with another interactor. A perspective defines a range of coordinates and a subrange for the portion of the total range that is currently visible. For example, the vertical range for a text editor might be the total number of lines in a file; the subrange would be the number of lines actually displayed in the editor's canvas.

A scroller displays a scroll box whose length reflects the fraction of the total perspective that is currently visible. The user can modify the perspective interactively through the scroller using the mouse. The perspective can also be changed by the interactor itself, for example, if the text editor adds a line to the file. When an interactor changes its perspective, the perspective in turn notifies its views that it has changed.

Other kinds of views of perspectives are possible. A panner, for example, supports movement in both dimensions from a single interface. Zooming can be supported by changing the size of the perspective's subrange. More than one view of the same perspective can be created. For instance a perspective could be modified by zoom and scroll buttons in addition to the scroll bar.

Buttons

A **button** is an interactor subclass that is a view of a **button state**. The user can "press" a button to set the associated button state to a particular value. Several buttons can be visible for the same button state, making it possible to use buttons to select from a discrete set of values (each button represents a different value). Like any subject, when a button state changes value it notifies all the buttons attached to it.

Three common kinds of buttons are provided, all derived from a **text button** class that defines behavior for labeled buttons. A **push button** has a round-cornered rectangle surrounding its label. The rectangle and label are drawn in reverse colors (background and foreground swapped) when the button is pressed. A **radio button** has a circle to the left of its label; the circle is filled when the button is pressed. A **check box** has a rectangle to the left of its label; the rectangle has an 'X' in it when pressed.

In addition to being attached to a button state, buttons can be attached to other buttons. If button *A* is attached to button *B*, then *A* is disabled while *B* is not pressed. A disabled button ignores input and draws itself with a gray pattern to show it is disabled.

Other Classes

InterViews includes a number of other classes that support user interfaces. A **text buffer** manages a two-dimensional array of characters. **Page** provides hierarchically structured text objects together with composition objects for a variety of layout styles.

A **banner** displays left-justified, centered, and right-justified headings. A **border** fills an area of a certain thickness; a **vborder** can be stretched vertically and the thickness determines its width; a **hborder** can be stretched horizontally and the thickness determines its height.

A **menu** is a box of **menu items**. When its `Popup` operation is called it inserts itself into the world, waits for the user to release a button, and returns the menu item that was chosen.

Picture is a base class for defining structured graphics objects. Subclasses of picture include basic graphics objects (such as **line**, **circle**, and **rectangle**) and **group** for representing a collection of pictures. Picture is a subclass of a **persistent** class so that picture data structures can be automatically stored on disk.

Rubberband is a base class for graphics objects that track user input. For example, a rubber rectangle can be used to drag out a new rectangle interactively. Another subclass, sliding rectangle, can be used to move around an existing rectangle. These classes complete isolate programmers from the device-dependent use of exclusive-or drawing or the use of an overlay plane.

WorldView is a base class for defining window managers. It provides operations that should only be used by a window manager, such as controlling input focus between several applications.

Workstation parameters are accessed using a predefined global object named **workstation**. The object is created when the associated world is created and can return information such as the physical dimensions of the display.

Example Usage

Squares is a demonstration program that uses many of the InterViews classes. The program contains a simple subject that manages a list of squares of different sizes and positions. The user interface is constructed from a view of the squares list, a frame around the view, and a dialog box for simple customization.

The frame surrounds a vertical box containing a banner and two horizontal boxes, all separated by horizontal borders. The upper horizontal box contains the squares view, a vertical border and and a vertical scroller. The lower horizontal box contains a horizontal scroller, a vertical border and a piece of glue. Figure 3.2 shows what a squares frame looks like; the code below shows the C++ code that constructs the frame:

```
frame = new VBox(
    banner,
    new HBorder(output),
    new HBox(
        view,
        new VBorder(output),
        new VScroller(view, vwidth, nil, output)
    ),
    new HBorder(output),
    new HBox(
        new HScroller(view, hwidth, nil, output),
        new VBorder(output),
        new HGlue(output, vwidth, 0)
    )
);
```

Using a pop-up menu, the user can create another view of the squares list, add a square to the list, open a dialog box to customize the squares frame, or

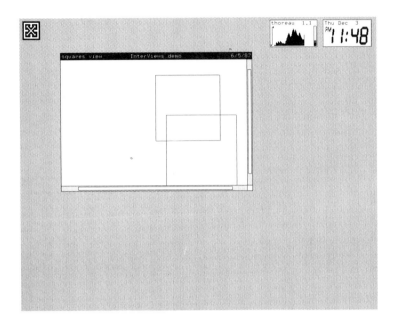

Figure 3.2
Screen dump of squares view

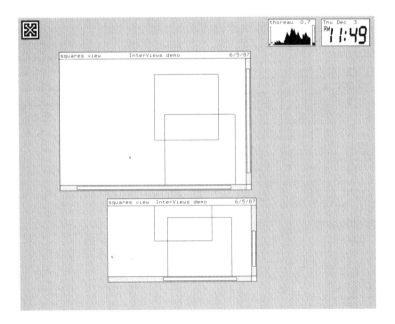

Figure 3.3
Second squares view

exit the program. Figure 3.3 shows the result of creating a second view and adding a square. The squares list notifies its views when the square is added, so that the new square is visible in both.

Figure 3.4 shows the dialog box used to customize the frame around a view. The dialog box contains check boxes for specifying the presence of scrollers, buttons for specifying attributes of the scrollers, and a confirmation button to indicate that customization is complete. The components of the dialog box are separated by glue objects. The glue above the "Horizontal Scroller" check box has high shrinkability, while the glue between the check box and the radio buttons has low shrinkability. If the vbox containing these objects is not given enough screen space to fit the natural sizes of their views, it will shrink the glue above the check box more than the glue below it. Figure 3.5 shows a resized dialog box.

Implementation

It took about three man-months to implement InterViews on top of X. In this section, we discuss some of the problems interfacing to X, the details of implementing boxes, and some reflections on using C++.

Interfacing to X

InterViews primitive class operations make direct X library calls to implement their semantics. The two main problems interfacing to X were managing windows and translating X input events into InterViews events.

Window Management

Each canvas is represented as an X window. The world's canvas is the root window for a display. The scene class contains operations to perform the creation, mapping, and configuration of windows. The two operations available to subclasses are `Place` and `UserPlace`. `Place` puts an interactor at a specific position in a scene, which is implemented by creating a subwindow of the scene's window and associated the subwindow with the interactor's canvas. `UserPlace` creates a window and lets the user interactively position it.

Input Events

The X model of input events is slightly different from the InterViews model. An important similarity is that associated with each X input event is a destination window. The interactor `Read` operation maps the window to an interactor through a global hash table maintained by scenes. The event is then checked against the interactor's current sensor to see if the interactor is interested in the event. Normally, we can tell X to ignore events that are not of interest; however, X cannot always distinguish events at the level we wish. For example, X cannot send events for the left mouse button and ignore events for the middle and right buttons.

X is very different from InterViews in the sizing and redrawing of windows. X represents the need to redraw part of a window as an input event; InterViews represents it as an out-of-band procedure call. When the `Read` operation sees a redraw event, it calls `Redraw` on the destination window and proceeds to read the next input event. Thus, a single InterViews read can result in reading multiple X events.

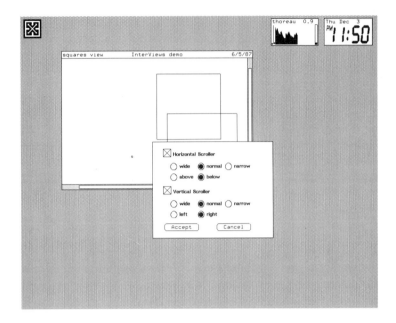

Figure 3.4
Squares metaview

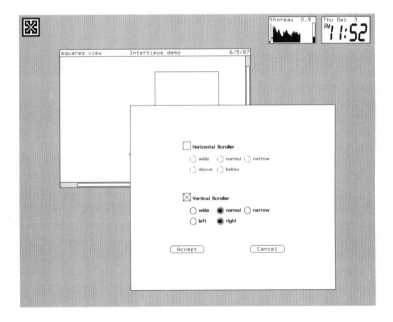

Figure 3.5
Resized metaview

The normal approach to processing X redraw events has an inherent performance problem. If a large number of windows need to be redrawn (in a hierarchy, for example), a large number of redraw events will be received. The result is a loop consisting of reading an event and redrawing part of a window in response. Because reading an event causes all pending output to be flushed, this loop defeats the X library buffering strategy and effectively increases the cost of every drawing operation. We solve this problem by storing redraw events on a queue instead of performing them directly. When an event read will block or the event is not a redraw, all of the redraw events on the queue are performed.

Boxes

An interesting aspect of implementing boxes is the computation of the shape of a box. A box must compute its own shape as a function of the shapes of the interactors inside it. Along the major axis (horizontal for an hbox, vertical for a vbox), the natural sizes, stretchabilities and shrinkabilities can simply be added.

Computing the parameters for the minor axis is more complicated. The natural size is the maximum of the component sizes. The minimum size is the maximum of the component minimum sizes, computed by subtracting their shrinkability from their natural size. The shrinkability of the box is therefore its natural size minus its minimum size.

The maximum size of the box is the minimum of the component maximum sizes, computed by adding their stretchability to their natural size. The stretchability of the box is therefore its maximum size minus its natural size.

C++ Experiences

Using C++ as the implementation language for InterViews has had several advantages and disadvantages. Inheritance and virtual functions simplify the structure of code and data that would otherwise need to use function variables and additional levels of indirection. C++ is also very portable, enabling us to bring up InterViews on Sun workstations in a matter of hours.

The major disadvantages we have found in using C++ are that it does not support multiple inheritance (yet) and the run-time system does not support garbage collection. Multiple inheritance is necessary for a clean class hierarchy and to facilitate shared behavior. For example, we have a subclass of frame, called **title frame**, that has a banner at the top. We cannot create a kind of banner that contains several interactors, because banner is not a subclass of scene. We cannot create a subclass of scene and use it in a title frame because it would not be type-compatible with banner. It would be incorrect for banner to be a subclass of scene, because the basic banner does not contain component interactors. With multiple inheritance, we could define a class that derived from both scene and banner.

Garbage collection would be very helpful because of object sharing. For a variety of reasons, it is beneficial to share objects in a user interface implementation. Sometimes the sharing is for the purposes of using the same output style; sometimes it simply eliminates the need to create new objects. When objects are shared, it becomes difficult to decide when the object should be destroyed. Our resource class solves the problem for a specific set of classes, but requires manual reference counting.

Current Status

InterViews currently runs on MicroVAX and Sun workstations on top of either X10 or X11. The library is roughly 15,000 lines of C++ source code. We have also implemented several applications on top of the library, including a reminder dialog box, a scalable digital clock, a drawing editor, a load monitor, a window manager, and a display of incoming mail. We are currently working on a more general drawing system, a structure editor, and a visual debugger as part of a C++ programming environment.

Conclusions

InterViews provides a relatively simple organization of user interface classes that is easy to use and extend via subclassing. The use of boxes and glue make it possible to define reusable user interface components.

The InterViews library completely hides the underlying window system from application programs. Our original reason for having this layer was that our model was different from X's, but in retrospect this approach has the added benefit that we can port InterViews applications to a new window system simply by porting the primitive classes.

Acknowledgments

Craig Dunwoody and John Vlissides participated in the design of InterViews. John implemented the drawing editor, the structured graphics classes, and coordinate transformations in the painter class. Paul Hegarty implemented the window manager. John Interrante helped write the reference manual.

References

[1] Goldberg, A., *Smalltalk-80: The Interactive Programming Environment*, Addison-Wesley, Reading, Massachusetts, 1984.

[2] Knuth, D., *The T_EX book*, Addison-Wesley, Reading, Massachusetts, 1984.

[3] R. W. Scheifler and J. Gettys, "The X Window System", *ACM Transactions on Graphics* Vol. 5, No. 2, April 1987, pp. 79-109.

[4] Schmucker, K. J., *Object-Oriented Programming for the Macintosh*, Hayden, Hasbrouck Heights, New Jersey, 1986.

[5] Stroustrup, B., *The C++ Programming Language*, Addison-Wesley, Reading, Massachusetts, 1986.

Chapter 4

Building Well-Behaved Type Relationships in C++

R. B. Murray

Introduction

The C++ programming language[1] allows the designer of a new user-defined type to define the conversions between that type and another type. When the arguments to a function call, overloaded operator, or initialization don't match a declaration exactly, the compiler can use these conversions to coerce arguments to make them match. If exactly one declaration can be matched using conversions, the compiler supplies the conversions automatically; otherwise it is a compile time error.

These *implicit type conversions* can make it easier to write more concise code; however, they can also create problems. The builder of a type structure is walking a thin line between supplying enough conversions to avoid frequent explicit casts, and supplying so many conversions that casts have to be added to resolve ambiguities. In addition, the type conversion rules of C++ make it possible for the addition of other declarations at a later time to break existing code. As the use of C++ libraries grows, these interactions between different packages are likely to become more common.

This paper will begin by reviewing the existing behavior of implicit type conversions in C++. We will then will suggest "rules of thumb" for avoiding unwanted interactions, both for the type designer, and for the type user.

Review: Type Conversions In C++

In both C and C++, the compiler understands how to make certain type conversions, and will quietly insert these conversions into the generated code when appropriate. For example, C and C++ compilers know how to convert an int into a double; so if a compiler is presented with the code fragment
```
double d;
d = 2;
```
it will quietly convert the int 2 into a double before assigning to d.

In C++, the designer of a user-defined type can specify conversions between that type and any other type. This can either be a specification of how to the convert this type into some other type, or how to convert some other type into this type. Either kind of conversion tells the compiler how to make one type into another; the difference is in which of the two types involved knows how to do the conversion.

From *USENIX 1988 C++ Conference Proceedings*, pp. 19-30.

Constructors

Conversion *from* another type From_type *to* a new type To_type is specified by supplying a *constructor* that takes exactly one argument, either of type From_type or From_type&:

```
class From_type {
    // ...
};
class To_type {
    // ...
public:
  To_type();
  To_type(From_type&);
};

To_type::To_type(From_type& o)
{
    // Do what it takes to make a From_type into this To_type
}
main(){
  From_type other_thing;
  To_type this_thing;
  this_thing = other_thing; // To_type(From_type&) called
}
```

Conversion Operators

Conversion *to* another type To_type *from* a type From_type is specified by supplying a member function (called a *conversion operator*) of the form operator To_type:

```
class To_type {
    // ...
};
class From_type {
    // ...
public:
  operator To_type();
};

From_type::operator To_type()
{
  // Do what it takes to make this From_type into a To_type
  // This function returns the new To_type
}
main() {
  From_type other_thing;
  To_type this_thing;
  this_thing = other_thing; // called From_type::operator named
                            //              To_type() called
};
```

Function Matching

The C++ compiler will attempt to use implicit type conversions when the arguments supplied to a function, overloaded operator, or initialization do not match any existing declaration exactly. (For the remainder of this paper, the term "function" will be used to include overloaded operators and initializations). The compiler may supply implicit type conversions in order to coerce one or more of the arguments to the types expected by the function.

For instance, if the function sqrt expects an argument of type double, but the call passes an int, the generated code will include a conversion of the int into a double and pass the result to sqrt. This is also true in Draft Proposed ANSI C[2]; however, C++ extends this behavior to include user defined types.

The C++ compiler will only call implicit type conversions if:

- no declaration for the function matches the argument list exactly, *and*
- there is exactly one such declaration for the function such that each argument either:

  o matches the corresponding argument in the function declaration exactly; *or*
  o has exactly one direct conversion that will change the argument into the type specified by the function declaration.

If there are no function declarations that can be made to match by adding conversions, or there are two or more, it is a compile time error. For example:

```
class Orange {
    // ...
};
class Apple {
    // ...
public:
  Apple();
  Apple(Orange&); //convert Orange to Apple
};
overload cross;
void cross(Orange,Apple);
void cross(Apple,Apple);

main(){
  Orange navel;
  Apple mcintosh;
  cross(navel,mcintosh);    // calls cross(Orange,Apple);
  cross(mcintosh,mcintosh); // calls cross(Apple,Apple);
  cross(mcintosh,navel);    // converts navel and
                            //      calls cross(Apple, Apple);
  cross(navel,navel);       // error: two possible conversions
};
```

The first two calls to cross match a declaration exactly, so no type conversions are called. Since the third call does not match any declaration exactly, and there is no way to make an Apple into an Orange, the third call can only be resolved by converting navel to an Apple and calling the cross(Apple,Apple) function. The fourth call also does not match any declaration exactly. The compiler could convert only the second argument (which would match cross(Orange,Apple), or it could convert both arguments (which would match cross(Apple,Apple). Since there is no exact match, and there is not exactly one declaration that can be made to match by supplying conversions, it is a compile time error.

Type Conversion Pitfalls

Implicit conversions can be convenient. However, if the class designer doesn't put some thought into their structure, they can cause troubles (in the form of compile-time errors) later. This section looks at some of the most common problems and describes ways to avoid them.

Multiple Owner Problem

This problem occurs when a conversion from S to T is necessary, and both `T::T(S)` (or `T::T(S&)`) and `S::operator T` exist. We call this the *multiple owner* problem because there are two "owners" for the conversion S → T:

```
            T::T(S)
   S ───────────────────► T
        S::operator T()
```

(In this picture, each arrow from type S to type T indicates that an implicit type conversion from S to T is declared.) It is never correct for both of these routines to exist.

This problem is minor because it cannot be introduced after the fact, since it requires that each class involved knows about the other. Normally this is only true when the same set of people is maintaining both classes, and it is therefore easily fixed by removing one of the conversions.

Ambiguous Type Structure

This error occurs when there is more than one possible set of conversions that will match the function being called:

```
class T1;
class T2;

overload func;
void func(T1);
void func(T2);

class S {
    // ...
public:
  operator T1();
  operator T2();
};

main(){
  S s;
  func(s);   // Error: two possible conversions
             // (S->T1 or S->T2)
};
```

In this case, there is no `func(S)`, and the type structure of the application allows either of two conversions to resolve the function call:

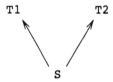

Avoiding the structural problem is harder, because it can be introduced after the fact. The later addition of a new type can cause existing code that depends on an implicit type conversion to no longer compile:

```
class Apple {
    // ...
public:
  Apple(int);
};

void peel(Apple);

main(){
  peel(2);   // calls peel(Apple(2));
};
```

The above code works, but if we later add another class that also defines peel we get a problem:

```
class Orange {
    // ...
public:
  Orange(int);
};
void peel(Orange);
```

When the new declarations (which are probably buried in a new header file) are added, all the calls to peel that depend on the implicit conversion int → Apple will no longer compile.

This problem will become more common in the future. As software development moves toward more aggressive reuse of code (as economics dictates that it must)[3], the percentage of code in an application that consists of libraries written by someone other than the application developer will grow. This both increases the chances of an accidental name collision and reduces the power of the victim to do anything about it (particularly if the victim does not have access to the library source). A lot of trouble can be avoided if some thought about type structures goes into the library design.

Rules For Designing Type Structures

The structure problem arises when there are two or more conversions *from* the same type. If we define the number of types that a type T can be implicitly converted *to* as the *fanout* of T, the number of opportunities for collision from structural problems is $O(fanout(T)^2)$. This is because a function name collision between any two types in the fanout is a possible structure error. So our first rule of thumb is:

Minimize the fanout in the type structure.

By avoiding multiple implicit conversions from a given type, the chances that ambiguities will be created are minimized. This does not mean that it should be impossible for users to convert a given type to more than one other type; the point is that no more than one of these conversions should be *implicit*. Other conversions should be normal member functions. For example, this type structure has high fanout:

```
class Thing { // ...  public:
  operator Another_thing();
  operator Still_another_thing();
  operator Yet_another_thing();
};
```

Rather than have implicit conversions to three other types, at most one of the types should be chosen for implicit conversions. In this case, suppose

`Another_thing` was the most common of the types involved; we should only supply a conversion operator for `Another_thing`:

```
class Thing {      // ...  public:
  operator Another_thing();
   Still_another_thing  cvt_Still_another_thing();
   Yet_another_thing  cvt_Yet_another_thing();
};
```

Conversions to `Still_another_thing` and `Yet_another_thing` will now require an explicit call to the appropriate member function.

Simplifying Conversions

Implicit type conversions are especially useful when one of the classes is an extension of the other. This may be an extension of the domain (e.g., `Complex` is an extension of double), or of the concepts (`String` is an extensionof char*). In these cases, the implicit conversion between the two classes should be from the extension to the simpler class; we call this a *no-value-added* conversion.

Why are no-value-added conversions better? In general, there will be more than one extension for a given simpler class. Implicit conversions from the extensions to the simpler class will fan *in* to the simpler class, which doesn't cause ambiguities:

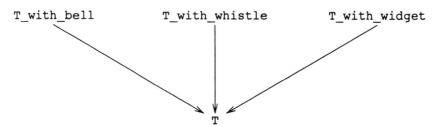

On the other hand, implicit conversions from the simpler class to the extensions (*value-added*) will fan *out*; there can be an ambiguity as to which extension the simpler type should be converted to:

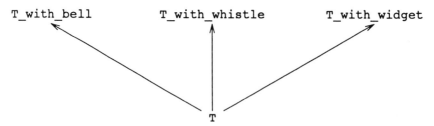

Since the simpler type should not know about the extension, no-value-added conversions will be conversion operators (as opposed to constructors). So the rule of thumb is:

Conversion operators should provide unique conversions to simpler types (no "value added").

Mutual Conversions Are OK

It may not always be obvious when one type is an extension of another. For example, consider the relationship between a type `Rational`, which implements rational numbers as the quotient of a pair of arbitrary precision integers, and the type `double`. Conceptually, the set of real numbers represented by `double` includes all rationals. However, since the implementation of most doubles is a fixed sized mantissa and a fixed size exponent, the set of data representable by `Rational` may in fact include all the data representable by `double`!

For situations like this, it is often simplest to use mutual conversions; each type can be implicitly converted to the other:

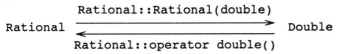

Surprisingly enough, this structure is not necessarily bad. If a function `f` accepts either a `Rational` or a `double`, any use of `Rational` or `double` will match exactly; if the function only accepts one of these types, the conversion will be called for the other type.

If In Doubt, Leave It Out

Every automatic type conversion opens up a new opportunity for error, either from multiple conversions requiring a new explicit cast, or (more sinister) from an unintended conversion causing the wrong function to be called when the right function declaration was missing. The most important rule of thumb is:

If an implicit conversion is not obviously necessary, leave it out.

Implicit Conversions In User Code

The user of a library needs to be aware that constructors often break the rule that implicit conversions should be unique, no-value-added conversions. Often, at least one form of the constructor for an extension will take, as its sole argument, the simpler type:

```
class T {
    // ...
};
class T_with_bell {
    // ...
public:
  T_with_bell(T);
};
```

The constructor `T_with_bell::T_with_bell(T)` defines an implicit value-added conversion. The designers of `T_with_bell` may not have intended their users to depend on this implicit conversion; it may simply exist because there is no way to specify a constructor of this form without also declaring an implicit conversion.

This is particularly common with constructors that take built in types. For example, a class that provides a buffer pool might have an integer parameter to the constructor that specifies an initial size of the pool:

```
class Buffer_pool {
    // ...
public:
  Buffer_pool(int);
};
```

The fact that this defines an implicit conversion from int to Buffer_pool is just an accident; users' code should not depend on it. For example, if there is a function

```
void flush(Buffer_pool);
```

which fills a Buffer_pool with available things, users should not call

```
flush(5);
```

with the intention of throwing away the next five things. This code depends on the conversion int → Buffer_pool to construct a temporary Buffer_pool of size 5, pass it to flush, and destroy it after the call returns. A compilation error can be introduced by the later addition of a constructor that takes int as its only argument if there is also a name collision on flush:

```
class Toilet {
    // ...
public:
  Toilet(int);
};

void flush(Toilet);
```

Now, flushing an int no longer works. The second example in the 'Ambiguous Type Structure', where code stopped working because an implicit conversion from int to Apple was broken by the subsequent addition of a conversion from int to Orange, is another example of this. So the rule of thumb here is:

Avoid the use of value-added conversions, even if they happen to be available. This is especially important for conversions from built in types.

Repairing A Broken Type Structure
If the user of a type gets bitten by a problem in the type structure, there are two ways to repair the problem in the users' code.

Provide Explicit Conversions
An ambiguity can be resolved by providing an explicit conversion in each function call:

```
class Orange {
    // ...
public:
  Orange(int);
};

class Apple {
    // ...
public:
  Apple(int);
};

overload peel;
void peel(Orange);
void peel(Apple);
```

```
main(){
  peel(Apple(2));
};
```

This has the advantage of making explicit an operation that may not have been obvious beforehand; but it also may clutter up the code, and can be a big effort. If there are few calls involved this is probably the simplest and clearest solution.

Provide Disambiguators

An alternative is to provide a *disambiguator* for the function involved:

```
inline void
peel(int i)
{
  peel (Apple(i));
}
```

Since the disambiguator is `inline`, there is no additional run time cost. This allows a fix to be made in one place, as opposed to being scattered throughout the code. However, we have added yet another inline function declarator to our headers. If there are many calls involved this is probably the easiest solution.

An Example

As an example, we'll consider a type structure for various kinds of numbers. The types involved will be:

- `int`;
- `Big_int`, supporting integers of arbitrary length;
- `Rational`, rational numbers (implemented as a pair of `Big_ints`);
- `double`;
- `Complex`, a complex number implemented as a pair of `doubles`.

We'll build this type structure in two steps. The first step is to figure out what conversions must exist, either because they are implied by constructors, or because they already exist:

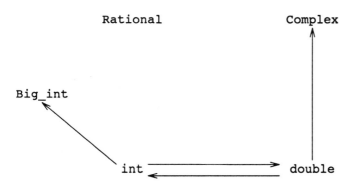

`int` and `double` are mutually convertible by the rules of C. We clearly need to initialize `Big_int` from an `int`, and it makes sense to initialize `Complex` from a `double`.

How do we initialize `Rational`? This is a little harder. The fact that `Rational` is implemented using `Big_int` is really an implementation detail;

you should not require the user of `Rational` to know about `Big_int` in order to use the package. However, we can imagine that a `Rational` could be initialized by `int`s, `double`s, or `Big_int`s, and we supply constructors for this:

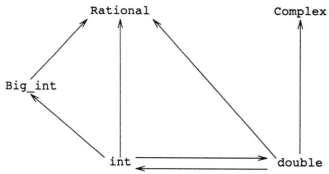

Having understood the conversions that exist because of constructors, the second step is to decide what simplifying (no-value-added) implicit conversions (using conversion operators) we should supply. We avoid implicit conversions when there are points in the domain that do not obviously map to the range; e.g. it's not obvious how to convert a `Complex` to a `double` when there is a nonzero imaginary part. However, there is a clear way to convert a `Rational` to a `double` (although we should be aware of possible loss of precision or range errors). So we add `Rational::operator double` to our type structure:

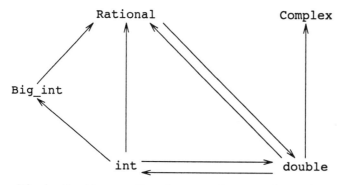

We don't add any other downward conversions, since that would increase the fanout from `Rational`. The high fanout from `int` and `double` is unavoidable (and is characteristic of built in types).

Suppose we want to convert a `Rational` to an `int` or a `Big_int`? Adding implicit conversions from `Rational` would increase the fanout; but we can imagine times when these conversions would be useful. The answer is to provide conversions that are normal member functions, without defining an implicit conversion:

```
class Rational {
// ...
public:
  Big_int cvt_Big_int();
  int cvt_int();
};
```

these allow users of `Rationals` to get the `Big_int` and `int` equivalents by making an explicit call.

We've avoided conversions between `Complex` and `int` or `Big_int` because we don't imagine this conversion happening very often (if it does, perhaps a version of Complex that uses `int` or `Big_ints` would be more appropriate), and can easily be done by converting to or from a double first. Since the conversion is not obviously necessary, we leave it out.

Summary

The moral of the story is: use implicit type conversions carefully, and with restraint. Every implicit type conversion has the potential for causing problems down the line. Think about the type structure as a whole, and look for ways to avoid fanout. The use of implicit type conversions from a simpler to a more complex type, even if the conversions are available, should be avoided; this is especially true if the simpler type is a built in such as `int`.

As software economics drives us toward more ambitious reuse of code, larger and larger parts of an application will consist of libraries written by someone other than the developer of the application. It is the responsibility of the library developer to make sure that the type structure provided by the library is as simple and small as is practical.

Acknowledgments

Helpful comments and suggestions were provided by Martin Carroll, Andrew Koenig, Stan Lippman, Barbara Moo, Jonathan Shopiro, and Bjarne Stroustrup.

References

[1] Stroustrup, B. *The C++ Programming Language*, Addison-Wesley, 1986.
[2] *Draft Proposed American National Standard for Information Systems-Programming Language C*, 5/13/88 draft, Doc. X3J11/88-090, J. Brodie, chair.
[3] Levy, L. *Taming the Tiger: Software Engineering and Software Economics*, Springer-Verlag 1987.

Part II
Multiple Inheritance

Chapter 5

The Case Against Multiple Inheritance in C++

T. A. Cargill

Abstract

Multiple inheritance (MI) is now part of C++. MI greatly complicates the language, burdening those who learn, write and read C++. The costs would be justified if MI enriched the language, making it easier to express programs. But the literature contains no convincing examples of MI solving programming problems. Still, the X3J16 ANSI standards committee for C++ has embraced MI by adopting Ellis & Stroustrup [1990] as a base document. Before imposing a standard that includes MI, the committee should justify the costs by publishing realistic sample programs that demonstrate a compelling need for MI.

Introduction

Originally C++ had single inheritance (SI): a derived class could have only a single base class, and a class inheritance hierarchy was a tree. Since the release of AT&T's C++ 2.0 (and compatible implementations) C++ has included multiple inheritance (MI): the number of base classes is unlimited, and in general, a class inheritance hierarchy is a directed acyclic graph (DAG).

Under MI, derived classes inherit all the members of all their base classes. The potential ambiguity arising from an identifier's use in more than one base class is resolved at compile time, usually by giving fully qualified names. A more subtle problem arises when an ancestor base class can be reached by more than one path through the DAG: should there be a unique shared instance of the base class or a distinct copy along each path? This issue is addressed by an additional inheritance mechanism: the virtual base class. Virtual ancestor base classes are shared; non-virtual bases are distinct. The semantics of MI in C++ and its possible implementations are discussed in depth in Stroustrup [1989b] and Ellis & Stroustrup [1990].

Programming Language Design

The primary purpose of programming languages is the writing of computer programs. Improvements in programming languages over the years have enabled us to program more effectively. Progress is made by identifying shortcomings in existing languages and experimenting with new languages or new language features. In this process, the perceived benefits of language features range from ease of learning for novice programmers to support for

From *Computing Systems*, Vol. 4, No. 1, pp. 69-82, 1991.

veterans maintaining aging code. Every feature added to a language incurs costs for programmers and implementors. The costs of each feature are weighed against its benefits, such as increased expressive power, safety or efficiency. Of course, the design process must consider not only each feature in isolation, but also the interactions between features.

In selecting language features, one simple criterion can be applied universally: it should be possible to use each feature to write practical programs that are improvements in some respect over the corresponding programs expressed without the feature. Programming language features should be useful for writing computer programs. I wish to apply this criterion to multiple inheritance in C++.

The Popular Perception

The popular perception is that MI is a valuable addition to C++. In books, magazines, and advertising copy, MI in C++ is described favorably, with phrases like

- learn how to create powerful hybrid classes using multiple inheritance
- a significant enhancement to the support of object-oriented programming
- one of the most important and fundamental changes to C++

[Weston 1990; Lippman 1990; Eckel 1989]. Unfortunately, those offering such opinions on the virtues of MI have not offered convincing evidence of those virtues.

The Costs of Multiple Inheritance

Multiple inheritance in C++ is complicated. It is complicated to learn, write and read. Each of these contributes to the cost of using C++.

With only one inheritance mechanism C++ would be a complex language. But a newcomer today is faced with six variants of inheritance: a choice of three access levels for each inheritance relationship (public, protected or private), and another choice of whether or not each base class is virtual. The real expressive power of inheritance is delivered by just one of the six variants: public inheritance from a non-virtual base. Yet we must learn the complexity of all six variants' interactions with other language features, such as initialization, virtual functions, overloading and conversions.

The evidence that MI is difficult to program is found in most of the published attempts to demonstrate its merits. Wiener and Pinson set out to exhibit a practical use of MI, but create an incorrect program that happens to produce the intended output on some hardware [Wiener & Pinson 1989]. Most textbook examples of MI are correct programs, but merely disguise aggregation as inheritance, for example [Dewhurst & Stark 1989; Pohl 1989; Stevens 1990]. It is unrealistic to believe that programmers at large will be more successful in using MI than the authors of text books.

Programs that use MI are hard to understand. For example, Shopiro describes the use of MI in the Iostream library [Shopiro 1989]. Shopiro's code, about one hundred source lines, has essentially the same architecture as

Iostream, simplified to reveal its use of MI. I have encountered several programmers who attempted to read the paper. Their talents are probably above
average in that they take the trouble to read *SIGPLAN Notices*. None managed
to understand the code. In my own case perseverance paid off on the third
reading. This measure may be unfair; more evidence, and of a more objective
nature, would be welcome. However, I doubt that anyone would argue that
MI is easy to read and comprehend. Skeptical readers should examine Shopiro
[1989] for themselves.

To illustrate the language complexity of MI in general, and virtual base
classes in particular, consider the following small program, adapted from
Stroustrup [1989b].:

```
class Top {
public:
virtual void f() { printf("Top::f()"); }
};

class Left : public virtual Top {
public:
        void g() { f(); }
};

class Right : public virtual Top {
public:
        void f() { printf("Right::f()"); }
};

class Bottom : public Left, public Right {
};

main()
{
    Bottom x;

    x.g();
    return 0;
}
```

Class Bottom inherits from both Left and Right, which have a common virtual base class, Top, as shown in Figure 5.1. The virtual function Top::f() is

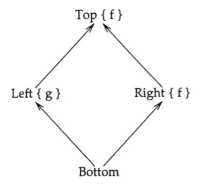

Figure 5.1
Inheritance hierarchy

redefined by Right. In main() the function Left::g() is invoked on x, an instance of Bottom. When f() is called from within Left::g(), should Top::f() or Right::f() be invoked?

The answer is Right::f()!!! (Triple exclamation marks appear in an earlier treatment of this phenomenon [Stroustrup 1989a], though not in its successor [Stroustrup 1989b].) If virtual base classes are used, determining which virtual function is called is much more complicated than under SI, where one need examine only classes that are reached by traversing up-paths and down-paths in the inheritance tree from the calling context. To understand the behavior of Left::g() we must examine the entire DAG reachable by traversing from any class derived from Left to any virtual base class of Left.

This example illustrates the complexity of part of the MI language mechanism in isolation. The complexity compounds when interactions with other language features, such as initialization and conversion, are considered. We must weigh the complexity and costs of MI in C++ against its benefits in terms of its assistance in writing programs. The benefits should be manifest in examples of C++ programs that use MI.

Examples of MI in the Literature

Most of the published examples of MI in C++ are just aggregation disguised as inheritance. Aggregation can be expressed more directly and naturally using the language mechanism intended for that purpose. It is better to express simple aggregation by embedding member objects than by pretending it is the richer relationship of inheritance.

Pohl [1989] contains a typical example:

```
class tools {
public:
     int      cost();
// ...
};

class labor {
public:
     int      cost();
// ...
};

class parts {
public:
     int      cost();
// ...
};

class plans : public tools, public parts, public labor {
public:
     int      tot-cost() { return (parts::cost() + labor::cost()); }
// ...
};
```

Without detriment, class plans can be re-expressed without MI–indeed without any inheritance–as follows.

```
class plans {
public:
    tools   t;
    labor   l;
    parts   p;
    int     tot-cost() { return (p.cost()+l.cost()); }
// ...
};
```

This example is representative of most attempts to demonstrate MI for the benefit of novice C++ programmers. Some similar examples are rewritten in Cargill [1990a].

Gorlen et al. [1990] use MI twice. Their first example (p. 295) uses inheritance to open the scope of classes serving as modules (that is, all members are static). The code has the following form:

```
class A {
// static data
public:
static void f();
static void g();
// ...
};

class B {
// static data
public:
static void f();
// ...
};

class M : public A, public B {
public:
    void    h();
};

void M::h()
{
//  ...
    B::f(); // just f() would be ambiguous
    g();    // unambiguously A::g()
//  ...
}
```

Because class M inherits from both A and B, member functions of A and B can be called from M's scope without name qualification, provided there is no ambiguity. Here MI is used to open other scopes and let the programmer write g() rather than A::g(). However, in general there is no saving. As Gorlen et al. themselves point out, when ambiguity arises scope resolution must be used to specify the function explicitly, e.g., B::f(). The call to g() is unambiguous only until a g() is added to B. It would be safer to write A::g() in the first place, making the inheritance redundant.

Gorlen, et al. also use MI to construct a class whose objects can be placed on two linked lists (p. 297), in the fashion described in Ellis & Stroustrup [1990, p. 199]. In the member functions of the derived class casts are used to select one of two auxiliary linked-list base classes. Ignoring the risks of using casts unnecessarily, such casts are equivalent to selection within an aggregate. A simpler equivalent class may be created using SI and aggregation, as shown in Cargill [1990b].

Weston uses MI to add an `ostream` (for debugging) to a text edit window [Weston 1990, p. 270]. The `ostream` could equally well be incorporated by aggregation as a member object. Indeed, using aggregation simplifies the cumbersome initialization code in the MI version.

As mentioned above, Shopiro describes the use of MI in Iostream [Shopiro 1989]. This is the most convincing example of MI published to date. An input-output (I/O) stream inherits from both an input and an output stream, each of which in turn inherits from a buffer management virtual base class. The weakness is that the I/O duality vanishes as soon as an operation is applied to an I/O stream. Any operation has the effect of selecting the input or the output half of the I/O stream. An alternative architecture that uses single inheritance and explicit aggregation is described in Cargill [1990a]. Moreover, the version of Iostream in the (December 1990) draft X3J16 library does not use MI [Schwarz 1990].

In summary, every published example of MI in C++ can be written just as easily without MI.

General Transformations

That all published MI programs can be transformed into equally simple SI programs might tempt one to look for a general procedure for eliminating MI. Strictly, such a procedure is trivial, but provides no insight. Since Cfront converts C++ to C, it could easily translate any C++ program into C++ without inheritance. But, as with the general algorithm for replacing `goto` by `while`, this approach would make no attempt to conserve structure. It therefore has no bearing on the question of writing real programs with or without MI.

In all but one of the examples above MI is eliminated by replacing inheritance with aggregation. But a general MI-eliminating transformation would have to do more than merely replace inheritance with aggregation. The MI in the following program schema cannot be converted to aggregation without serious distortion.

```
class B1 {
public:
virtual void f1();
};

class B2 {
public:
virtual void f2();
};

class M : public B1, public B2 {
public:
        void f1();
        void f2();
};

void M::f1()
{
    ...
    f2();
    ...
}
```

```
void M::f2()
{
    ...
    f1();
    ...
}
```

In this schema the virtual functions `M::f1()` and `M::f2()` are redefined such that they mutually depend on each other. This schema cannot easily be expressed using only aggregation and single inheritance. The schema demonstrates the expressive power of MI, but only in a hypothetical setting. If MI were widely used in this manner in real programs, my thesis would collapse. However, this style of MI is not found in any of the published examples.

MI in Other Languages

A popular thesis is that MI has proven its worth in other languages and therefore C++ was incomplete without it. Such feature-by-feature reasoning between languages is spurious. The effectiveness of features depends on how they interact with other features as much as on their intrinsic properties.

Examples of MI in Eiffel [Meyer 1988] do not map directly into C++ because of other features in Eiffel. The scope system of Eiffel means that inheritance is needed for access to the equivalent of a public static member in C++. But, as discussed above, C++'s regular scope resolution is a simpler solution than inheritance. MI is also used in Eiffel in combination with generic classes. A proposal for adding generic classes to C++ ("parameterized types") has been adopted by the ANSI committee. At present, the interaction between MI and the forthcoming generics in C++ is no more than the subject of speculation. (Of course, I question the wisdom of standardizing extensions before better understanding the basis.)

MI is used in CLOS [Bobrow et al. 1988] for creating "mix-in" classes. However, the type system and binding mechanisms of CLOS are radically different from those of C++. The run-time method selection algorithm of CLOS is comparable with the compile-time overloading resolution algorithm of C++. Ellis and Stroustrup observe that mix-ins do not work in C++ [Ellis & Stroustrup 1990, p. 202].

Curry and Ayers [1984] discuss the use MI in the Traits language for the Xerox Star workstation. Their conclusions about MI are mixed. MI was used many times, but not to much advantage:

> Although [. . .] many of the classes used multiple subclassing, very few used multiple subclassing in an intrinsic or unavoidable way; minor rearrangements of the traits graph, not costly either in program logic or in class data space, could eliminate the multiple inheritance.

A comprehensive study of the use of MI in other languages, with attempts to map programs into C++, might yield further insight into the interaction between MI and the type and scope mechanisms of C++.

Virtual Base Classes

Inheritance from multiple independent class libraries is often cited as the case for MI in C++. C++ can be significantly simplified by the elimination of virtual base classes and still be sufficient for independent multiple inheritance. Virtual base classes are only meaningful when the different paths through an inheritance DAG are designed as a whole. Virtual bases cannot be exploited when multiply inheriting from independently developed libraries.

There is therefore perhaps a technical middle ground to explore. We may discover that MI is indeed useful, but that virtual base classes are unnecessary. For example, MI is used in the C++ Booch Components [Booch & Vilot 1990]. Few details have been published, but it appears to make no use of virtual base classes. Most of the complexity of MI in C++ is due to virtual bases. Determining that the benefits of virtual bases do not justify their costs would be progress, even if the larger question of MI in general were left unresolved.

Programming Language Research

Critics may observe that I was among the first to call for MI in C++ [Cargill 1986]. In that paper I was calling for an opportunity to conduct research on the question of MI in C++. I believe that research in programming languages must involve programming experiments. Aesthetically elegant ideas do not always work well in practice. For example, Algol 60's call-by-name was mathematically sound, but impractical, and is not found in modern programming languages. When I called for investigation of MI in C++ my concluding remark on the subject was:

> Of course, the success of multiple inheritance cannot be guaranteed without practical experience, but it is certainly worth pursuing.

At that time I hoped that MI would appear in an experimental implementation, where programmers could explore and evaluate the idea, but that did not happen. The first working implementations were closely followed by compiler products and the ANSI committee's adoption of MI in a base document. We must question the diligence of the C++ technical community in conducting our research.

Conclusion

The evidence to date is that multiple inheritance is not useful in writing C++ programs. It should not become part of the ANSI C++ standard before convincing examples of its use are published. If multiple inheritance is a mistake, programmers will pay the price of using an unnecessarily complicated language for years to come.

Acknowledgements

My thanks to Carol Meier and Rob Pike for their suggestions about this paper.

References

D. G. Bobrow, et al., *The Common Lisp Object System*, Technical Report 88P002R, X3J13 Committee, ANSI, 1988.

G. Booch, M. Vilot, The Design of the Booch Components, *Proceedings OOPSLA/ECOOP 90, Sigplan Notices*, 25(10), October 1990.

T. A. Cargill, Pi: A Case Study in Object-Oriented Programming, *Proceedings OOPSLA 86, Sigplan Notices*, 21(11), November 1986.

T. A. Cargill, Does C++ Really Need Multiple Inheritance?, *Proceedings of the USENIX C++ Conference, San Francisco,* April 1990a.

T. A. Cargill, We Must Debate Multiple Inheritance, C++ *Journal,* 1(2), Fall 1990b.

G. A. Curry, R.A. Ayers, Experience with Traits in the Xerox Star Workstation, *IEEE Transactions on Software Engineering,* SE-10(5), September 1984.

S. C. Dewhurst, K. T. Stark, *Programming in C++,* Prentice Hall, 1989.

B. Eckel, *Using C++,* Osborne McGraw-Hill 1989.

M. A. Ellis, B. Stroustrup, *The Annotated C++ Reference Manual,* Addison-Wesley, 1990. K. E. Gorlen, S. M. Orlow, P. S. Plexico, *Data Abstraction and Object-Oriented Programming in C++,* Wiley, 1990.

S. B. Lippman, C++: How Release 2.0 Differs from Release 1.2, *The C++ Journal,* 1(1), Summer 1990.

B. Meyer, *Object-Oriented Software Construction,* Prentice-Hall, 1988.

I. Pohl, C++ *for C Programmers,* Benjamin Cummings, 1989.

J. S. Schwarz, Personal Communication, December 1990.

J. E. Shopiro, An Example of Multiple Inheritance in C++: A Model of the Iostream Library, *Sigplan Notices,* 24(12), December 1989.

A. Stevens, *Teach Yourself C++,* MIS Press, 1990.

B. Stroustrup, The Evolution of C++: 1985 to 1989, *Computing Systems,* 2(3), Summer 1989a.

B. Stroustrup, Multiple Inheritance for C++, *Computing Systems,* 2(4), Fall 1989b.

D. Weston, *Elements of C++ Macintosh Programming,* Addison-Wesley, 1990.

R. S. Wiener, L. J. Pinson, A Practical Example of Multiple Inheritance in C++, *Sigplan Notices,* 24(9), September 1989.

Chapter 6

The Case For Multiple Inheritance in C++

Jim Waldo

Abstract

Multiple inheritance is a difficult and complex feature added to C++ at release 2.0. Cargill argues that the addition was a step backward in that the feature adds complexity to the language without adding functionality. His basis for the latter half of this claim is that no example of multiple inheritance has been given which cannot be rewritten into a functionally equivalent example which uses single inheritance and aggregation instead of multiple inheritance.

I examine Cargill's arguments, and then sketch an example which uses multiple inheritance but which cannot be rewritten to be functionally equivalent by using single inheritance and aggregation. I then distinguish among three forms of inheritance, and argue that most attempts to give an example of multiple inheritance have attempted to use the one form which is the least likely to need that feature.

Introduction

Cargill has argued [1991] that multiple inheritance in C++ complicates the language without adding anything that can be shown to be of use. He backs up his claim by showing that all existing examples of the use of multiple inheritance in the current literature can be executed just as well without using multiple inheritance. His conclusion is that

> the evidence to date is that multiple inheritance is not useful in writing C++ programs. It should not become part of the ANSI C++ standard before convincing examples of its use are published...

This is not the first time that Cargill has argued that multiple inheritance is not a useful addition to the C++ programming language (other examples of the argument can be found in Cargill 1990a and Cargill 1990b).

The purpose of this article is threefold. First, I will attempt to clarify what the argument is by restating what I take Cargill to be saying. I will then sketch an example of a use of multiple inheritance that I believe does show that the feature is needed in the language to solve a certain set of problems. Finally, I will try to explain why convincing examples of multiple inheritance have not appeared before.

From *Computing Systems*, Vol. 4, No. 2, pp. 156-170, 1992.

Cargill's Argument

Before attempting to sketch an example of a use of multiple inheritance in C++ that could not be programmed in some other way, I think it would be useful to look at just exactly what Cargill's argument is. The main argument is basically laid out as having three premises that lead to the conclusion quoted above. These premises are

1. Multiple inheritance in C++ is complicated. It is complicated to learn, write, and read;
2. Multiple inheritance is not (strictly) needed in C++, i.e., there is nothing that can be done with the feature that cannot be done without it;
3. If a feature is complicated and not needed in a language, it should not be a part of that language.

Therefore

4. Multiple inheritance should be removed from C++.

The first of these is stated overtly and is backed up in a section of Cargill's paper. The second is not stated but is the obvious conclusion of the other sections of Cargill's paper. The third premise of the argument is a general principle that is never overtly stated but is clearly argued for in the section of Cargill's paper on Programming Language Design.

Certainly, the main argument is valid; that is, if (1) through (3) are true, we must accept the conclusion. While the position that multiple inheritance is complicated to learn, write, and read could be disputed, I believe that if that were the only weakness of the argument I would probably side with Cargill. I will, therefore, accept (1) as true, and turn my attention to (2) and (3).

The second premise is itself the conclusion of an argument that has the form

5. No one has given a good reason for multiple inheritance in C++;
6. If no one has shown a reason to include a feature in a programming language, then that feature is not needed by the language;

Therefore,

7. Multiple inheritance is not needed in C++.

Statement (5) is proved by exhaustion. Cargill goes through the various examples and arguments given for including multiple inheritance in C++ and shows that the arguments are either flawed or the examples could be accomplished more easily using single inheritance and aggregation. (6) is again not explicitly stated, but seems to be one allied with (3) as a general principle of programming language design that Cargill tries to express in his section on that activity.

Having misspent my youth as a logician, I feel compelled to point out that the arguments that Cargill is putting forward are perilously close to having the form of the *ad ignoratium*, or appeal to ignorance, fallacy, in which one concludes that a proposition is false because no one has shown it to be true. However, I take Cargill to be making a more interesting claim. Rather than claiming that multiple inheritance is not and never could be useful in writing a C++ program, he has made the weaker claim that no one has shown it to be useful. The interesting part of his claim is that he moves from that proposition to the claim that the feature should not be part of the language.

The real unstated principle behind Cargill's attacks on multiple inheritance in C++ appears to be a sort of Occam's razor applied to programming languages. Occam's razor, applied to metaphysics, states that one should not multiply entities needlessly, and is generally interpreted as holding that simpler systems are to be preferred to more complex ones. Applied to programming languages, this interpretation would hold that less is more, and that languages should only be made more complex if the added complexity allows one to do something with the language that could not be done without the feature being added.

While this principle sounds like one that we would all accept without question, I believe that it is far less absolute than most of us would like to admit. For example, I have seen introductory programming students struggle with the for loop construction in C. The construction is actually quite complex, having non-trivial entry and exit conditions, variable scoping conditions, and genuinely complex rules for determining the state of variables when the loop is terminated in some irregular fashion. Further, anything that can be done with a for loop can be done with a while loop. Therefore, by the principle of simplicity that I am ascribing to Cargill, the for loop is a genuine candidate for being banished from the ANSI C++ standard for exactly the same reasons as multiple inheritance. I take this to be an argument that is more damaging to the principle stated in (6) than to the for loop construction.

Whether Cargill's argument carries the logical weight it should, the fact remains that it is somewhat puzzling that no one seems to be able to give an example that uses multiple inheritance in C++ that is both convincing and understandable. One reason for this might well be that multiple inheritance is not the sort of thing that lends itself to examples. The real use of multiple inheritance is found in large systems, not small examples.

However, in the next section I will attempt to sketch an example that does require the use of multiple inheritance. The example will not be a full, compilable chunk of C++ but rather a part of a much larger system. It will also appear to be a rather odd use of inheritance, having little to do with the inheritance most C++ programmers are used to. The reasons for this will be discussed in the last section of this paper.

An Example of Multiple Inheritance

Before laying out some class definitions, let me begin by giving a brief explanation of the purpose of the example. In what follows, I will sketch a system with three sorts of objects. One is the usual C++ object, which exists when it is created and ceases to exist when it is freed (if it was created by a call to new) or when it goes out of scope (if it was created by entry into a scope).

The second sort of object is like the first but exists from one run of a program to another; it is a persistent object. In this design, persistence is treated as type.[1] The notion of persistence being talked about is not terribly

---

[1]I realize that this is not the only way to deal with persistence. Others, such as Atwood [private discussion], argue that the best approach to persistence is to consider it a storage class, analogous to automatic. This debate is only slightly relevant to the current debate, and would require a change in the language . The example outlined above may take the wrong approach, but can be implemented within the current definition of the language.

sophisticated, only allowing the saving of state into some entity in a file system. Indeed, we will not really talk about how the persistence works, appealing to magic in the details of the actual mechanism for saving and restoring the state.

The third sort of object can be thought of as a remote pointer to the first or second sorts; I will refer to it as a surrogate for an object that exists in a different address space (perhaps on a different machine). This object's purpose is to cloak the difference between local and remote objects. In the discussion of remoteness, I will assume that there is some underlying RPC mechanism that allows the sending of a message to an object in a different address space. While this is an interesting subject, it is not the subject of this paper, and so the details of how this is done will not be discussed here.[2]

The purpose of this system is to isolate the programmer from having to distinguish between purely local objects, persistent objects, and remote objects. Such isolation is not always possible; there will be times that the programmer will need to know what kind of object is being manipulated. But the overall goal is to allow the same code to manipulate all three.

We start, then, with a class definition for a persistent object, which will look something like the following:

```
class persist
{
 protected:
  char            *where,
   .
   .
   .
 public:
  virtual save() = 0;
  virtual restore() = 0;
}
```

This is, admittedly, a rather odd class definition, consisting of a string (which we can assume is the name of the file in which the persistent state is stored) and two virtual functions, which are not implemented at this level. There might be other data (offsets into the persistent file, whatever) that are used to help in the implementation, but exactly what such data would be is not of interest to this example. This class doesn't look particularly useful, and indeed in its current state it is not. But bear with me.

Equally useless looking is the second class I will define, which is the base class for surrogates to remote objects:

```
class remote
{
 protected:
  objid_t   object,
   .
   .
   .
};
```

This class contains an objid_t, which is used to locate and identify the object for which this is a surrogate. The exact nature of this type would depend on the underlying RPC system used. Note that the class contains no public data or function members. By itself, this is not a very interesting class.

---

[2]This is not a particularly novel approach to remote objects. See, for example, [Tiemann 1988], [Seliger 1990], or [Martin 1991].

To get something that is of some interest, we need a class that does something. For the purpose of this example, even this class will not be very interesting–I will use the old standard of an employee class. Employees will be characterized by an employee name and an employee number. Again, remember that all I am trying to do is to sketch an example of multiple inheritance, not an interesting or useful example.

While the employee class may not be very interesting, the way I get to the definition of the class is not the standard way. I begin by defining what I will call the employee interface class, which looks like:

```
class employee_if
{
  public:
   virtual
   char*
          get_name() = 0;
   virtual
   void
          set_name(
           char    *new_name
            ) = 0;
   virtual
   int     get_num() = 0;
   virtual
   void
          set_num(
           int        new_num
            ) = 0;
};
```

The reason for calling this the employee interface class is now clear. This class defines the set of calls that can be made on classes that derive from it, establishing an interface between the rest of the world and objects that are of this class. However, there is no data associated with instances of this class, and there is no implementation of any of the functions in the interface supplied by this class.

Now I can define some classes that actually do some work. As might be expected, I will define three classes of employee objects. The first will be just like a standard C++ object, in that it will be within a particular address space and will not persist beyond the time the program is running. I will call this class the temporary employee (in all senses of the term):

```
class employee_t :
   public employee_if
{
  char    *name;
  int        number;
  public:
  employee_if();
  ~employee_if();
 };
```

This class contains only two functions in addition to those that were declared in the `employee_if` class; a constructor and a destructor for the instances of the class.[3] The implementation of the class will, of course, have to supply code for all of the virtual functions in the `employee_if` class.

---

[3]Of course, if this were a real chunk of code rather than an example, there would be other functions declared, such as a copy constructor and assignment function. While such calls would be

The second class we will define is our first use of multiple inheritance. This class defines the set of persistent instances of employees. These are instances that can be written to long term storage and read back from that store. The idea for such objects is that they are only restored when needed; if they are never accessed they are never restored. Such a class would be defined as:

```
class employee_persist :
        public employee_if,
        public persist
{
  employee_t        *local_inst;
 public:
  employee_t(
        char      *in_store
        );
  ~employee_t();
};
```

The persistent employee class contains all of the functions in the employee interface class and the save and restore functions of the persistent class. It also contains its own constructor and destructor. Implementations of all of these functions will need to be supplied; no implementation is or can be inherited.

The idea behind the employee_persist class is that the implementation of all of the functions inherited from the employee_if class

The destructor for the persistent version of the employee should call the save function that will pickle the current state of the local_inst and save it to persistent storage. Other functions might also call the save function; for example, if the class is being used in a situation where it would be bad to lose any changes, the save function could be called as part of the implementation of the set functions that change the data.

The final part of the example constructs a class of employees that live, potentially, outside of the address space of the current application (and perhaps on another machine). The idea for this class is much like that found in the persistent class; the class structure looks like:

```
class employee_remote :
  public employee_if,
  public remote
{
 public:
  employee_remote(
        objid_t    far_emp
        );
  ~employee_remote();
};
```

Note that this class adds no new functions to the employee interface class other than a constructor and a destructor (like the local employee case) and adds no new data members.

The virtual functions inherited from the employee_if class would be implemented in the employee_remote class as RPC calls to some actual employee object. That object would receive the RPC call would be determined

---

needed, they are not needed to show the requirement for multiple inheritance. Making this into a genuinely useful C++ class is an exercise left to the reader.

by the object identifier that is the only data member of instances of this class, that was assigned as part of the constructor for the object.

One of the ways in which this example differs from others given of multiple inheritance in C++ is that none of the derived classes listed above inherit any code from a base class. Indeed, the functions in the base classes are all explicitly defined as empty.

This is not an artifact of the example being merely sketched. No code can be given to implement the persistent base class, as the two functions that constitute that class are dependent on the data that is added by the derivation. There are no functions to implement in the `remote` class; that class simply provides a way of storing the data needed to give the underlying RPC a handle to contact a remote object. The `employee_if` class implements no functions, since that class has no data associated with it.

Sharing code among these classes was not the reason for constructing this particular class hierarchy. The reason for this hierarchy is to share code that *manipulates* instances of these classes. With the above hierarchy, for example, I can write a single `print_employee_name` function, that will work on all three kinds of employee objects: local, persistent, and remote. In the same way, we can pass lists of pointers to `employee_if` objects to functions that sort by name or employee number and then list the names of the employees in that order. In short, we have provided a way of writing code that handles three kinds of employees at the same time when the differences between those employees are hidden (as it should be) by the encapsulation offered by the `employee_if` abstraction.

In the same way, I could write routines that work on all persistent objects, whether they be employee objects or, say, inventory objects. These could be ways to force save the objects, or ways or doing batch restores. The main point is that whatever else these objects are, there are certain functions that require only that they be persistent. For those functions, being derived from the `persist` class is enough to allow the object to be passed into and be manipulated by them.

It is this reuse of code that manipulates the objects that keeps the example from being reducible by the Cargillian technique of aggregation to an equivalent example that uses single inheritance. The signature of a function that prints all employee names would be:

```
void
print_emp_name(
  employee_if    *to_print
);
```

to allow the printing of names of local, persistent, and remote employees. The signature of a routine that forced the saving of a persistent object would be something like:

```
void
force_save(
  persist        *to_save
);
```

To allow a single object to have its address passed into either routine requires that we use multiple inheritance.

Multiple Inheritance for Multiple Inheritances

What is really going on in this example is that we are using different kinds of inheritance for different purposes. The C++ language doesn't help us here, for all inheritance in C++ appears to be of a single kind–a derived class inherits from its base class, and that's all there is to it. Unfortunately, this hides a distinction between at least three different kinds of inheritance, all of which look like they are simple cases of a class deriving from another class.

In the C++ literature, most examples of inheritance are examples of what I will call implementation inheritance. Implementation inheritance is characterized as the relationship a derived class has with its base class when some of the functions of the derived class are delegated to functions that have been implemented in the base class. The derived class inherits code from the base class.

This sort of inheritance is one that most programmers from outside the object-oriented paradigm can immediately appreciate. It's easy to see the advantages implementation inheritance gives you, because you can produce a new object without writing very much code. So it isn't surprising that most of the books that attempt to teach C++ center on this sort of inheritance.

Unfortunately, implementation inheritance is probably the most difficult kind of inheritance to use if one wishes to give an example in which multiple inheritance is needed. The actual implementation of some code is tied rather closely to the particulars of some class, and can usually only be reused if the class derived from the base class differs only in a fairly small way from the original class. Put another way, implementation inheritance works well only in cases when the derived class is a subset of the base class, i.e., it differs from the base class only by being more restrictive. The implementation of functions in the base class that are irrelevant to the restriction can then be reused (inherited), because the things that make the derived class different from the base are irrelevant to those implementations.

The subset relation holding between a derived class and its base class is a characteristic of single inheritance. Multiple inheritance allows (and, in fact, generally requires) that the derived class be a superset of any of its base classes. In a single inheritance system, if A is derived from B you can be sure that A is just a more restrictive kind of B. In a multiple inheritance system, if A is derived from B and C you cannot be sure that A is just a more restrictive kind of B. In fact, you know that it isn't–it is both a B and a C. So it is not surprising that any code implemented for something that is only a B would not work well for something that is both a B and a C.

A second sort of inheritance is the reason for the `employee_if` class in the example. This sort of inheritance is often called interface inheritance,[4] because the reason for using this sort of inheritance is to allow the same functional interface to be presented by all objects that are members of classes that derive from that class.

The `employee_if` class can be thought of as a class that exists purely for the purpose of interface inheritance. It has no data associated with it, and there is no implementation of any of the functions that are the only real meat of the

---

[4]There are a number of authors who identify this sort of inheritance with this name; see, for example, Dewhurst and Stark [1989].

class. In effect, the class is a contract between any class that derives off of it and the rest of the world, saying that since the class derives off of the `employee_if` class, it thereby contracts to allow the calling of any and all of those functions.

The final kind of inheritance is what I will label data inheritance; it is the kind of inheritance used in the `remote` class in the example. This is sort of the flip-side of interface inheritance–while the latter gives functional interfaces without any data or implementation, the pure case of data inheritance allows the derivation of a new class that shares only data members with no implication that the functions that can be called on instances of such a derived class or the behavior of those instances will have anything in common with the base. In our example, the remote class was defined only so that all remote objects, no matter what their behavior or interface, could inherit the same data layout, that in turn would allow the RPC mechanism to work.

These last two sorts of inheritance, interface inheritance and data inheritance, are far more likely than implementation inheritance to require support for multiple inheritance in the language. Each of these is of limited use by itself, but gains power when allowed to be part of an inheritance graph. These other sorts of inheritance allow the specification of relationships between classes of objects that are more subtle than those that are given by the use of implementation inheritance, and allow the same code to use different sorts of objects based on their similarities.

The reason that no examples of multiple inheritance have been given thus far has much to do with the obvious power of implementation inheritance. Implementation inheritance is an obvious win, for it allows new classes of objects to be created that only need to have code written for a small part of their functionality. Showing examples of implementation inheritance is a good way to win over programmers who are unfamiliar with object oriented programming to the paradigm, for they see that they can do more with less code.

No such obvious savings are seen when interface or data inheritance is used. It is only when looking at the larger system, the part of the system that uses the objects of the classes that are created, that the payoff of these other kinds of inheritance become obvious. Since this payoff requires seeing the use of multiple inheritance within the context of a full system, and since the gains in such systems come about only when the systems themselves become large or complex, it is difficult to give examples that are both easily understood and obviously useful that use these other forms of inheritance.

Once we understand this, it is not surprising that no simple example of multiple inheritance has been given showing a need for the feature. However, to argue that because an example is lacking the feature should not be put into the language misses the distinction between the various forms of inheritance. Accepting such an argument is tantamount to saying that the language should contain only implementation inheritance. This would weaken the language significantly.

To say that a language feature should be taken out if no one can provide a simple example of the feature's use is justified if the language is being designed to support the construction of examples. However, for a language like C++, which has been designed for production work, the lack of a simple example does not show that the feature is not needed. It only shows that the feature may not be simple.

References

T. A. Cargill, Does C++ Really Need Multiple Inheritance, *Proceedings of the USENIX C++ Conference, San Francisco,* April 1990. (A)

T. A. Cargill, We Must Debate Multiple Inheritance, *C++ Journal,* 1(2), Fall 1990. (B)

T. A. Cargill, Controversy: The Case Against Multiple Inheritance in C++, *Computing Systems 4.1* (1991).

S. C. Dewhurst, K. T. Stark, *Programming in C++,* Prentice Hall, 1989.

Bruce Martin, The Separation of Interface and Implementation in C++, *Proceedings of the USENIX C++ Conference, Washington, D.C.,* April 1991.

Robert Seliger, Extended C++, *Proceedings of the USENIX C++ Conference,* San Francisco, April 1990.

Michael D. Tiemann, Wrappers: Solving the RPC Problem in GNU C++, *Proceedings of the USENIX C++ Conference, Denver,* October 1988.

Chapter 7

Signature-Based Polymorphism for C++

Elana D. Granston and Vincent F. Russo

Abstract

Polymorphism is defined as the potential for a variable or function parameter to have a value of one type at one point in time, and a value of a different type at another. In this paper, we propose an extension to the C++ language that offers the polymorphism flexibility of multiple inheritance without its software engineering disadvantages. Rather than relying on inheritance, our extension allows polymorphism to be achieved by explicitly defining the *signature* (public class interface) a variable or formal parameter is required to have at a set of usage or call sites. Any object whose class *conforms* to the designated signature can be bound to such a variable or formal parameter. Our conformance rule is independent of the class hierarchy from which such objects are instantiated. When a member function is invoked on a pointer or reference with a signature as its declared type, the corresponding member function of the referenced object's actual class is invoked. The class's member functions that correspond to the signature's member functions can be `virtual`, `inline`, neither or both.

Introduction

A fundamental feature of object-oriented programming[8, 4] is *polymorphism*[2]. Polymorphism is the potential for a variable or function parameter to have a value of one type at one point in time, and a value of a different type at another. At present, inheritance coupled with virtual functions is the *only* mechanism for achieving such polymorphism in C++[3]. With single inheritance, the range of polymorphism that can be supported is limited. Multiple inheritance extends this range, but not without incurring several software engineering disadvantages.

In this paper, we propose an extension to the C++ language that offers greater polymorphism flexibility than multiple inheritance without incurring its disadvantages. Rather than relying on inheritance, our extension allows polymorphism to be achieved by explicitly defining the *signature* (public class interface) a variable or formal parameter is required to have at a set of usage or call sites. *Any* object whose class *conforms* to the designated signature can be bound to such a variable or formal parameter. When a member function is invoked on a pointer or reference with a signature as its declared type, the corresponding member function of the referenced object's actual class is

From *USENIX 1990 C++ Conference Proceedings*, pp. 65-79.

invoked. The class's member functions that correspond to the signature's member functions can be `virtual`, `inline` neither or both.

The remainder of this paper is organized as follows. The second section defines polymorphism and discusses the disadvantages and limitations of existing C++ polymorphism mechanisms. The third section introduces our language extension. The fourth section proposes a naive implementation. The fifth section discusses the performance tradeoffs of our proposed implementation relative to existing methods. The sixth section discusses potential extensions. Finally, the last section draws conclusions as to the relative efficacy of our proposed language feature.

Mechanisms for Achieving Polymorphism in C++

Inheritance coupled with virtual functions provides the basic form of polymorphism in C++. For example, consider the following two classes:

```
class ListOfInt {
        ...
public:
        ...
        virtual void add( int x );
};
class OrderedListOfInt : public ListOfInt {
        ...
public:
        ...
        void add( int x );
};
```

We can define a function `initialize` with a formal parameter of the type `ListOfInt` as follows:

```
void
initialize( ListOfInt * aList, int n )
{
    while( int i = 0; i < n; i++ ) {
            aList->add( random() );
    };
}
```

Although the formal parameter `aList` is defined with type `ListOfInt`, the actual arguments to `initialize()` can either have type `ListOfInt` or type `OrderedListOfInt`. Hence, `initialize` is polymorphic with respect to the formal parameter `list`.

Since `add()` is virtual, C++ retains sufficient knowledge regarding the actual class of any argument bound to the formal parameter `list` so that it can be determined at run-time whether to call `ListOfInt::add()` or `Ordered-ListOfInt::add()`. This run-time binding is what makes polymorphism work in C++.

In the above example, polymorphism is supported through single inheritance. However, there are many cases where single inheritance is insufficient to achieve the desired polymorphic behavior. For example, suppose that we have two libraries containing hierarchies of classes for X-Windows display objects. One hierarchy is rooted at `OpenLookObject` and the other at `MotifObject`. Further assume that all the classes in each hierarchy implement the `display()` and `move()` member functions. Finally, suppose that we obtained the libraries from two separate vendors and that only header files and binaries have been provided. Can a display list of objects be constructed that can contain objects from *both* class libraries *simultaneously*? An obvious solution would be to alter the two implementations so that the roots of both existing hierarchies were derived from a common base class. However, since source code is not available for the two libraries, such *retroactive* inheritance is not possible.

An extremely inelegant solution can be effected by declaring each element of the display list to be a discriminated union (i.e., union plus tag field) as follows:

```
struct displayListElement {
    int tag;
    union {
        MotifObject * pMotifObject;
        OpenLookObject * pOpenLookObject;
    };
};
...
displayListElement displayList[NELEMENTS];
```

Since an assignment to a union causes C++ to lose information about the actual type of an object, a tag must be explicitly set on assignment to indicate whether the object is from the MotifObject hierarchy or the OpenLookObject hierarchy. This information is needed to determine whether to call the displayList[i].pMotifObject->display() function or the displayList[i].pOpenLookObject->display() function. This solution violates good object-oriented programming style.

Multiple inheritance [6] can also be used to solve this problem. First, we construct a new class XWindowsObject that defines virtual functions display() and move() as follows:

```
class XWindowsObject {
public:
    virtual void display() = 0;
    virtual void move() = 0;
};
```

Next, we create a set of new classes, where each class corresponds to an existing library class. Each new class multiply inherits from XWindowsObject and its corresponding library class, and redefines display() and move() to call the corresponding function in the library class. For example,

```
class XOpenLookCircle :
        public OpenLookCircle, public XWindowsObject {
public:
    void display() { OpenLookCircle::display(); }
    void move( int x, int y ) { OpenLookCircle::move( x, y ); }
};
```

and

```
class XMotifSquare : public MotifSquare, public XWindowsObject {
public:
    void display() { MotifSquare::display(); }
    void move( int x, int y ) { MotifSquare::move( x, y ); }
};
```

Finally, we can create the display list as follows:

```
XWindowsObject * displayList[NELEMENTS];
```

The task of creating these classes can be simplified by using templates [7, 3]. For example given the template

```
template<class T>
class XWindowsObjectTemplate : public XWindowsObject, public T {
public:
    void display() { T::display(); }
    void move( int x, int y ) { T::move( x, y ); }
};
```

the necessary classes could be created as follows:

```
typedef XWindowsObjectTemplate<MotifSquare> XMotifSquare;
typedef XWindowsObjectTemplate<OpenLookCircle> XOpenLookCircle;
```

Even with templates, this option entails substantial software engineering costs. Building all these extra classes is tedious at best, and muddles the program name space with a superfluous set of new classes. Despite these drawbacks, however, this option is currently the *only* method for achieving the desired results in C++ given the specified limitations.

Note that in the above example, it is the multiple inheritance and not the templates that permit the polymorphic behavior of the new leaf classes. While templates are useful for many purposes, they *cannot* be used to achieve polymorphism. Templates allow the same body of source code (function or class implementation) to be instantiated with one of many types. They do not allow the same body of source code to be used in a single instantiation with multiple, unrelated types (no common base class). For example, templates can be used to create a generic display list class `DisplayList<`*type*`>` parameterized by the type of elements in the list. This template can then be instantiated as either a list of `MotifObjects` (i.e., `DisplayList<MotifObject>`) or `OpenLookObjects` (i.e., `DisplayList<OpenLookObject>`), but *not* both simultaneously. In other words, `DisplayList<OpenLookObject` *and/or* `MotifObject>` is impossible.

The difficulty in creating a display list that can contain both `MotifObjects` and `OpenLookObjects` is that C++ constrains the type of an object reference or pointer to a class type, providing only one mechanism (inheritance coupled with virtual functions) to achieve polymorphism of this form. Consequently, even if every class in both libraries implements the `display()` and `move()` functions with the same interface, C++ does not enable us to express that this is the *only* requirement for addition to our display list.

Signatures

To address the problems discussed in the previous section, we propose augmenting the current C++ type system to allow *signature conformance* to be explicitly specified. We define the signature of a class X (`sigof(X)` in our notation) to be the member functions (along with their return types and argument types) in the public interface of X. The signature of a class includes public member functions defined by the class, as well as those inherited from its base classes. Therefore, `sigof(X)` specifies the *interface provided by* class X, as opposed to an *instance of* class X (or any derived class of X). Our definition of conformance is that class Y conforms to `sigof(X)` if for each member function in the public interface of X, there is a member function in the public interface of Y with the exact same name, return type, number of arguments, ordering of arguments, and argument types. Since there is assumed to be a canonical ordering of signature functions which does not necessarily equal the lexical order of the associated declaration, the ordering of the member function declarations in either class is irrelevant. It should be noted that a class's signature does *not* include its constructor, but does include its destructor. The only thing special about the destructor is that any destructor conforms to any other destructor. In other words, the name of the destructor (only) is ignored when checking conformance.

For example, given the two class definitions

```
class A {
public:
    A();
    ~A();
    virtual int a();
    void b( int );
    float f;
};
```

and

```
class B {
private:
    void c( int );
    int d;
public:
    void b( int );
    int a();
    B();
    ~B();
};
```

sigof(A) is equivalent to sigof(B) and the two signatures can be used interchangeably.

Only references and pointers to type sigof(X) are allowed. These have type "sigof(X) * " or "sigof(X) & ". Attempting to create an instance of sigof(X) is meaningless and therefore, invalid. The address of any variable whose nominal type conforms to the signature of class X is an acceptable r-value for an assignment to a variable of type sigof(X) *. Likewise, any variable that conforms can be assigned to a sigof(X) &. By nominal type, we mean the static type (type declared in the code) of the r-value. Due to inheritance, the actual type of the object may be a derived class of the nominal type.

We also allow pointers and references with base type sigof(Y) to be assigned to those with base type sigof(X), providing Y's signature conforms to X's. If Y is a derived class of X this happens automatically since Y inherits all the members functions of X. However, this form of signature conformance is not restricted to derived classes. For example, given the two unrelated classes:

```
class W {
    ...
public:
    int a();
    void b( int );
};
```

and

```
class Z {
    ...
public:
    int a();
    char * c();
    void b( int );
};
```

the assignment

```
sigof(Z) * aZ = ...;
sigof(W) * aW = aZ;
```

is valid even though there is no class inheritance relationship between W and Z at all. The reverse assignment is obviously invalid.

When a member function of a signature pointer or reference is called, the implementation of that function defined by the referenced object's actual class is invoked. Our mechanism places no restrictions on the actual implementation and/or declarations of the member functions in either a class being used for its signature, or the class of an object being assigned to such a variable. The member functions can be virtual, inline, neither, or both. It is interesting to note that our technique allows variables and functions with signature arguments to behave polymorphically even when the referenced objects do not have virtual functions.

To motivate signatures further, let us return to the example introduced in the second section. Recall that we have two class hierarchies for displaying objects on an X-Windows display, one rooted at MotifObject and the other at OpenLookObject. Our signature proposal allows variables of type sigof(XWindowsObject) * or sigof(XWindowsObject)& to be declared, and instances of *any* class that conforms to this signature to be assigned to them. Unlike multiple inheritance, our language extension allows such conformance to be inferred by the compiler. Explicitly coded inheritance is not required. For example, we could simply declare the display list as

```
sigof(XWindowsObject) * displayList[NELEMENTS];
```

and directly assign existing classes from either library as follows

```
displayList[1] = new MotifSquare();
displayList[2] = new OpenLookCircle();
```

In this way we achieve the same result as the multiple inheritance solution without cluttering the program with placeholder classes like XMotifSquare and XOpenLookCircle, and without modifying existing code to retroactively inherit from a new base class.

An additional disadvantage to the multiple inheritance solution lies in the implementation of multiple inheritance itself and the inefficiencies it introduces[1]. In particular, objects instantiated from the new leaf classes have multiple virtual function tables so each object is increased by the space to store the extra table reference(s). The signature based solution we propose provides this same flexibility with none of these disadvantages. Objects do not grow at all in size, no existing code needs to be modified, and no new subclasses need to be introduced.

Implementation

The implementation of our technique centers around the representation of a signature pointer sigof(C) * or signature reference sigof(C) & as a pair *(optr,sptr)*, in which *optr* is a pointer to the object bound to the pointer or reference and *sptr* is a pointer to a signature-specific function lookup table *stbl*.[1]

---

[1]This implementation precludes a signature pointer from being cast to an int, or other integral type, and back, however we believe that this will not be a significant limitation in practice. Note that there is already a precedent for such tuple pointers in C++. Some implementations require double wide pointers to member functions[3].

When a signature reference is constructed, either as the result of an assignment or as the result of passing a conforming object to a function with a signature argument, the object's address is assigned to the *optr* field and the proper signature function lookup table is assigned to the *sptr* field. We propose to use a "thunk" technique that allows the signature table and thunk for any valid assignment to be constructed at compile time and, when necessary, filled in at link time. The *stbl* table is filled with the addresses of thunks. Each thunk indirectly invokes the object class's corresponding function after first updating the this pointer to point to the object rather than the signature reference or pointer. If necessary, multiple inheritance adjustments of the object pointer are also done in these thunks.

Calling a member function of a signature reference proceeds similarly to a C++ virtual function call except that the address of the function to call is obtained by indexing through the table pointed to by the *sptr* field of the signature reference or pointer, rather than indexing through the object's virtual function table (if it even has one). The thunk is called by passing the address of the signature reference as the this pointer (this indirection is stripped off by the thunk), and passing the remaining arguments as if calling a normal member function. For example, given:

```
class X {
        ...
public:
        void a( int, int );
        void b( );
} anX;

sigof(X) * pX = &anX;
```

the call

```
pX->a( 10, 20 );
```

would compile to code approximating

```
(* pX.sptr[n ])( &pX, 10, 20 );
```

where n is the index into the signature table corresponding to the member function called. These indices are assigned similarly to those for classes with virtual functions.

All signature thunks are all basically of the form

```
this = optr;
branch function entry point;
```

The first statement removes the level of indirection the signature reference or pointer introduces, and the second statement branches to the proper function's entry point. The code generated by the compiler is assumed to otherwise leave the stack and all registers unchanged, so when the actual class function is called, the proper arguments are supplied in the proper places.

A signature table and its corresponding thunks must be constructed for each unique signature/class pair resulting from assignments in a given compilation unit. In cases where an object being assigned to a signature pointer or reference has no virtual functions, the signature function lookup table and thunks are simple to construct because the addresses of all the functions referenced via the thunks are known at compile time (or link time). Hence, no run time penalty is incurred for creating either the thunks or the *stbl* tables. For example, given the class X defined earlier, and the pointer

```
sigof(X) * pX;
```

the assignment

```
pX = &anX;
```

would yield the situation shown in Figure 7.1. If an instance of another class meeting X 's signature, say

```
class Y {
        ...
public:
        int a( int, int );
        char * c( int );
        void b( );
} aY;
```

were assigned to pX, the situation in Figure 7.2 would result.

If the object's class defines a member function corresponding to an inline signature function, a non-inline version of the function is compiled and the

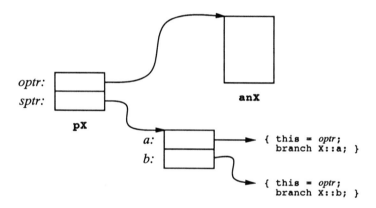

Figure 7.1
Result of assigning &anX to pX

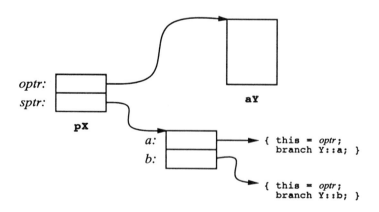

Figure 7.2
Result of assigning &aY to pX

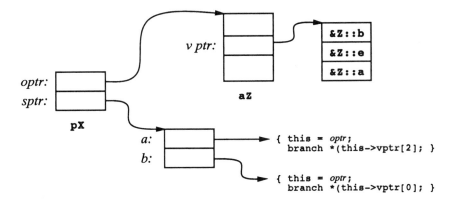

Figure 7.3
Result of assigning &aZ to pX

address of this version is used in the thunk.[2] Alternately, the body of the inline function can be expanded into the thunk.

When a function is defined as virtual in the class of the r-value object, the virtual function table of the object must be indexed at run time. Such a thunk has the following structure:

```
this = optr;
branch *(this->vptr[n ]);
```

Signature tables and thunks are generated based on the nominal type of the r-value of the assignment to a signature pointer or reference. During compilation, every assignment to a signature pointer or reference lexically encountered in a compilation unit causes a signature function table and corresponding thunks to be generated as necessary. Since a class fixes the offsets of virtual functions pointers in the virtual function table for all its subclasses, the nominal type of the r-value of an assignment is sufficient to both determine the offset of the virtual function table pointer from the this pointer and to index into the table. As with virtual functions in C++, all the information necessary to construct the thunks and *stbl* tables is available at compile time.

For example, given

```
        ...
public:
        virtual void b();
        virtual void e();
        virtual int a( int, int );
        int d();
} aZ;
```

the assignment pX = &aZ would yield the situation shown in Figure 7.3.

The last case of interest occurs when one signature pointer or reference is assigned to another. This is only valid when the r-value signature conforms to the l-value signature. In this case, the *optr* field of the l-value is set to the

---

[2]This is similar to the case when a member function is declared to be both virtual and inline in existing C++ compilers.

r-value and the thunks referenced by the l-value's *stbl* index into the *stbl* of the r-value to obtain the next level of thunk. For example,

```
this = optr;
branch *(this->sptr[n ]);
```

In other words, an extra level indirection is performed for each level of additional signature qualification added to an object. Each higher level thunk simply strips off a level of indirection and then branchs to the next level of thunk. Eventually, this chain of indirection terminates, and the actual member function is reached by one of the two earlier mechanisms. In theory, this recursion is bounded by the number of levels of signature qualification which in turn is bounded by the maximum number of public member functions in any class. In practice, the depth of this recursion is not expected to exceed one or two levels in most cases.

```
class U {
        ...
public:
        int a();
        int b();
};
```

and

```
class V {
        ...
public:
        int a();
        virtual int b();
        int c();
};
```

the statements

```
V aV;
sigof(U) * pU;
sigof(V) * pV;
...
pV = &aV;
pU = pV;
```

would yield the situation show in Figure 7.4.

One danger of this "chaining" of signature objects is that the intervening objects may have been stack allocated. Returning a signature typed value from a functions could, therefore, result in dangling pointers to old activation records. One solution to this problem is to do the necessary closure analysis and then heap, rather than stack, allocate signature object which might escape the current function. We are currently exploring this and other solutions to this problem.

Possible Extensions

Three possible extensions to our proposed language feature are:

- extending signatures to include public *data* members,
- allowing aliasing of the names in a signature,
- allowing the builtin types to conform to certain signatures.

Extending Signatures to Include Data Members
sigof(X) could be extended to include not only the function members in the public interface of X but *also* any *data* members in the public interface of X. Implementing this would be straightforward and likely involve either storing offsets to access the given variable in the *stbl* table for a signature pointer or reference, or providing thunks to access the variables. This latter case would likely be necessary for situations where the data is available through a virtual base class. It is interesting to note that the latter case reduces to the same code as if the programmer had supplied functions to access the variables. However, the usefulness of allowing data in signatures seems somewhat dubious because it seems to confuse implementation with interface. Good programming practice stresses the separation of these two.

Aliasing of Signature Names
Suppose that in the examples in third section, MotifObject named the function to display the object show(), rather than display(). In this case, MotifObject would no longer conform to sigof(XWindowsObject), even though it logically has all the proper operations. For this reason, it might be desirable to extend C++ syntax to allow member aliases to be specified. For example, XWindowsObject could be defined as

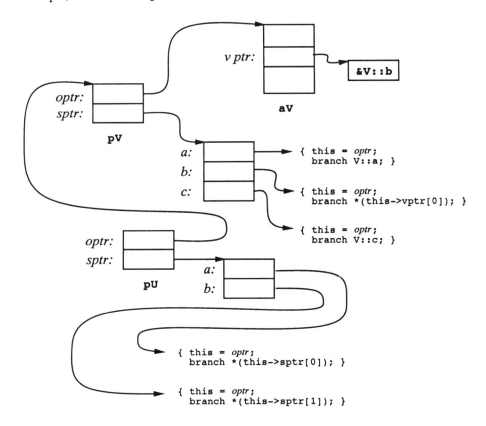

Figure 7.4
Result of assigning pV to pU

```
class XWindowsObject {
public:
        virtual void display();
        virtual void move( int, int );

        alias show display;
};
```

This would be interpreted to mean that given window with type XWindowsObject *, the calls window->display() and window->show() are equivalent operations. We could then extend signature conformance to mean that any class with either move and display or move and show in its interface conforms to sigof(XWindowsObject).

Including the Builtin Types

the builtin types (int, char, short) are considered to have signatures as well, they may conform to certain other signatures. For example, the builtin type int logically conforms to sigof(Counter) if Counter is defined as:

```
class Counter {
public:
    operator ++();
    operator --();
    operator int();
};
```

Other classes implementing the Counter signature could also be constructed. For example, AtomicCounter could implement a counter in a multiprocessor environment, or RangeCheckedCounter could check that a counter never exceeds a maximum value. If a variable with type sigof(Counter) * or sigof(Counter) & is used in a piece of code, instances of AtomicCounter, RangeCheckedCounter, or and ordinary int could be assigned to the variable. The implementation of this would involve the employment of more sophisticated thunks that contain code to perform the operations on the primitive types directly, since corresponding member functions do not exist.

Conclusion

We have discuss the limitations of existing techniques for supporting polymorphism and code reuse in C++. We have proposed a new language extension that allows polymorphism to exist without relying on inheritance. We have outlined a naive implementation of our technique, and analyzed its performance. Many optimizations are possible, but these are beyond the scope of this paper.

Our proposal allows forms of polymorphism to be provided which presently can only be achieved in C++ by using (multiple) inheritance and modifying existing code or by introducing new leaf classes. We consider this to be a major software engineering disadvantage. Due to its limited overhead, we believe that our technique has significant advantages over multiple inheritance solutions for supporting polymorphism in C++.

We note that this paper presents a "blue sky" language extension to C++. Further evaluation of its usefulness in practice is necessary. We solicit comments as to the perceived usefulness of our technique. An implementation of this extension in the GNU C++ compiler is currently in progress.

Acknowledgements

We would like to thank Doug Lea for his insightful comments on an earlier version of this paper. We would also like to thank Ralph Johnson for helping us clarify some of the terminology used in this paper, and (unbeknown to him) for inspiring the original idea for this work through his work on type-checking Smalltalk. Other inspiration for this work comes from the Emerald[5] programming language.

This work was done while Elana Granston was affiliated with the University of Illinois at Urbana-Champaign Center for Supercomputing Research and Development and was supported by the Department of Energy under Grant No. DE-FG02-85ER25001 and Cray Research Inc. Vincent Russo was affiliated with the Purdue University department of Computer Sciences and was supported by grants from Hewlett-Packard Laboratories and the Purdue Research Foundation.

Bibliography

[1] T. A. Cargill. Does C++ Really Need Multiple Inheritance? In *1990 USENIX C++ Conference*, pages 315-323, 1990.

[2] Luca Cardelli and Peter Wegner. On Understanding Types, Data Abstraction, and Polymorphism. *ACM Computing Surveys*, 17(4):471-522, December 1985.

[3] Margaret A. Ellis and Bjarne Stroustrup. *The Annotated C++ Reference Manual*. Addison-Wesley, Reading, Massachusetts, 1990.

[4] Daniel C. Halbert and Patrick D. O'Brien. Using Types and Inheritance in Object-Oriented Programming. *IEEE Software*, pages 71-79, September 1987.

[5] Eric Jul, Henry Levy, Norman Hutchinson, and Andrew Black. Fine-Grained Mobility in the Emerald System. In *Proceedings of the Eleventh ACM Symposium on Operating System Principles*, pages 62-74, November 1987.

[6] Bjarne Stroustrup. Multiple Inheritance for C++. In *EUUG Spring '87 Conference*, 1987.

[7] Bjarne Stroustrup. Parameterized Types for C++. In *1988 USENIX C++ Conference*, pages 1-18, 1988.

[8] Peter Wegner. Dimensions of Object-Based Language Design. In *Proceedings of the 1987 OOPSLA Conference*, pages 168-182, 1987.

Part III
Exception Handling

Chapter 8

Exception Handling for C++

Andrew Koenig and Bjarne Stroustrup

Abstract

This paper outlines a design for an exception handling mechanism for C++. It presents the reasoning behind the major design decisions and considers their implications for implementation alternatives. The mechanism is flexible, comparatively safe and easy to use, works in a mixed language execution environment, and can be implemented to run efficiently. Two implementation strategies are described in some detail.

Introduction

The author of a library can detect errors, but does not in general have any idea what to do about them. The user of a library may know how to cope with such errors, but cannot detect them – or else they would have been handled in the user's code and not left for the library to find.

The primary purpose of the exception handling mechanism described here is to cope with this problem for C++ programs; other uses of what has been called exception handling in the literature are considered secondary. See the references for discussions of exception handling techniques and mechanisms.

The mechanism described is designed to handle only synchronous exceptions, such as array range checks. Asynchronous exceptions, such as keyboard interrupts, are not handled directly by this mechanism.

A guiding principle is that exceptions are rare compared to function calls and that exception handlers are rare compared to function definitions. We do not wish to use exception handling as a substitute for more conventional control structures. Further, we do not want to require the vast majority of functions to include code specifically relating to exception handling for a program to benefit from exception handling.

The mechanism described here can be implemented in several different ways. In particular, we outline a portable implementation based on C's setjmp/longjmp mechanism and an implementation that has no run-time costs when exceptions do *not* occur.

C++ is designed to coexist with other languages that do not support exception handling. Consequently, we rejected any ideas for exception handling that would have required all functions in a program to be written in C++.

This paper is a revised version of a paper with a similar title presented at the USENIX 1990 C++ Conference.

After the presentation of the exception handling scheme we discuss its use compared to 'traditional' error handling techniques. Many details that we felt to be important, yet not essential to appreciate the fundamentals of the exception handling scheme, are placed in appendices.

This paper is written to stimulate discussion of exception handling in C++. The mechanisms described here are not part of C++ and might never become part of C++. Previous versions of these mechanisms were presented at the C++ *at Work* conference in November 1989[8] and the Usenix C++ Conference in San Francisco in April 1990[9]. The scheme described here owes much to the discussion generated by those presentations. In particular, the present scheme provides a greater degree of protection against mistakes by transferring more obligations from the programmer to the language implementation. A more formal description of the scheme can be found in [3].

An Example

Suppose that an exception called xxii can occur in a function g() called by a function f(). How can the programmer of f() gain control in that case? The wish to 'catch' the exception xxii when it occurs and g() doesn't handle it can be expressed like this:

```
int f()
{
    try {
        return g();
    }
    catch (xxii) {
        // we get here only if 'xxii' occurs
        error("g() goofed: xxii");
        return 22;
    }
}
```

The text from catch to the next close brace is called a *handler*[1] for the kind of exception named xxii. A single *try-block* can have handlers for several distinct exceptions; a handler marked by the ellipsis, ..., picks up every exception not previously mentioned. For example:

```
int f()
{
    try {
        return g();
    }
    catch (xx) {
        // we get here only if 'xx' occurs
        error("g() goofed: xx");
        return 20;
    }
    catch (xxii) {
        // we get here only if 'xxii' occurs
        error("g() goofed: xxii");
        return 22;
    }
```

---

[1]The grammar for the exception handling mechanism can be found in Appendix B.

```
catch (...) {
    // we get here only if an exception
    // that isn't 'xxii' or 'xx' occurs
    error("g() goofed");
    return 0;
    }
}
```

The series of handlers is rather like a switch statement. The handler marked
(...) is rather like a default. Note, however, that there is no 'fall through'
from one *handler* to another as there is from one case to another. An alternative and more accurate analogy is that the set of handlers looks very much like
a set of overloaded functions. However, unlike a set of overloaded functions,
the try clauses are checked in the sequence in which they appear.

An exception handler is associated with a try-block and is invoked whenever
its exception occurs in that block or in any function called directly or indirectly
from it. For example, say in the example above that xxii didn't actually occur
in g() but in a function h() called by g():

```
int g() { return h(); }

int h()
{
    throw xxii();        // make exception 'xxii' occur
}
```

The handler in f() would still handle the exception xxii.

We will use the phrase 'throwing an exception' to denote the operation of
causing an exception to occur. The reason we don't use the more common
phrase 'raising an exception' is that raise() is a C standard library function
and therefore not available for our purpose. The word signal is similarly
unavailable. Similarly, we chose catch in preference to handle because
handle is a commonly used C identifier.

A *handler* looks a lot like a function definition. A *throw-expression* looks
somewhat like both a function call and a return statement. We will see
below that neither similarity is superficial.

Because g() might be written in C or some other language that does not
know about C++ exceptions, a fully general implementation of the C++ exception mechanism cannot rely on decorations of the stack frame, passing of hidden arguments to functions not in C++, or other techniques that require
compiler cooperation for every function called.

Once a handler has caught an exception, that exception has been dealt with
and other handlers that might exist for it become irrelevant. In other words,
only the active handler most recently encountered by the thread of control will
be invoked. For example, here xxii will still be caught by the handler in f():

```
int e()
{
    try {
        return f();      // f() handles xxii
    }
    catch (xxii) {       // so we will not get here
        // ...
    }
}
```

Another way to look at it is that if a statement or function handles a particular
exception, then the fact that the exception has been thrown and caught is

invisible in the surrounding context – unless, of course, the exception handler itself notifies something in the surrounding context that the exception occurred.

Naming of Exceptions

What is an exception? In other words, how does one declare an exception? What do exception names, such as xxii above, really identify?

Perhaps the most important characteristic of exceptions is that the code that throws them is often written independently from the code that catches them. Whatever an exception is must therefore be something that allows separately written programs to communicate.

Moreover, it should be possible to define 'groups' of exceptions and provide handlers for such groups. For example, it should be possible for a single handler to cope with all exceptions coming from a major sub-system such as the file system, the stream I/O system, the network software, and so on. In the absence of such a mechanism, systems relying of large numbers of exceptions (say, hundreds) become unmanageable.

Finally, we want to be able to pass arbitrary, user-defined information from the point where an exception is thrown to the point where it is caught.

Two suggestions have been made for C++:

1. that an exception be a class, and
2. that an exception be an object.

We propose a combination of both.

Exceptions as Classes

Suppose an exception is a class. That would allow us to use inheritance to group exceptions. For instance, one can imagine an Overflow exception that is a kind of Matherr exception. Inheritance is a natural way to express such a relationship and this seems to support the notion that exceptions should be classes.

Closer inspection, however, raises a question. Throwing an exception passes information from where it is thrown to where it is caught. That information must be stored somewhere. This implies that we need a run-time representation of an exception, that is, an object representing the exception. In C++, a class is a type – *not* an object. Classes do not carry data; objects do. Also, if an exception is a class, it seems natural to declare objects of that class. If the classes themselves are used to express throwing and catching of exceptions, what good are the objects?

Exceptions as Objects

If exceptions are objects, what kind of objects? The simplest possibility is to make them integers whose values identify the kind of exception. The trouble with that is that it is difficult for people working apart to choose such integer values without clashing. I may choose the unlikely number 299793 to represent my exception, but so may you and when some unlucky third person tries to use our programs together trouble starts. It would seem more sensible to use the *identity* (that is, the address) of the exception object, rather than its *value*, to denote the particular exception being thrown.

But this raises problems as well. If we use the identity of an object to 'name' an exception, which particular object do we want to catch? The object presumably identifies the kind of exception that interests us, but that exception hasn't been thrown yet, so how can the object exist? Alternatively, if what we catch is a pre-existing object, do we throw that object as well? If so, the object probably needs to be external, but how do we throw an external object without guaranteeing trouble in an environment where multiple processes share a single address space? See [8] for a C++ exception handling scheme based on object identities.

Exceptions as Classes and Objects
It appears, therefore that the most natural way to describe exceptions is to *throw* objects and *catch* classes. A *copy* of the object thrown is passed to the handler.

Given that, it is possible to use any type in a *handler* and any object as the argument in a *throw-expression*. For example:

```
// add with overflow checking

// a class for integer overflow exception handling:
struct Int_overflow {
    const char* op;
    int operand1, operand2;
    Int_overflow(const char* p, int q, int r):
        op(p), operand1(q), operand2(r) { }
};

int add(int x, int y)
{
    if (x > 0 && y > 0 && x > MAXINT - y
     || x < 0 && y < 0 && x < MININT + y)
        throw Int_overflow("+", x, y);
    // If we get here, either overflow has
    // been checked and will not occur, or
    // overflow is impossible because
    // x and y have opposite sign
    return x + y;
}
```

If the arguments to this add function are out of range, it creates an Int_overflow object to describe what went wrong and makes (a copy of) that object available to a corresponding *handler*. The exception thus thrown can be caught like this:

```
main()
{
    int a, b, c;
    cin >> a >> b;
    try {
        c = add(a,b);
    }
    catch (Int_overflow e) {
        cout << "overflow " << e.op << '('
             << e.operand1 << ',' << e.operand2
             << ")\n";
    }
    // and so on
}
```

When the *handler* is entered, e will be a copy of the `Int_overflow` object that was created inside the add function to describe what went wrong.

The parallel to function calls is now almost exact: The *throw-expression* passes an `Int_overflow` object to the *handler* declared to accept objects of class `Int_overflow`. The usual initialization semantics are used to pass this argument. The type of the object thrown is used to select the handler in approximately the way the arguments of a function call is used to select an overloaded function. Again, a slightly different way of looking at the *throw-expression* is as a `return` statement where the argument is not only passed back to the caller, but is also used to select which caller to return to.

C++ supports the definition of classes and the use of objects of classes. Using a class to describe the kind of exception expected simplifies type checking between a *throw-expression* and a *handler*. Using an object to describe the exception itself makes it easy to pass information safely and efficiently between those two points. Relying of such fundamental and well-supported language concepts rather than inventing some special "exception type" ensures that the full power of C++ is available for the definition and use of exceptions.

Grouping of Exceptions

Exceptions often fall naturally into families. For example, one could imagine a `Matherr` exception that includes `Overflow`, `Underflow`, and other possible exceptions.

One way of doing this might be simply to define `Matherr` as a class whose possible values include `Overflow` and the others:

```
enum Matherr { Overflow, Underflow, Zerodivide, /* ... */ };
```

It is then possible to say

```
try {
    f();
}
catch (Matherr m) {
    switch (m) {
    case Overflow:
        // ...
    case Underflow:
        // ...
    // ...
    }
    // ...
}
```

In other contexts, C++ uses inheritance and virtual functions to avoid this kind of switch on a type field. It is possible to use inheritance similarly to describe collections of exceptions too. For example:

```
class Matherr { };
class Overflow: public Matherr { };
class Underflow: public Matherr { };
class Zerodivide: public Matherr { };
// ...
```

Such classification is particularly convenient because of the desire to handle similarly any member of a collection of exceptions: it is easy to imagine many reasons why one might want to recover from any kind of `Matherr` without caring precisely which kind it was. Using inheritance in this way makes it possible to say

```
try {
    f();
}
catch (Overflow) {
    // handle Overflow or anything derived from Overflow
}
catch (Matherr) {
    // handle any Matherr that is not Overflow
}
```

Here an `Overflow` is handled specifically, and all other `Matherr` exceptions will be handled by the general case. Of course, a program that says `catch(Matherr)` will not know what kind of `Matherr` it has caught; whatever it was, its copy will be a `Matherr` by the time the handler is entered. We will see later how a program can cater to a potentially unknown set of exceptions by catching a *reference* to an exception.

There are cases where an exception can reasonably be considered to belong to two or more groups. For example:

```
class network_file_err : public network_err ,
                         public file_system_err { };
```

Obviously, this too is easily handled without language extensions.

Naming the Current Exception
We name the current exception analogously to naming the argument of a function:

```
try { /* ... */ } catch (zaq e) { /* ... */ }
```

This is a declaration of e with its scope identical to the body of the exception handler. The idea is that e is created using the copy constructor of class `zaq` before entering the handler.

Where there is no need to identify the particular exception, there is no need to name the exception object:

```
try { /* ... */ } catch (zaq) { /* ... */ }
```

This again is similar to the technique of not naming unused function arguments in a function definition.

As with functions, the argument declaration (...) accepts any call, so that

```
catch (...) { /* any exception will get here */ }
```

will catch every exception. There is no way of finding out what exception caused entry into such a handler. Were such a way provided, type safety would be compromised and the implementation of exception handling complicated.

When a handler is done with an exception, it may sometimes want to re-throw that exception, whatever it was, without caring what kind of exception it was. To do this, say `throw` without specifying an exception:

```
catch (...) {
    // do something
    throw;      // re-throw current exception
}
```

Such a re-throw operation is valid only within a handler or within a function called directly or indirectly from a handler.

Because of things like (...) clauses, this kind of *throw-expression* offers a facility that cannot be simulated by other means. While this facility is sometimes essential, we will in the sixth section demonstrate how most problems typically solved by a re-throw operation can be solved more elegantly by careful use of destructors.

Note that

```
try { /* ... */ } catch (zaq e) { throw zaq; }
```

is *not* equivalent to

```
try { /* ... */ } catch (zaq e) { throw; }
```

In the first example, the usual rules of initialization ensures that if the exception originally thrown was an object of a class derived from zaq, then it will be "cut down" to a zaq when used to initialize e. In the second example, the original exception – possible of a class derived from zaq – is re-thrown.

Order of Matching
The *handlers* of a *try-block* are tried in order. For example:

```
try {
    // ...
}
catch (ibuf) {
    // handle input buffer overflow
}
catch (io) {
    // handle any io error
}
catch (stdlib) {
    // handle any library exception
}
catch (...) {
    // handle any other exception
}
```

The type in a catch clause matches if either it directly refers to the exception thrown or is of a base class of that exception, or if the exception thrown is a pointer and the exception caught is a pointer to a base class of that exception.

Since the compiler knows the class hierarchy it can warn about sillinesses such as a (...) clause that is not the last clause or a clause for a base class preceding a clause for a class derived from it. In both cases the later clause(s) could never be invoked because they were masked.

No Match
Where no match is found, the search for a handler continues to the calling function. When a handler is found and entered, the exception is no longer considered thrown. After dropping off the end of a *handler* the computation continues after the complete *try-block*. For example,

```
void f()
{   try {
        // ...
    }
    catch (x) {
        // handle exception 'x'
    }
    catch (...) {
        // do nothing
    }
```

```
    // whatever happens (short of hardware failure
    // terminate(), abort(), etc.) we'll get here
    h();
}
```

If the try-block raises exception x, the first handler will be executed. Any exception other than x will execute the second, empty handler. If execution continues at all, it will continue with the call to h().

Exception Types
Any pointer type or type with a public copy constructor can be used to name an exception in a *handler*. When an exception of a derived class is thrown directly, the use of the copy constructor implies that the exception thrown is 'cut down' to the exception caught. For example:

```
class Matherr { /* .... */ };

class Int_overflow: public Matherr {
public:
    char* op;
    int operand1, operand2;
    // ...
};

void f()
{
    try {
        g();
    }
    catch (Matherr m) {
        // ...
    }
}
```

When the Matherr handler is entered, m is a Matherr object, even if the call to g() threw Int_overflow.

For some applications, it may be useful to use virtual functions to deal with exceptions whose type is not statically known at the point where the exception is caught. One way to do that is to use references to exceptions:

```
void g()
{
        if ( /* ... */ ) throw Int_overflow( /* arguments */ );
}

void f()
{
    try {
        g();
    }
    catch (Matherr& m) {
        // ...
        mp.vfun();
    }
}
```

In order for this to work, the Int_overflow object being thrown must remain in existence until after the corresponding handler has exited. This implies that throwing an exception to a handler that expects a reference might require allocation of memory on the heap. It is therefore unwise to use references to exceptions to deal with memory exhaustion.

The only conversions applied to exception objects are the derived class to base class conversions (for objects, references, and pointers) and conversions that add const or volatile to the subjects of pointers or references. Other standard conversions, even ones like int to long, are not applied.

Access to Local Variables

Since a *throw-expression* is an exit from a block and typically also a return from one or more functions, one cannot pass information stored in local variables in the block where the throw occurs — or in automatic (local) variables in functions returned from by the throw. For example:

```
void f()
{
    try { g(); }
    catch (int* p) {
        if (*p == 0) // ...
    }
}
void g()
{
    int a = 0;
    throw &a;    // unwise
}
```

This is logically equivalent to returning a pointer to a local variable from a function using the normal function return mechanism.

Handling of Destructors

Consider what to do when an exception is thrown and we need to pass 'up' through a function or block to find a handler. This is commonly called 'stack unwinding.' If a local object has a destructor, that destructor must be called as part of the stack unwinding. This can be done by implicitly providing a handler that calls the destructor when an exception is thrown after construction but before destruction of the local object. Such destructor calls are done before entry into a handler. For example, if classes A and B have destructors,

```
void f()
{
    A a;
    B b;
    g();
}
```

might be implemented in the following equivalent way:

```
void f()    // pseudo code
{
    try {
        A a;
        try {
            B b;
            try {
                g();
            }
            catch (...) {
                        // destroy 'b'
                        // destroy 'a'
                throw;
            }
        }
```

```
        catch (...) {
            // exception occurred during the construction of 'b'
            // destroy 'a'
            throw;
        }
    }
    catch (...) {
        // exception occurred during
        // the construction of 'a'

        throw;
    }
    // destroy 'b'
    // destroy 'a'
}
```

This looks horrendously complicated and expensive. Fortunately, a user will never have to write it, and in fact, there is an implementation technique that (in addition to the standard overhead of establishing a handler) involves only minimal overhead. Here is an example of C code that might be generated for the example above:

```
void f()      // generated code
{
    int __counter = 0;
    struct A a;
    struct B b;

    A::A(&a);
    __counter++;        /* one object created */

    B::B(&b);
    __counter++;        /* two objects created */

    g();

    __counter = 3;      /* no exception occurred */
__catch:
    switch (__counter) {
    case 3:
    case 2: b.B::~B();  /* fall through */
    case 1: a.A::~A();
    }

    if (__counter == 3) return;
    throw;              /* or whatever the corresponding C is */
}
```

For this to work we assume two things: a way of getting to the label __catch in case an exception is thrown in g(), and a way of re-throwing the exception at the end of f() if an exception caused transfer of control to __catch.

The problem becomes somewhat more complicated in the face of arrays of objects with destructors, but we do not believe that dealing with these complications is any more than tedious.

Suppressing Destructor Calls

It has been observed that for many objects destruction is irrelevant once an exception is thrown and that an exception may be thrown precisely under conditions where it would be dangerous to run the destructor for certain objects. One could therefore imagine facilities for specifying that objects of certain classes should not be destroyed during the stack unwinding caused by exception handling. Such facilities could lead to faster and safer exception handling and more compact code.

Nevertheless, lack of experience argues that we should not immediately include specific facilities for that. Where necessary, the user can simulate the effect of such facilities by inserting suitable checks in destructors. Should experience show that such code proliferates, and especially if experience shows such code to be baroque, we should revisit the question of a facility for selectively suppressing destructor calls.

Throwing Exceptions in Destructors

Naturally, a destructor can throw an exception. In fact, since destructors often call other functions that may throw exceptions it cannot be avoided. Throwing exceptions during a "normal" invocation of a destructor causes no special problems. Throwing an exception during the execution of a destructor that was called as part of the stack unwinding caused by an exception being thrown may be another matter. This should be allowed to avoid putting artificial constraints on the writing of destructors.

Only one restriction is needed: If a destructor invoked during stack unwinding throws an exception, directly or indirectly, that propagates uncaught back through that destructor itself, the exception will be turned into a call of `terminate()`. The default meaning of `terminate()` is `abort()`; see Appendix G. Without this restriction the implementation of exception handling would be needlessly complicated and it would not be at all clear what exception should be considered thrown: the original exception or the one thrown by the destructor? We see no general rule for resolving that question.

Handling of Constructors

An object is not considered constructed until its constructor has completed. Only then will stack unwinding call the destructor for the object. An object composed of sub-objects is constructed to the extent that its sub-objects have been constructed.

A well written constructor should ensure that its object is completely and correctly constructed. Failing that, the constructor should restore the state of the system after failure to what it was before creation. It would be ideal for naively written constructors always to achieve one of these alternatives and not leave their objects in some 'half-constructed' state.

Consider a class X for which a constructor needs to acquire two resources x and y. This acquisition might fail and throw an exception. Without imposing a burden of complexity on the programmer, the class X constructor must never return having acquired resource x but not resource y.

We can use the technique we use to handle local objects. The trick is to use objects of two classes A and B to represent the acquired resources (naturally a single class would be sufficient if the resources x and y are of the same kind). The acquisition of a resource is represented by the initialization of the local object that represents the resource:

```
class X {
    A a;
    B b;
    // ...
    X()
        : a(x), // acquire 'x'
          b(y)    // acquire 'y'
    {}
    // ...
};
```

Now, as in the local object case, the implementation can take care of all the bookkeeping. The user doesn't have to keep track at all.

This implies that where this simple model for acquisition of resources (a resource is acquired by initialization of a local object that represents it) is adhered to, all is well and – importantly – the constructor author need not write explicit exception handling code.

Here is a case that does not adhere to this simple model:

```
class X {
    static int no_of_Xs;
    widget* p;
    // ...
    X() { no_of_Xs++; p = grab(); }
    ~X() { no_of_Xs--; release(p); }
};
```

What happens if grab() throws some exception so that the assignment to p never happens for some object? The rule guaranteeing that an object is only destroyed automatically provided it has been completely constructed ensures that the destructor isn't called – thus saving us from the release() of a random pointer value – but the no_of_Xs count will be wrong. It will be the programmer's job to avoid such problems. In this case the fix is easy: simply don't increase no_of_Xs until the possibility of an exception has passed:

```
X::X() { p = grab(); no_of_Xs++; }
```

Alternatively, a more general and elaborate technique could be used:

```
X::X()
{
    no_of_Xs++;
    try {
        p = grab();
    }
    catch (...) {
        no_of_Xs--;
        throw;        // re-throw
    }
}
```

There is no doubt that writing code for constructors and destructors so that exception handling does not cause 'half constructed' objects to be destroyed is an error-prone aspect of C++ exception handling. The 'resource acquisition is initialization' technique can help making the task manageable. It should also be noted that the C++ default memory allocation strategy guarantees that the code for a constructor will never be called if operator new fails to provide memory for an object so that a user need not worry that constructor (or destructor) code might be executed for a non-existent object.

Termination vs. Resumption

Should it be possible for an exception handler to decide to resume execution from the point of the exception? Some languages, such as PL/I and Mesa, say yes and [11] contains a concise argument for resumption in the context of C++. However, we feel it is a bad idea and the designers of Clu, Modula2+, Modula3, and ML agree.

First, if an exception handler can return, that means that a program that throws an exception must assume that it will get control back. Thus, in a context like this:

```
if (something_wrong) throw zxc();
```

it would not be possible to be assured that something_wrong is false in the code following the test because the zxc handler might resume from the point of the exception. What such resumption provides is a contorted, non-obvious, and error-prone form of co-routines. With resumption possible, throwing an exception ceases to be a reliable way of escaping from a context.

This problem might be alleviated if the exception itself or the throw operation determined whether to resume or not. Leaving the decision to the handler, however, seems to make programming trickier than necessary because the handler knows nothing about the context of the throw-point. However, leaving the resumption/termination decision to the throw-point is equivalent to providing a separate mechanism for termination and resumption – and that is exactly what we propose.

Exception handling implies termination; resumption can be achieved through ordinary function calls. For example:

```
void problem_X_handler(arguments)    // pseudo code
{
    // ...
    if (we_cannot_recover) throw X("Oops!");
}
```

Here, a function simulates an exception that may or may not resume. We have our doubts about the wisdom of using *any* strategy that relies on conditional resumption, but it is achievable through ordinary language mechanisms provided there is cooperation between the program that throws the exception and the program that handles it. Such cooperation seems to be a prerequisite for resumption. Pointers to such "error handling" functions provide yet another degree of freedom in the design of error handling schemes based of the termination-oriented exception handling scheme presented here.

Resumption is of only limited use without some means of correcting the situation that led to the exception. However, correcting error conditions after they occur is generally much harder than detecting them beforehand. Consider, for example, an exception handler trying to correct an error condition by changing some state variable. Code executed in the function call chain that led from the block with the handler to the function that threw the exception might have made decisions that depended on that state variable. This would leave the program in a state that was impossible without exception handling; that is, we would have introduced a brand new kind of bug that is very nasty and hard to find. In general, it is much safer to re-try the operation that failed from the exception handler than to resume the operation at the point where the exception was thrown.

If it were possible to resume execution from an exception handler, that would force the unwinding of the stack to be deferred until the exception handler exits. If the handler had access to the local variables of its surrounding scope without unwinding the stack first we would have introduced an equivalent to nested functions. This would complicate either the implementation/semantics or the writing of handlers.

It was also observed that many of the "potential exceptions" that people wanted to handle using a resumption-style exception handling mechanism where asynchronous exceptions, such as a user hitting a break key. However, handling those would imply the complications of the exception handling mechanism as discussed in the ninth section.

Use of a debugger can be seen as constituting a special form of resumption: Where a debugger is activated because an exception has been thrown but not caught, the user expects to find the program in a state where the local variables at the throw-point are accessible. After inspecting and possibly modifying the state of the program, the programmer might want to resume. This special case of resumption can be supported with minor overhead in the case where a debugger is active (only). Modifications of the program's behavior in this case are of the same kind as any other modifications of a program's state using a debugger; they are extra-linguistic and defined as part of a programming environment rather than as part of the language.

Safety and Interfaces

Throwing or catching an exception affects the way a function relates to other functions. It is therefore worth considering if such things should affect the type of a function. One could require the set of exceptions that might be thrown to be declared as part of the type of a function. For example:

```
void f(int a) throw (x2, x3, x4);
```

This would improve static analysis of a program and reduce the number of programmer errors[5, 6]. In particular, one could ensure that no exception could be thrown unless there were a matching handler for it.

Static Checking

Compile and link time enforcement of such rules is ideal in the sense that important classes of nasty run-time errors are completely eliminated (turned into compile time errors). Such enforcement does not carry any run-time costs – one would expect a program using such techniques to be smaller and run faster than the less safe traditional alternative of relying on run-time checking. Unfortunately, such enforcement also has nasty consequences.

Suppose a function f() can throw an exception e:

```
void f() throw (e)
{
    // ...
}
```

For static checking to work, it must be an error for a function g() to call f() unless either g() is also declared to throw e or g() protects itself against f() throwing e:

```
void g() throw (h)
{
    f();         // error: f() might throw e

    try {
        f();     // OK: if f() throws e, g() will throw h
    }
    catch (e) {
        throw h;
    }
}
```

To allow such checking *every* function must be decorated with the exceptions it might throw. This would be too much of a nuisance for most people. For example:

```
#include <stream.h>
main()
{
    cout << "Hello world\n"; // error: might throw an exception!
}
```

Preventing such compile-time errors would be a great bother to the programmer and the checking would consequently be subverted. Such subversion could take may forms. For example, calls through C functions could be used to render the static checking meaningless, programmers could declare functions to throw all exceptions by default, and tools could be written to automatically create lists of thrown exceptions. The effect in all cases would be to eliminate both the bother and the safety checks that were the purpose of the mechanism.

Consequently, we think the only way to make static checking practical would be to say that undecorated functions can potentially throw any exception at all. Unfortunately, that again puts an intolerable burden on the programmer who wishes to write a function that is restricted to a particular set of exceptions. That programmer would have to guard *every* call to *every* unrestricted function – and since functions are unrestricted by default, that would make restricted functions too painful to write in practice. For instance, *every* function that did not expect to throw I/O exceptions would have to enumerate every possible I/O exception.

Dynamic checking

A more attractive and practical possibility is to allow the programmer to specify what exceptions a function can potentially throw, but to enforce this restriction at run time only. When a function says something about its exceptions, it is effectively making a guarantee to its caller; if during execution that function does something that tries to abrogate the guarantee, the attempt will be transformed into a call of unexpected(). The default meaning of unexpected() is terminate(), which in turn normally calls abort(); see Appendix G for details.

In effect, writing this:

```
void f() throw (e1, e2)
{
    // stuff
}
```

is equivalent to writing this:

```
void f()
{
    try {
        // stuff
    }
    catch (e1) {
        throw;   // re-throw
    }
    catch (e2) {
        throw;   // re-throw
    }
    catch (...) {
        unexpected();
    }
}
```

The advantage of the explicit declaration of exceptions that a function can throw over the equivalent checking in the code is not just that it saves typing. The most important advantage is that the function *declaration* belongs to an interface that is visible to its callers. Function *definitions*, on the other hand, are not universally available and even if we do have access to the source code of all our libraries we strongly prefer not to have to look at it very often.

Another advantage is that it may still be practical to detect many uncaught exceptions during compilation. For example, if the first f() above called a function that could throw something other than e1 or e2, the compiler could warn about it. Of course the compiler has to be careful about such warnings. For example, if every integer addition can potentially throw Int_overflow, it is important to suppress warnings about such common operations. Programmers do not appreciate being showered by spurious warnings.

Detecting likely uncaught exceptions may be a prime job for the mythical lint++ that people have been looking for an excuse to design. Here is a task that requires massive static analysis of a complete program and does not fit well with the traditional C and C++ separate compilation model.

Type Checking of Exceptions
If a list of exceptions is specified for a function, it behaves as part of the function's type in the sense that the lists must match in the declaration and definition. Like the return type, the exception specification does not take part in function matching for overloaded functions.

A function declared without an exception specification is assumed to throw every exception.
```
int f();        // can throw any exception
```
A function that will throw no exceptions can be declared with an explicitly empty list:
```
int g() throw ();   // no exception thrown
```
The list of exceptions could be part of the function's signature so that type-safe linkage could be achieved. This, however, would require sophisticated linker support so the exception specification is better left unchecked on systems with traditional linker (just as the return type is left unchecked). Simply forcing a re-write and recompilation whenever an exception specification changed would cause the users to suffer the worst implications of strict static checking.

For example, a function must potentially be changed and recompiled if a function it calls (directly or indirectly) changes the set of exceptions it catches

or throws. This could lead to major delays in the production of software produced (partly) by composition of libraries from different sources. Such libraries
would *de facto* have to agree on a set of exceptions to be used. For example, if
sub-system X handles exceptions from sub-system Y and the supplier of Y
introduces a new kind of exception, then X's code will have to be modified to
cope. A user of X and Y will not be able to upgrade to a new version of Y
until X has been modified. Where many sub-systems are used this can cause
cascading delays. Even where the 'multiple supplier problem' does not exist
this can lead to cascading modifications of code and to large amounts of
re-compilation.

Such problems would cause people to avoid using the exception specification
mechanism or else subvert it. To avoid such problems, either the exceptions
must not be part of a function's signature or else the linker must be smart
enough to allow calls to functions with signatures that differ from the expected
in their exception specification only.

An equivalent problem occurs when dynamic checking is used. In that case,
however, the problem can be handled using the exception grouping mechanism presented in the fourth section. A naive use of the exception handling
mechanism would leave a new exception added to sub-system Y uncaught or
converted into a call to unexpected() by some explicitly called interface.
However, a well defined sub-system Y would have all its exceptions derived
from a class Yexception. For example

```
class newYexception : public Yexception { /* ... */ };
```

This implies that a function declared

```
void f() throw (Xexception, Yexception, IOexception);
```

would handle a newYexception by passing it to callers of f().

Exception handling mechanisms descending from the Clu mechanism tend to
provide a distinguished *failure* exception that is raised (that is, thrown) when
an unexpected exception occurs. In that case, the scheme presented here calls
unexpected(). This is a more serious response to an unexpected exception
since a call of unexpected() cannot be caught the way an exception can and
is intended to trigger a program's response to a catastrophic failure. This
choice partly reflects the observation that in a mixed language environment it
is not possible to intercept all exceptional circumstances so it would be
dangerous to encourage programmers to believe they can. For example, a C
function may call the standard C library function abort() and thus bypass
attempts to intercept all returns from a call to a subsystem. Having a distinguished failure exception also allows easy subversion of interfaces by providing a single catch-all for (almost) every kind of unexpected event. Stating
that a function raises only a specific set of exceptions becomes less meaningful
because one must always remember "and failure" – and failure can be caught
elsewhere leaving a program running "correctly" after the explicit assumption
of an interface specification has been violated. In other words, the motivation
for not having a failure exception is that in our model, raising it would always
indicate a design error and such design errors should cause immediate
termination whenever possible.

The grouping mechanism provided for C++ allows programmers to use
separate exception classes for major sub-systems, such as basic I/O systems,
window managers, networks, data base systems, etc. By deriving the individual exceptions thrown by such a sub-system from the sub-system's "main

exception," that main exception becomes the equivalent to a failure exception for that sub-system. This technique promotes more precise and explicit specification of exceptions compared with the unique distinguished failure exception technique. Having a universal base class for exceptions, which one might call failure, would simulate the Clu technique and is consequently not recommended.

Occasionally, the policy of terminating a program upon encountering an unexpected exception is too Draconian. For example, consider calling a function g() written for a non-networked environment in a distributed system. Naturally, g() will not know about network exceptions and will call unexpected() when it encounters one. To use g() in a distributed environment we must provide code that handles network exceptions – or rewrite g(). Assuming a re-write is infeasible or undesirable we can handle the problem by redefining the meaning of unexpected(). The function set_unexpected() can be used to achieve that. For example:

```
void rethrow() { throw; }

void networked_g()
{
    PFV old = set_unexpected(&rethrow);
    // now unexpected() calls rethrow()
    try {
        void g();
    }
    catch (network_exception) {
        set_unexpected(old);
        // recover
    }
    catch (...) {
        set_unexpected(old);
        unexpected();
    }
}
```

See Appendix G for details and for a more elegant way of setting and restoring unexpected().

Asynchronous Events

Can exceptions be used to handle things like signals? Almost certainly not in most C environments. The trouble is that C uses functions like malloc that are not re-entrant. If an interrupt occurs in the middle of malloc and causes an exception, there is no way to prevent the exception handler from executing malloc again.

A C++ implementation where calling sequences and the entire run-time library are designed around the requirement for reentrancy would make it possible for signals to throw exceptions. Until such implementations are commonplace, if ever, we must recommend that exceptions and signals be kept strictly separate from a language point of view. In many cases, it will be reasonable to have signals and exceptions interact by having signals store away information that is regularly examined (polled) by some function that in turn may throw appropriate exceptions in response to the information stored by the signals.

Concurrency

One common use of C++ is to emulate concurrency, typically for simulation or similar applications. The AT&T task library is one example of such concurrency simulation[16]. The question naturally arises: how do exceptions interact with such concurrency?

The most sensible answer seems to be that unwinding the stack must stop at the point where the stack forks. That is, an exception must be caught in the process in which it was thrown. If it is not, an exception needs to be thrown in the parent process. An exception handled in the function that is used to create new processes can arrange that by providing a suitable exception handler.

The exception handling scheme presented here is easily implemented to pass information from the throw-point to handlers in a way that works correctly in a concurrent system; see Appendix A for details. The 'resource acquisition is initialization' technique mentioned in the sixth section can be used to manage locks.

C Compatibility

Since ANSI C does not provide an exception handling mechanism, there is no issue of C compatibility in the traditional sense. However, a convenient interface to the C++ exception handling mechanism from C can be provided. This would allow C programmers to share at least some of the benefits of a C++ exception handling implementation and would improve mixed C/C++ systems. In 'plain' ANSI C this would require tricky programming using the functions implementing the C++ exception handling mechanism directly. This would, however, still be simpler and better than most current C error handling strategies. Alternatively, C could be extended with a `try` statement for convenience, but if one were going that far there would be little reason not to switch completely to C++.

Standard Exceptions

A set of exceptions will eventually be standard for all implementations. In particular, one would expect to have standard exceptions for arithmetic operations, out-of-range memory access, memory exhaustion, etc. Libraries will also provide exceptions. At this point we do not have a suggested list of standard exceptions such as one would expect to find in a reference manual.

This paper describes a set of language mechanisms for implementing error handling strategies – not a complete strategy.

So How Can We Use Exceptions?

The purpose of the exception handling mechanism is to provide a means for one part of a program to inform another part of a program that an 'exceptional circumstance' has been detected. The assumption is that the two parts of the program are typically written independently and that the part of the program that handles the exception often can do something sensible about it.

What kind of code could one reasonably expect to find in an exception handler? Here are some examples:

```
int f(int arg)
{
    try {
        g(arg);
    }
    catch (x1) {
        // fix something and retry:
        g(arg);
    }
    catch (x2) {
        // calculate and return a result:
        return 2;
    }
    catch (x3) {
        // pass the bug
        throw;
    }
    catch (x4) {
        // turn x4 into some other exception
        throw xxii;
    }
    catch (x5) {
        // fix up and carry on with next statement
    }
    catch (...) {
        // give up:
        terminate();
    }
    // ...
}
```

Does this actually make error handling easier than 'traditional techniques?' It is hard to *know* what works without first trying this exact scheme, so we can only conjecture. The exception handling scheme presented here is synthesized from schemes found in other languages and from experiences with C++, but learning from other people's mistakes (and successes) is not easy and what works in one language and for a given set of applications may not work in another language for different range of applications.

Consider what to do when an error is detected deep in a library. Examples could be an array index range error, an attempt to open a non-existent file for reading, falling off the stack of a process class, or trying to allocate a block of memory when there is no more memory to allocate. In a language like C or C++ without exceptions there are only few basic approaches (with apparently infinite variations). The library can

1. Terminate the program.
2. Return a value representing 'error.'
3. Return a legal value and leave the program in an illegal state.
4. Call a function supplied to be called in case of 'error.'

What can one do with exceptions that cannot be achieved with these techniques? Or rather – since anything can be fudged given sufficient time and effort – what desirable error handling techniques become easier to write and less error-prone when exceptions are used?

One can consider throwing an exception as logically equivalent to case [1]: 'terminate the program' with the proviso that if some caller of the program thinks it knows better it can intercept the 'terminate order' and try to recover.

The *default* result of throwing an exception is exactly that of termination (or entering the debugger on systems where that is the default response to encountering a run-time error).

Exception handling is not really meant to deal with 'errors' that can be handled by [4] 'call an error function.' Here, a relation between the caller and the library function is already established to the point where resumption of the program is possible at the point where the error was detected. It follows that exception handling is not even as powerful as the function call approach. However, should the 'error function' find itself unable to do anything to allow resumption then we are back to cases [1], [2], or [3] where exceptions may be of use.

Case [2], 'returning an error value,' such as 0 instead of a valid pointer, NaN (not a number, as in IEEE floating point) from a mathematical function, or an object representing an error state, implies that the caller will test for that value and take appropriate action when it is returned. Experience shows that

1. There are often several levels of function calls between the point of error and a caller that knows enough to handle the error, and
2. it is typically necessary to test for the error value at most intermediate levels to avoid consequential errors and to avoid the 'error value' simply being ignored and not passed further up the call chain. Even if error values such as NaN can be propagated smoothly, it can be hard to find out what went wrong when a complicated computation produces NaN as its ultimate result.

Where this is the case one of two things happens:

1. Sufficient checking is done and the code becomes an unreadable maze of tests for error values, or
2. insufficient checking is done and the program is left in an inconsistent state for some other function to detect.

Clearly, there are many cases where the complexity of checking error values is manageable. In those cases, returning error values is the ideal technique; in the rest, exception handling can be used to ensure that [2], 'insufficient checking,' will not occur and that the complexity induced by the need for error handling is minimized through the use of a standard syntax for identifying the error handling code and through a control structure that directly supports the notion of error handling. Using exception handling instead of 'random logic' is an improvement similar to using explicit loop-statements rather than gotos; in both cases benefits only occur when the 'higher level' construct is used in a sensible and systematic manner. However, in both cases that is easier to achieve than a sensible and systematic use of the 'lower level' construct.

Case [3], 'return a legal value leaving the program in an illegal state,' such setting the global variable errno in a C program to signal that one of the standard math library functions could not compute a valid result relies on two assumptions

1. that the legal value returned will allow the program to proceed without subsequent errors or extra coding, and
2. someone will eventually test for the illegal state and take appropriate action.

This approach avoids adding complex error handling tests and code to every function, but suffers from at least four problems:

1. Programmers often forget to test for the error state.
2. Subsequent errors sometimes happen before the execution gets back to the test for the error condition.
3. Independent errors modify the error state (e.g. overwrite `errno`) so that the nature of the problem encountered becomes confused before getting back to the error test. This is particularly nasty where several threads of control are used.
4. Separate libraries assign the same values (error states) to designate different errors, thus totally confusing testing and handling of errors.

Another way of describing the exception handling scheme is as a formalization of this way of handling errors. There is a standard way of signaling an error that ensures that two different errors cannot be given the same 'error value,' ensures that if someone forgets to handle an error the program terminates (in whichever way is deemed the appropriate default way), and (since the ordinary execution path is abandoned after an exception is thrown) all subsequent errors and confusion will occur in exception handling code – most of which will be written specifically to avoid such messes.

So, does the exception handling mechanism solve our error handling problems? No, it is only a mechanism. Does the exception handling mechanism provide a radically new way of dealing with errors? No, it simply provides a formal and explicit way of applying the standard techniques. The exception handling mechanism

1. Makes it easier to adhere to the best practices.
2. Gives error handling a more regular style.
3. Makes error handling code more readable.
4. Makes error handling code more amenable to tools.

The net effect is to make error handling less error-prone in software written by combining relatively independent parts.

One aspect of the exception handling scheme that will appear novel to C programmers is that the default response to an error (especially to an error in a library) is to terminate the program. The traditional response has been to muddle on and hope for the best. Thus exception handling makes programs more 'brittle' in the sense that more care and effort will have to be taken to get a program to run acceptably. This seems far preferable, though, to getting wrong results later in the development process (or after the development process was considered complete and the program handed over to innocent users).

The exception handling mechanism can be seen as a run-time analog to the C++ type checking and ambiguity control mechanisms. It makes the design process more important and the work involved in getting a program to compile harder than for C while providing a much better chance that the resulting program will run as expected, will be able to run as an acceptable part of a larger program, will be comprehensible to other programmers, and amenable to manipulation by tools. Similarly, exception handling provides specific language features to support 'good style' in the same way other C++ features support 'good style' that could only be practiced informally and incompletely in languages such as C.

It should be recognized that error handling will remain a difficult task and that the exception handling mechanism while far more formalized than the techniques it replaces, still is relatively unstructured compared with language features involving only local control flow.

For example, exceptions can be used as a way of exiting from loops:

```
void f()
{
    class loop_exit { };
    // ...
    try {
        while (g()) {
            // ...
            if (I_want_to_get_out) throw loop_exit();
            // ...
        }
    }
    catch (loop_exit) {
        // come here on 'exceptional' exit from loop
    }
    // ...
}
```

We don't recommend this technique because it violates the principle that exceptions should be exceptional: there is nothing exceptional about exiting a loop. The example above simply shows an obscure way of spelling goto.

Conclusions

The exception handling scheme described here is flexible enough to cope with most synchronous exceptional circumstances. Its semantics are independent of machine details and can be implemented in several ways optimized for different aspects. In particular, portable and run-time efficient implementations are both possible. The exception handling scheme presented here should make error handling easier and less error-prone.

Acknowledgements

Michael Jones from CMU helped crystallize early thoughts about exception handling in C++ and demonstrate the power of some of the basic exception handling implementation techniques originating in the Clu and Modula2+ projects. Jim Mitchell contributed observations about the problems with the Cedar/Mesa and Modula exception handling mechanisms. Bill Joy contributed observations about interactions between exception handling mechanisms and debuggers. Dan Weinreb provided the 'network file system exception' example.

Jerry Schwarz and Jonathan Shopiro contributed greatly to the discussion and development of these ideas. Doug McIlroy pointed out many deficiencies in earlier versions of this scheme and contributed a healthy amount of experience with and skepticism about exception handling schemes in general. Dave Jordan, Jonathan Shopiro, and Griff Smith contributed useful comments while reviewing earlier drafts of this paper.

Discussions with several writers of optimizing C compilers were essential.

A discussion in the `c.plus.plus/new.syntax` conference of the BIX bulletin board helped us improve the presentation of the exception handling scheme.

The transformation of the exception handling scheme presented at the C++ *at Work* conference into the scheme presented here owes much to comments by and discussions with Toby Bloom, Dag Bruck, Peter Deutsch, Keith Gorlen, Mike Powell, and Mike Tiemann. The influence from ML is obvious.

We are also grateful to United Airlines for the period of enforced airborne idleness between Newark and Albuquerque that gave us the time to hatch some of these notions.

References

[1] L. Cardelli, J. Donahue, L. Glassman, M. Jordan, B. Kalsow, G. Nelson: *Modula-3 Report*. DEC Systems Research Center. August 1988.

[2] Flaviu Cristian: *Exception Handling*. in *Dependability of Resilient Computers*, T. Andersen Editor, BSP Professional Books, Blackwell Scientific Publications, 1989.

[3] Margaret A. Ellis and Bjarne Stroustrup: *The Annotated C++ Reference Manual*. Addison Wesley 1990.

[4] J. Goodenough: *Exception Handling: Issues and a Proposed Notation*. CACM December 1975.

[5] Steve C. Glassman and Michael J. Jordan: *Safe Use of Exceptions*. Personal communication.

[6] Steve C. Glassman and Michael J. Jordan: *Preventing Uncaught Exceptions*. Olivetti Software Technology Laboratory. August 1989.

[7] Griswold, Poage, Polonsky: *The SNOBOL4 Programming Language*. Prentice-Hall 1971

[8] Andrew Koenig and Bjarne Stroustrup: *Exception Handling for C++*. Proc. C++ at Work Conference, SIGS Publications, November 1989.

[9] Andrew Koenig and Bjarne Stroustrup: *Exception Handling for C++ (revised)*. Proc. USENIX C++ Conference, San Francisco, April 1990.

[10] Bertrand Meyer: *Object-oriented Software Construction*. Prentice Hall. 1988.

[11] Mike Miller: *Exception Handling Without Language Extensions*. Proceedings of the 1988 USENIX C++ Conference.

[12] B. Milner, M. Tofte, R. Harper: *The Definition of Standard ML*. MIT Press 1990.

[13] James G. Mitchell, William Maybury, and Richard Sweet: *Mesa Language Manual*. Version 5.0. April 1979. XEROX PARC CSL-79-3.

[14] Barbara Liskov and Alan Snyder: *Exception Handling in CLU*. IEEE ToSE. November 1979.

[15] Paul Rovner: *Extending Modula-2 to Build Large, Integrated Systems*. IEEE Software Vol.3 No.6 November 1986. pp 46-57.

[16] Jonathan Shopiro and Bjarne Stroustrup: *A Set of C++ Classes for Co-Routine Style Programming*. Proc USENIX C++ Workshop. Santa Fe, NM. November 1987.

[17] Sun Common Lisp Advanced User's Guide. Section 3: *The Error Handling Facility*.

[18] David Waitzman: *Exception Handling in Avalon/C++*. CMU Dept. of Computer Science. August 6. 1987.

[19] USA Department of Defense: *Reference Manual for the ADA Programming Language*. ANSI/MID-STD-1815A-1983.

[20] Shaula Yemini and Daniel M. Berry: *A Modular Verifiable Exception-Handling Mechanism*. ACM ToPLaS. Vol.7, No.2, April 1985, pp 214-243. San Francisco, April 1990.

Appendix A: Implementations

We have described the design of an exception handling mechanism. Several different implementations are possible. In particular, it is possible to write an implementation that is fully portable in the sense that it produces ANSI C (only) and also to write an implementation that is close to ideal in its use of run-time.

Run-time representation of Types
All implementations must provide a way of representing the type of the exception thrown for matching with the types specified in the handlers. At the point where an exception is thrown, the compiler might give to the library functions that search for a handler a pointer to a string that names the exception class and all its base classes, along with a pointer to the copy constructor for each. A variant of the encoding of types used to achieve type-safe linkage on systems with traditional linkers could be used. For example:

```
class X { /* ... */ };
class Y : public X { /* ... */ };
class A { /* ... */ };
class Z : public Y : public A { /* ... */ };
```

could be represented as:

type	run-time representation
X	"_1X"
Y	"_1Y:_1X"
Z	"_1Z:(_1Y:_1X,_1A)"
Y&	"R_1Y:_1X"
Z*	"P_1Z:(_1Y:_1X,_1A)"
const char*	"PCc"

The reason that strings are a reasonable representation and that the complete inheritance hierarchy is needed is that separate compilation of the *throw-expression* and the *handler* will be the norm and that the resolution must be done at run time.

Schemes based on other kinds of objects representing the classes are of course also feasible and will be more appropriate than strings in some environments. Whatever representation is chosen should be suitably encapsulated in a class. It will also be necessary to define a set of C functions for creating and using such run-time representations. We present the string encoding scheme simply as an existence proof.

Exception Temporaries
Another issue that every implementation must face is the need to introduce a "temporary object" to hold the current exception during stack unwinding and during the execution of a handler (in case a re-throw operation occurs in the handler or in a function called by the handler). The use of such a temporary object is completely under control of the exception handling mechanism. One strategy would be to allocate such objects using the general purpose free store mechanisms. However, that could make the exception handling mechanism vulnerable to free store corruption and exhaustion. A better strategy would be to allocate such objects out of a pre-allocated pool of storage used only by the exception handling mechanism and maybe also optimize away the "temporary object" for exceptions passed by value and not re-thrown.

Outline of a Portable Implementation
Here we describe an implementation that is fully portable in the sense that it makes it possible to generate ANSI C (only) from a C++ program. The importance of such an implementation is that it allows programmers to experiment

with C++ exception handling without waiting for implementations to be specifically tuned for their particular system and guarantees portability of programs using exception handling across a greater range of machines than would be economically feasible had each machine required a 'hand crafted' implementation. The price of such an implementation is run-time cost. We have no really good estimates of that cost but it is primarily a function of the cost of setjmp() and longjmp() on a given system.

To simplify the discussion, we need to define a few terms. A *destructible object* is an object that has a non-empty destructor or contains one or more destructible objects. The *destructor count* of a class is the number of destructors that must be executed before freeing an object of that class, including the destructor for the class itself. The destructor count of an array is the number of elements in the array times the destructor count of an element.

The general strategy is to lay down a destructor for every destructible object, even if the user did not specify one (for example, consider an object without an explicit destructor that contains two objects with destructors). Every destructible object on the stack acquires a *header* containing a pointer to the destructor for that object, a pointer to the next most recently created automatic destructible object, and a *skip count* that indicates how much of that object has been constructed:

```
struct _header {
    void* destructor;
    void* backchain;
    unsigned skipcnt;
};
```

Thus, for example, a C++ class that looks like this:

```
class T {
public:
    T();
    ~T();
};
```

will be augmented internally to look like this:

```
class T {
    _header _h;
public:
    T();
    ~T();
}
```

Every _header object is part of some other object. All destructible objects on the stack therefore form a chain, with the most recent first. The head of that chain is a (single) global variable created for the purpose, initially null.

Therefore, to construct an automatic object, the implementation must make the object header point to the destructor for that object, set the skip count to indicate that construction has not yet started, and link the header into the global chain. If the variable that heads the chain is called _DO_head (DO stands for 'destructible objects'), the following code would be inserted into T::T() to maintain the chain:

```
_h.backchain = _DO_head;
_h.skipcnt = 1;    // destructor count of T
_h.destructor = (void*) &T::~T();
_DO_head = &h;
```

We will use this chain *only* to destroy objects while unwinding the stack; we do not need it when a destructor is called during normal exit from a block. However, an exception could occur in a destructor during normal block exit, so it is necessary to keep the global chain header up to date while destroying objects. The safest way to do this is probably for the compiler to avoid following the actual chain. Instead, the compiler should point the chain header directly at each object it is about to destroy.

In other words, rather than generating code inside `T::~T()` to update `_DO_head`, the compiler should reset `_DO_head` explicitly and then call the relevant destructor where possible:

```
_DO_head = previous value;
t->T::~T();
```

The skip count indicates how many destructors have to be skipped when destroying an object. When we are about to begin constructing an object, we set its skip count to its destructor count. Each constructor decrements the skip count, so that a completely constructed object has a skip count of zero.

The elements of an object are destroyed in reverse order. Each destructor *either* decrements the skip count *or* destroys its associated object if the skip count is already zero.

To do all this, we give every constructor and destructor the address of the skip count as an 'extra' argument. If the object is not on the stack, we pass the address of a dummy word.

For example, code generated for the destructor `T::~T()` might look like this:

```
T_dtor(/* other args */, unsigned* skipcnt) /* generated code */
{
    if (*skipcnt)
        --*skipcnt;
    else {
        /* destroy '*this' */
    }
}
```

If destructors leave a zero skip count untouched, we can safely give a destructor for an off-stack object the address of a static zero word somewhere. Having a destructor do this costs little, as destructors must test for zero, anyway.

The test is presumably unnecessary for constructors, and it would be a shame to have to include it anyway just to avoid having a constructor for an off-stack object scribble a global value. However, we can use a different global value for constructors. We don't care what the value is, so all constructors can safely scribble it. By making all skip counts `unsigned`, we can avoid the possibility of overflow or underflow.

The actual stack unwinding must be done by `longjmp` and takes place in two stages. First we track back through the stack object chain, calling destructors along the way. After that, we execute the C `longjmp` function to pop the stack.

What is the overhead of this scheme? Every constructor gets an extra argument (which takes one instruction to push it) and has to decrement the skip count (one or two instructions, two memory references). Every destructor gets an extra argument (one instruction to push it) and has to decrement and test the skip count (three or four instructions). In addition, each destructible object gets three extra words (which takes three instructions to fill them) and the list head must be updated when the object is created (one instruction). There is no extra overhead for classes, such as Complex, that do not have destructors.

Thus the overhead per destructible object is somewhere near 10-12 instructions. This overhead decreases if constructors or destructors are inline: the skip counts can be set directly instead of indirectly and the inline destructors don't even have to test them. It is still necessary to lay down an out-of-line destructor with full generality.

Outline of an Efficient Implementation
Here we outline an implementation technique (derived from Clu and Modula2+ techniques) that has close to ideal run-time performance. This means that (except possibly for some table building at startup time), the implementation carries absolutely no run time overhead until an exception is thrown; every cycle spent is spent when exceptions are thrown. This could make throwing an exception relatively expensive, but that we consider a potential advantage because it discourages the use of exception handling where alternative control structures will do.

Since this implementation requires detailed knowledge of the function calling mechanism and of the stack layout on a particular system, it is portable only though a moderate amount of effort.

The compiler must construct, for each block, a map from program counter values to a 'construction state.' This state is the information necessary to determine which objects need to be destroyed if execution is interrupted at the given point.

Such a table can be organized as a list of address triples, the first two elements representing a region in which a particular destruction strategy is appropriate, and the third element representing a location to which to jump if execution is interrupted in that region. The number of entries in such tables could be greatly reduced (typically to one) at a modest execution cost by adding a fourth element to entries and using the __counter trick presented in the fifth section.

This table is searched only if an exception is thrown. In that case, the exception dispatcher unwinds the stack as necessary, using the appropriate table for each stack frame to decide how to destroy objects for that stack frame. The dispatcher can regain control after each level of unwinding by 'hijacking' the return address from each frame before jumping to the destruction point.

It is possible to merge all pre-frame exception tables into a single table either at run time or compile time. Where dynamic linking is used such table merging must be done at run time.

As before, the decision about whether to enter an exception handler can be made by code generated for the purpose, the address of which can be placed in the table in place of the destruction point for those blocks with exception handlers.

The only overhead of this scheme if exceptions are not used is that these tables will take up some space during execution. Moreover, the stack frame layout must be uniform enough that the exception dispatcher can locate return addresses and so on.

In addition, we need some way of identifying these tables to the exception dispatcher. A likely way to do that while still living with existing linkers is to give the tables names that can be recognized by a suitable extension to the munch or `patch` programs.

Appendix B: Grammar

In the C++ grammar, the exception handling mechanism looks like this:

> *try-block:*
>   `try` *compound-statement handler-list*
>
> *handler-list:*
>   *handler handler-list*
>
> *handler:*
>   `catch` (*exception-declaration*) *compound-statement*
>
> *exception-declaration:*
>   *type-specifier-list declarator*
>   *type-specifier-list abstract-declarator*
>   *type-specifier-list*
>   ...

A *try-block* is a *statement*.

> *throw-expression:*
>   `throw` *expression*

A *throw-expression* is a *unary-expression* of type `void`.

A *exception-specification* can be used as a suffix in a function declaration:

> *exception-specification:*
>   `throw` (*type-list*)
>
> *type-list:*
>   *type-name*
>   *type-list* , *type-name*

Appendix C: Local Scope Issues

Allowing the exception handling code in a *handler* to access variables in the `try` block to which it is attached would violate the notion that a block establishes a scope. For example:

```
void f(int arg)
{
    int loc1;

    try { int loc2; /* ... */ g(); } catch (x1) { /* ... */ }
    try { int loc3; /* ... */ g(); } catch (x2) { /* ... */ }
}
```

Here, both exception handlers can access the local variable `loc1` and the argument `arg`, but neither of them can get at `loc2` or `loc3`.

Disallowing access to variables in the block to which the handler is attached is also important to allow good code to be generated. For example:

```
void f(int arg)
{
    int loc1;
    // ...
    try {
        int loc2 = 1;
        g1();
        loc2++;
        g2();
    }
```

```
catch (x1) {
    if (loc2 == 1) // ...
}
}
```

Were this allowed, the compiler and run-time systems would have to ensure that the value of `loc2` is well defined upon entry to the handler. On many architectures, this implies that its value must be allocated in memory before the calls of `g1()` and `g2()`. However, this involves an increase of the size of the generated code and poor use of registers. One could easily lose a factor of two in run-time performance while at the same time enlarging the code significantly.

Access to local variables in the surrounding scope (including the function arguments) is allowed and is important in the cases where recovery is possible. For example:

```
void f(int arg)
{
    // ...

    try {
        // ...
    }
    catch (x1) {
        // fix things
        return f(arg);  // try again
    }
}
```

When re-trying this way, one should beware of the infinite recursion that can occur in case of repeated failure.

Naturally, the value of local variables accessible from a handler, such as `arg`, must be correct upon entry of the handler. This implies compilers must take a certain amount of care about the use of registers for such variables.

Appendix D: Syntax Details

It might be possible to simplify the
```
try { ... } catch (abc) { ... }
```
syntax by removing the apparently redundant `try` keyword, removing the redundant parentheses, and by allowing a handler to be attached to any statement and not just to a block. For example, one might allow:

```
void f()
{
    g(); catch (x1) { /* ... */ }
}
```
as an alternative to
```
void f()
{
    try { g(); } catch (x1) { /* ... */ }
}
```
The added notational convenience seems insignificant and may not even be convenient. People seem to prefer syntactic constructs that start with a prefix that alerts them to what is going on, and it may be easier to generate good code when the `try` keyword is required. For example,

```
void f(int arg)
{
    int i;
    // ...
    try { /* ... */ } catch (x) { /* ... */ }
    // ...
}
```

Here, the `try` prefix enables a single-pass compiler to ensure, at the beginning of the block with a handler, that local variables in the surrounding block are not stored in registers. Without the prefix, register allocation would have to be postponed until the end of the function. Naturally, optimal register allocation based on flow analysis does not require `try` as a hint, but it is often important for a language design to enable simple code generation strategies to be applied without incurring devastating run-time penalties.

Allowing exception handlers to be attached to blocks only and not to simple statements simplifies syntax analysis (both for humans and computers) where several exceptions are caught and where nested exception handlers are considered (see Appendix E). For example, assuming that we allowed *handlers* to be attached to any statement we could write:

```
try try f();
    catch (x) { ... } catch (y) { ... } catch (z) { ... }
```

The could be interpreted be in at least three ways:

```
try { try f(); catch (x) { ... } }
                catch (y) { ... } catch (z) { ... }
try { try f(); catch (x) { ... } catch (y) { ... } }
                                        catch (z) { ... }
try { try f(); catch (x) { ... }
    catch (y) { ... } catch (z) { ... } }
```

There seems to be no reason to allow these ambiguities even if there is a trivial and systematic way for a parser to chose one interpretation over another. Consequently, a `{` is required after a `try` and a matching `}` before the first of the associated sequence of `catch` clauses.

Appendix E: Nested Exceptions

What happens if an exception is thrown while an exception handler is executing? This question is more subtle than it appears at first glance. Consider first the obvious case:

```
try { f(); } catch (e1 e) { throw e; }
```

This is the simplest case of throwing an exception inside an exception handler and appears to be one of the more common ones: a handler that does something and then passes the same exception on to the surrounding context. This example argues strongly that re-throwing e1 should not merely cause an infinite loop, but rather that the exception should be passed up to the next level.

What about throwing a different exception?

```
try { f(); } catch (e2) { throw e3; }
```

Here, if exception e2 occurs in `f()`, it seems to make sense to pass e3 on to the surrounding context, just as if `f()` had thrown e3 directly. Now, let's wrap a block around this statement:

```
try {
    try { f(); }
    catch (e2) { throw e3; }
    catch (e3) {
        // inner
    }
}
catch (e3) {
    // outer
}
```

If f() throws e2, this will result in the handler for e3 marked 'outer' being entered.

From the language's perspective an exception is considered caught at the point where control is passed to a user-provided handler. From that point on all exceptions are caught by (lexically or dynamically) enclosing handlers.

The handling of destructors naturally gives raise to a form of nested handlers – and these *must* be dealt with. Nested handlers may naturally occur in machine generated code and could conceivably be used to improve locality of error handling.

Appendix F: Arguments to Throw Operations

We expect that it will be commonplace to pass information from the point where an exception is thrown to the point where it is caught. For example, in the case of a vector range exception one might like to pass back the address of the vector and the offending index. Some exception handling mechanisms provide arguments for the throw operation to allow that[13, 14, 15]. However, since (in the scheme presented here) exceptions are simply objects of user-defined types, a user can simply define a class capable of holding the desired information. For example:

```
class Vector {
    int* p;
    int sz;
public:
    class Range {
        Vector* id;
        int index;
    public:
        Range(Vector* p, int i): id(p), index(i) { }
    };
    int& operator[](int i)
    {
        if (0<=i && i<sz) return p[i];
        throw Range(this, i);
    }
};
void f(Vector& v)
{
    try { do_something(v); }
    catch (Vector::Range r) {
        // r.id points to the vector
        // r.index is the index
        // ...
    }
}
```

This solution works nicely even under a system with concurrency. Throwing an exception involves creating a new object on the stack; catching it involves unwinding the stack to the catch point after copying the exception object into the handler. Neither of these operations is a problem for a system that can handle concurrency at all.

Appendix G: `terminate()` *and* `unexpected()`

Occasionally, exception handling must be abandoned for less subtle error handling techniques. Examples of this are when the exception handling mechanism cannot find a handler for a thrown exception, when the exception handling mechanism finds the stack corrupted, and when a destructor called during stack unwinding cause by an exception tries to exit using an exception. In such cases

```
void terminate();
```

is called.

One other kind of error is treated specially: when a function tries to raise an exception that it promised in the *throw-clause* in its declaration not to raise. In that case

```
void unexpected();
```

is called. This case does not necessarily call `terminate()` because although the failure is severe in some sense, its semantics are well defined and it may therefore be possible to recover in a reliable way.

The `terminate()` function executes the last function given as an argument to the function `set_terminate()`:

```
typedef void(*PFV)();
PFV set_terminate(PFV);
```

The previous function given to `set_terminate()` will be the return value.

Similarly, the `unexpected()` function executes the last function given as an argument to the function `set_unexpected()`.

This enables users to implement a stack strategy for using `terminate()` or `unexpected()`:

```
class STC { // store and reset class
    PFV old;
public:
    STC(PFV f) { old = set_terminate(f); }
    ~STC() { set_terminate(old); }
};
void my_function()
{
    STC xx(&my_terminate_handler);

    // my_terminate_handler will be called in case of
    // disasters here

    // the destructor for xx will reset the terminate handler
}
```

This is an example of using a local object to represent the acquisition and relinquishing of a resource as mentioned in the sixth section. Without it, it guaranteeing the reset of the function to be called by `terminate()` to its old value would have been tricky. With it, `terminate()` will be reset even when `my_function()` is terminated by an exception.

We avoided making STC a local class because with a suitable name it would be a good candidate for a standard library.

By default unexpected() will call terminate() and terminate() will call abort(). These default are expected to be the correct choice for most users.

A call of terminate() is assumed not to return to its caller.

Note that the functions abort() and terminate() indicate abnormal exit from the program. The function exit() can be used to exit a program with a return value that indicates to the surrounding system whether the exit is normal or abnormal.

A call of abort() invokes no destructors. A call of exit() invokes destructors for constructed static objects only. One could imagine a third way of exiting a program where first constructed automatic objects were invoked in (reverse) order and then then destructors for constructed static objects. Such an operation would naturally be an exception. For example:

```
throw Exit(99);
```

where Exit must be defined something like this:

```
class Exit {
public:
    int val;
    Exit(int i) { val=i; }
};
```

One might further define the invocation of a C++ program like this:

```
void system()    // pseudo code
{
    try {
        return main(argv,argc);
    }
    catch (Exit e) {
        return (e.val);
    }
    catch (...) {
        return UNCAUGHT_EXCEPTION;
    }
}
```

Chapter 9

An Exception Handling Implementation for C++

Michael D. Tiemann

Abstract

This paper outlines a design for an exception handling mechanism that has been implemented in GNU C++, a free, native-code C++ compiler. Various alternatives for handling exceptions are presented. An abstraction is derived which solves problems with existing C/C++ solutions. The abstraction is flexible, type-safe, and works in a mixed language execution environment. Two implementations are presented: one which can be implemented by a C++ to C translator, the other which can be implemented to run efficiently under a native-code compiler. This paper concludes with a brief survey of other exception handling designs.

Introduction

Program behavior is divided into two categories: normal operation and exceptional circumstances. The C++ programming language was designed to support programming under normal conditions. Unfortunately, exceptional circumstances (hereafter called *exceptions*) do arise, and when they do, most C++ programs are poorly equipped to deal with them, mainly because doing so is hard without language support.

This paper presents an extension to the language which supports programming in the presence of exceptions. It provides the programmer with a disciplined way of dealing with exceptions that is portable, type-safe, works in a mixed-language execution environment, and can be implemented to execute efficiently.

The presentation begins with a motivation for adding exception handling to C++. With that background, it then shows how the design of a particular exception handling design evolved. The use and utility of this design is then shown. Finally, the design is targeted to two different compiler platforms: a C++ to C translator and a native-code compiler. The paper concludes with a brief comparison of this exception handling design with previous designs.

Why Handle Exceptions?

Reliable programs must be able to expect the unexpected. When a subroutine encounters a situation with which it cannot cope, three alternatives are traditionally used in C/C++:

From *USENIX 1990 C++ Conference Proceedings*, pp. 215-240.

1. Set a flag and return an error code;
2. Abort the program;
3. Print an error message and continue, hoping for the best.

These alternatives are not attractive for these respective reasons:

1. The domain of every return type must include an error code, and every value returned by a function must be checked against this code;
2. The program, at some higher level, may be prepared to deal with the problem;
3. A program that has been poisoned is dangerous; it should be cured or killed.

We therefore conclude that existing C/C++ mechanisms are not sufficient to deal effectively with exceptional events (such as running out of memory or trying to write to a file that no longer exists). Given the propensity for exceptional events to occur, and a desire to write programs that don't crash (such as operating systems) a more reliable mechanism is needed.

An Abstraction for Exception Handling

The characteristic of the exceptions treated here is that they show up in one place, but must be handled in another. While it is perfectly valid to consider an exception within a C function that must be handled in another place within that same function, we consider for now that such a case is largely solved by using a goto statement. What has not been solved is when a function f is active, and wants to raise exception EX to be handled by one of the functions that (transitively, at the time f is active) called f, i.e., we are concerned with exceptions that cross function-call boundaries. In this paper, solutions for inter-function exception handling can be trivially generalized to intra-function exception handling.

We begin by examining the properties of function calls and control transfer.

Solutions in C

The C programming language, and by extension C++, has a very simple function-call model. Informally, a C function call takes a (possibly empty) list of arguments, and returns a (possibly void) value. The point of return is always to the point of invocation.[1] In the parsimonious world of C and C++ programming, error values or exception values are not usually in the domain of the return type, so it is often not possible to "return" an error code. To handle exceptions, then, the return mechanism must be augmented.

Multiple return values (i.e., a normal return value and an error code) can be simulated by returning aggregate values, though with some performance penalty. The use of aggregate return values would also clutter code with temporary variables: what was once the use of a function call as an expression would have to become the initialization of a temporary variable via a function call, followed by a test of that variable's return status code. If the return status

---

[1]Except for longjmp, which is not really a C function anyway.

code signified that things are ok, the remainder of the temporary would be used for the function return value. If the return status code signified an exception, then exception handling would have to be initiated at that point.

Handling exceptions by using multiple return values would change code that looks like this:

```
int f (int), g (int), gronk (int, int);
int i = gronk (f (1), g (2));
```

into this:

```
enum error_code { OK = 0, ... };
struct aggr { error_code err; int val;};
void handle (aggr);
aggr f (int), g (int), gronk (int, int);

aggr t1 = f (1);
if (t1.err != OK) handle (t1);

aggr t2 = g (2);
if (t2.err != OK) handle (t2);

aggr t3 = gronk (t1.val, t2.val);
if (t3.err != OK) handle (t3);

int i = t3.val;
```

The overhead includes one extra value assignment and one extra conditional test per function call. Also, on many machines (depending mostly on the compiler), it might mean that all function calls would have to return values through memory rather than through registers. All in all, such a solution would add noticeably to execution time, and program size.

The use of side-effects is an alternative to returning aggregate values, as shown in the following code typifying the UNIX solution:

```
enum error_code { OK = 0, ...};
error_code errno;
int f (int), g (int), gronk (int, int);

int i = gronk (f (1), g (2));

// which function set ERRNO???
if (erno == EIEIO)
moo ();
```

Notice that this technique is not reentrant, and highly error-prone, since the type system does not give the user a way to automatically check that s/he has tested all variables that a program might be using to store exception information. So while this solution has reduced apparent overhead, it has done so at the cost of code safety.

A Better Solution

The C function-call model is based upon a fixed, typed, immutable *continuation*. The continuation is the pair <return value, return address> and cannot be changed or extended by the programmer. It is maintained by the compiler, and incurs very little overhead: on the average machine the cost is a push to save the return value, and the setting of a register to communicate the return value. The continuation is activated by a simple "return from subroutine" instruction. All this simplicity is nice for the compiler writer, but a pain for the programmer: in order to control behavior of the program across function call boundaries, the programmer must set state variables and interpret them manually (i.e., compare a global variable against zero, etc.).

With more general continuation model, the programmer would have the ability to pass control structures across function-call boundaries. In particular, it would be possible to have a function return to multiple places by building a continuation which encapsulates different points of return:

```
// cont is a first-class continuation
int f (int, cont), g (int, cont), gronk (int, int, cont);
cont k1, k2;

int i = gronk (f (1, k1), g (2, k1), k2); ... // normal return
// ok to use 'i' here

ki (int x):
// deal with one kind of problem involving X

k2 (int x, int y):
// deal with another kind of problem involving X and Y
```

where a function's C continuation (returning to the point of invocation) is considered implicit.

This gives us the following advantages:

- continuations make control transfer for exceptions explicit;
- use of continuations can be type-checked;
- continuations provide an encapsulation for environments which must share information;
- the same continuation can be used in many places within the program.

with the following disadvantages:

- additional overhead for function calls;
- nontrivial extension to C.

A good design would therefore provide the advantages without imposing the disadvantages.

Mapping Continuations to C

First-class continuations as provided by languages like Scheme are not easily added to C. However, one can approximate a first-class continuation using the setjmp/longjmp mechanism. The setjmp function establishes a continuation, and a call to longjmp "returns" to it. There are significant constraints as to how these continuations can be set up, and modification of these continuations is not defined. Using C, we have:

```
int f (int, jmp_buf), g (int, jmp_buf), gronk (int, int, jmp_buf);
jmp_buf j1, j2;

if (setjmp (j1)) goto k1;
if (setjmp (j2)) goto k2;

int i = gronk (f (1, j1), g (2, j1), j2);
    ...
// normal return

k1: // deal with one kind of problem

k2: // deal with another kind of problem
```

As can be seen, the syntax is clumsy, requiring lots of "continuation" declarations in addition to the calls to setjmp everywhere. Control transfer has been made explicit, but at the cost of code legibility. Because the programmer must still manually set up the continuation her/himself, it is still all too possible to write code that will go haywire when calling longjmp on an uninitialized jmp_buf. It would also be easy to call setjmp on the wrong jmp_buf, clobbering a valid continuation.

Using this model, there is no easy general solution to passing information from the exception raiser to the exception handler without extra mechanism. Non-reentrant techniques are rejected because they defeat the requirement of this design. Non-portable solutions, such as using the return value of setjmp to pass back a pointer to a block of arguments, cannot be accepted either.

Finally, in passing around the continuation, there is still the overhead of passing an extra parameter to every exception-handling function call.

The Need for Special Syntax

To implement an exception handling mechanism which is compatible with C++, two criteria must be met: exceptions must interact properly with existing C++ constructs and they must be implementable in an efficient way. The major interaction which must be preserved is that when a binding contour is exited, destructors for objects in that contour must be called. As it is, longjmp makes no such guarantees, so longjmp alone is not sufficient.

Due to a concession made by the ANSI C committee, longjmp may return to an environment established by setjmp in which registers at the point of the call to setjmp will have different values than just after the longjmp. For this reason, setjmp and longjmp can interfere with, if not completely defeat register-based optimizations that the compiler might perform. Therefore, it is desirable to be able to base an exception handling implementation using continuations that can be implemented by something other than setjmp and longjmp (though setjmp and longjmp will certainly work).

A system which has a high-level notion of exception handling is now considered. For this system, setjmp and longjmp are used only to describe semantics; there is no stipulation that they must be used.

In the following code, the try block establishes an exception handler. Exceptions raised within the try block will be handled by handlers appearing at the end of the try block. In this model, EX and EY name exceptions, and the catch statements combine with them denote continuations. That is, if a function raises the EX exception, then control will logically "throw" to the handler labeled catch EX. Similarly for EY.

```
int f (int) raises EX, g (int) raises EX;
int gronk (int, int) raises EY;

try {
    int i = gronk (f (1), g (2));
    ... // normal execution
}
catch EX // deal with one kind of problem
{
}
catch EY // deal with another kind of problem
{
}
...
// normal return
```

Implementing the example code using the above model makes control transfer explicit, satisfying the first of the three desiderata.

The model is strongly typed in that the declaration of a continuation is matched with its handler, so the programmer is not in a position to make mistakes with setjmp/label: pairs. Additionally, functions which raise exceptions can make that fact explicit in their type signature, aiding program documentation and making it possible for the compiler to check consistency of interfaces.

It should be noted that by a simple translation process, this structure can be implemented with C semantics using setjmp and longjmp,[2] hence no extensions to a C-based model are necessary. Furthermore, because the model uses specify exception-related semantics without specifying a corresponding implementation, optimizations are possible when considering target implementations beyond the C language. In particular, a mechanism can be implemented in such a way that there is no overhead for establishing try blocks.

Extensions to the Model

The model of the previous section lacks a means to pass information from the exception's raiser to the exception's handler (beyond the raised exception's name). The model also does not treat relationships between exceptions, specifically subclassing. The following section explains the key observation which unifies the solution we have with a C++ implementation.

The Environment Abstraction

A binding contour maps names to locations, and is the mechanism by which global variables, parameters, and local variables are supported in C and C++. Characteristics of these binding contours are:

- they *nest* in a particular order;
- they are *static* (as opposed to *dynamic*);
- they are not first-class objects

These characteristics imply that binding contours cannot be passed from one function to another, and that they cannot be modified at run-time. A function f can pass information to another function g only by modifying the values mapped by f's binding contour, but it cannot pass its own binding contour for f to use. For completeness, it is noted that parameter lists can be passed around via the varargs mechanism, but that that mechanism is very primitive, and does not permit parameter locations to be named outside their containing function's scope.

In the Scheme world, environments and continuations go hand in hand. An *environment* is a generalization of a binding contour. When a continuation is called, the arguments to the continuation become part of the resulting (callee's) environment. A similar feat can be performed using objects.

---

[2]In fact, such an implementation exists in GNU C++ 1.37.1.

Sharing Environments

It is appropriate to begin with the age-old question "what's in a name?". Specifically, is the name of an exception sufficient to pass to the handler all the information needed to handle the exception? In general, the answer is no. It will certainly do for coarse-grained exception handling to have the name encode all that needs to be know, for example DIV_BY_0. But consider the case of a process requesting exclusive access to a set of resources. If some subset of those resources are unavailable (since granting them might cause a deadlock), the requestor might like to know which ones are causing trouble, rather then handling an otherwise uninformative EDEADLOCK exception.

To review C-style mechanisms which will not solve this problem, we begin by noting that we have already rejected the simplest mechanism of encoding semantic information in the exception name.

The use of global variables to hold the exception environment is rejected because it provides poor encapsulation for the exception handler (thereby violating the object-oriented programming paradigm). It is also not reentrant, making it difficult if not impossible to use in a parallel processing environment.

Passing a local environment down the call chain to be filled in by the raiser of an exception would add overhead to all calls to functions active between the raiser and handler. The overhead must be paid whether or not exceptions are raised at run-time. Such a solution reintroduces the efficiency problem that we worked so hard to remove. It also requires the programmer to write and maintain a lot of extra code. The extra work means that the programmer will probably not bother with it, and choose instead to write programs limited to name-based exception handling. If the difficulty of using the exception handling mechanism discourages programmers from using it to solve common exception-based problems, then its design should be rethought or scrapped.

Environments and Objects

In general, lexical closures, hence environments, can be first-class objects, and can therefore be shared by functions in the same way that a pointer can be shared. This section describes how the environments between exception raiser and exception handler can be shared using objects.

Objects are interesting in that they define a lexical closure which is distinct from the standard C lexical closures (the global binding level, the function parameter level, and inner program blocks). In contrast to these closures, which are static, the lexical closure of an object is dynamic. In other words, C binding contours stay in one place; to access their elements, the user must be brought into their context. On the other hand, the environment of an object moves around with the object, and to access its elements, the object need only be brought to the user. For this reason, information encapsulated within the environment of an object can be shared between two viewpoints separated across function boundaries, while information encapsulated in static environments (except the global one) cannot.

It is precisely this use of encapsulation that makes objects a uniquely suitable vehicle for solving the communication problem between exception raiser and exception handler. No other part of the language solves this problem so elegantly:

```
exception { int i; char *p; } EX;
exception { String s; } EY;
int f (int) raises EX, g (int) raises EX;
int gronk (int, int) raises EY;
try {
    int i = gronk (f (1), g (2));
    ...          // normal execution
}
except ep {
    EX {
        // use exception parameters
        if (ep .i) printf (ep.p);
    }
    EY {
        // use other exception parameters
        raise EY (ep.s + " raise ");
    }
    default {
        // default exception, parameters are invisible
        raise ep;
    }
    ...
// normal return
```

We can therefore pass information from exception raiser to exception handler by passing an object encapsulating the raiser's environment as part of the continuation.

Exceptions and Inheritance

Inheritance has been identified as one of the central concepts of object oriented programming. In this exception handling design, types play a key role in the specifications and use of exceptions. This design would be incomplete without discussing how these new kinds of types interact with or relate to inheritance.

Just as with normal programming, one can imagine uses for exceptions which can be handled by general handlers (base handlers) or can be handled by more specialized handlers (derived handlers). We first consider how normal inheritance is used in normal programming contexts. We then show how inheritance is used under exceptional circumstances, and conclude with a design that satisfies our minimal requirements.

As pointed out previously, normal type relations are static. Objects of base type and objects of derived type can be constructed such that the type of the object (often implemented by its virtual function table) remains constant throughout the object's lifetime. In particular, how the object reacts to method calls is invariant of the object (except during construction and destruction, which are special cases).[3]

For exceptions, the way in which exceptions are handled is not an invariant of the exception; rather it is a function of both the exception being raised and the dynamic context (i.e., the current lexical contours and/or current call chain). Thus, it is not possible to talk of inheritance strictly as a function of the exception type.

---

[3]Actually, this is not true for non-virtual methods, but we consider such cases anomalies.

The reasons for using inheritance in handling exceptions are the same reasons for using inheritance in normal programming. Namely, to support (and promote) code reuse by writing general handlers which can be specialized as programs evolve. For example, when using an I/O package, one should expect to handle I/O errors. Initially, the program will handle very general I/O errors, but as the program evolves, it might handle them at a finer grain of detail. If the package raises `FileScrambled_error`, it would be nice to be able to catch either *IO_error*, *File_error*, or *FileScrambled_error*. With inheritance of exceptions, one handler could catch all three, or the most specialized handler could be applied. Thus it is easy to write a prototype program which is still robust.

Seeing the utility of inheritance of exceptions, the question arises of how to support it. Two possibilities spring to mind: the first is to implement inheritance of exceptions directly; the second is to use inheritance as provided by objects. We consider both implementations and choose the one which delivers all the features we want without compromising the efficiency of the implementation.

The interesting implementation of inheritance for objects is provided via the objects virtual function table(s). Irrespective of where a virtual method call is made to an object, the object responds to the call in the same way. Thus the virtual function table serves to encode part of the object's behavior. (In contrast, non-virtual method calls are more a function of the object's lexical environment-whether the object is seen by the compiler as a being of base or derived type.)

Since the handling of exceptions is a function of the dynamic call chain, an exception cannot itself encode an action to perform in the event that it is raised. An exception therefore needs a means of identifying itself so that the run-time exception mechanism can know which handler should handle the exception. Without inheritance of exceptions, the name of an exception was sufficient to identify the exception. With inheritance of exceptions, a more complicated encoding is needed.

An inheritance tree can be encoded as a tree of names in the inheritance tree. This tree, like the name, can be built at compile or link time, and can even take advantage of structure-sharing techniques. Multiple inheritance can also be handled by constructing a directed acyclic graph (DAG) instead of a tree. The search mechanism can optionally be enhanced to optimize a search of the DAG; otherwise, it will search it as a tree, visiting some subgraphs more than once.

As usual, the search mechanism must be written to find the best match among a list of potential handlers. When the exact handler appears, that match must be found first. After that, it is up to the exception matcher to find the best alternative. In some cases, an exact match against a derived handler might be preferable to a match against a base handler closer on the call chain. In other cases, the first handler that can match at all is the wanted one. Such flexibility can be achieved by associating a matcher with the exception being raised.

This implementation provides the features of inheritance that we want, but at a price which is the complexity of the search mechanism. Since exceptions are considered exceptional, the speed with which an exception can be handled is not of primary importance. But it is not desirable to add a lot of code and data overhead to implement features that will not (or need not) be used.

A second implementation is much simpler. Under this implementation, inheritance of exceptions is provided via existing mechanisms. Exception types *per se* are not inheritable, but the parameters to the exceptions can be types which obey inheritance. Thus, the system works with a small number of primitive, general exceptions, and special behavior is provided by objects which may be parameters to exceptions.

In C++:

```
exception { class base *b; ... } IO;
class File : public virtual base { ... };
class Network : public virtual base { ...};
class NetworkFile : public File, public Network { ... };

int foo ()
{
    ...
    try
    {
        fd = open ("bar", "xyzzy");
    }
    except ep
    {
        IO {
            (ep.b)->handle (fd);
        }
    }
}
```

The second implementation provides access to the use of inheritance for exceptions without requiring any further extension or complication of the original model. It is also a proper subset of the implementation which permits explicit inheritance of exceptions. Since it provides the features we want without extra complexity, and since it is upwards compatible with a more complicated mechanism, we choose it as the best way to provide inheritance to users of exceptions.

Implementation

This section described two possible implementations: one for a C++ to C translator and one for a native-code C++ compiler. The exception mechanism presented in this paper can be implemented as follows:

The declaration of an exception such as:

```
exception { T1 p1; T2 p2; } EX;
```

results in the following:

```
long exception_EX; // used to identify exception.

class EX {
    public:
    T1 i1;
    T2 i2;
    EX (T1 p1, T2 p2) { i1 = p1; i2 = p2; }
    ~EX () {}
};
```

The representation of an exception handler is as follows:

```
class ExceptionHandler {
    // enclosing handler
    ExceptionHandler *prev;

    // see setjmp/longjmp
    jmp_buf handler;

    // exception name
    long *name;

    // pointer to parameter object
    void *parameters;

    // constructor and destructor for handler
    ExceptionHandler ();
    ~ExceptionHandler ();
}
```

The constructor for an exception handler initialized the fields and links the new handler on the top of the exception handler stack. The destructor unlinks it and releases the storage for the handler object.

The `try` statement expands into the following code:

```
{                       // start of new block for handler
    ExceptionHandler eh (); // allocation handler
    if (setjmp (eh.handler) == 0)
    {
        // statements
    }
    else {
        exceptionHandlerStack = exceptionHandlerStack->prev;
        if (eh.name == &exception_EX) {
            // handler for exception EX; access parameters by
            // casting eh.parameters to class EX*
        }
        else if /* look for other exceptions ... */
        else {
            // either default handler or reraise using
            // eh.name and eh.parameters.
        }
    }
}
```

The `raise` statement expands into the following code:

```
exceptionHandlerStack->parameters = (void *)new EX (parameters);
exceptionHandlerStack->name = &exception_EX;
DoDestructors (); // run all destructors necessary
longjmp (exceptionHandlerStack->handler);
```

For native code compiler, a similar structure is used, but calls to `setjmp` are not needed. Instead, the compiler notices `try` statements, and emits code indicating their boundaries. The linker builds tables which map program counter ranges to specific handler addresses. When an exception is raised, the run-time system looks in the tables to find the appropriate handler, and sends the execution thread to that location. Thus, the overhead of a `try` statement is reduced to nothing at runtime. The overhead of a `raise` statement might be higher, but since `raise` is expected very infrequently, this is not considered a problem.

A Survey of Other Designs

The differences between exception handling implementations can be distinguished in two interesting ways: differences in policy and differences in mechanism. This section is far too brief, but is included in the hopes that it provides some completeness.

In the Mesa system, exception handling was introduced for two primary purposes. The first was to make if easy for the programmer to be able to program as though things that were not really supposed to happen could be treated as though they never would, and secondly, as a form of documentation of behavior. For example, when the programmer wants to use the Mesa storage allocator, s/he can program as though it never returns NULL. The exception handling mechanism handles the rare instances when it does, but otherwise, there is no need to test the return value against NULL. Mesa takes advantage of this fact, and optimized the implementation so that overhead is actually reduced in the normal case (though raising exceptions might be very expensive). In terms of program documentation, explicit language constructs clearly differentiate normal from exceptional program conditions.

In languages like CLU, exceptions are more a control structure than an exception handling mechanism. They are implemented very efficiently, and extensive analysis is performed by the compiler and the linker to transform the exception control construct into a simpler one (like if-then-else). In CLU, a common use of exceptions is to exit from a loop iterating across an array. The loop never explicitly tests the iteration variable against the array bounds. When the Bounds exception is raised (by accessing an element beyond the legal bounds of the array), the loop is exited. In this respect, one cannot reliably tell that an exception is really all that exceptional.

In LISP systems, exceptions implemented with CATCH and THROW primitives, which are similar to the catch and raise primitives in this C++ design except that THROW does not take arguments whereas exceptions raised in this design can. One interesting feature of the LISP exception handling mechanism is the interaction between signaling an exception and the unwind-protect construct. The way in which LISP systems must "clean up" their frames before exiting them is also a requirement in C++ where destructors must be called for objects that were constructed in that scope.

In Scheme, continuations are provided naturally by the language. Exception handling is therefore provided directly to the user. A global error continuation handles generic errors (such as trying to take the CAR of an atom). The programmer can handle error exceptions in special ways by establishing a new error continuation has as one of its continuations the previous error continuation. Thus, the exception handler stack is built from control constructs rather than data.

The other C++ exception handling proposal that has appeared to date (Koenig and Stroustrup) takes a very different view exceptions. The major differences between that design and the one presented in this paper are with the way exceptions relate to the type system and the object system. Koenig and Stroustrup chose to make exceptions variables, and extend the language only to catch exceptions. They assume that exception is a base type for implementing exception types, and that the raise method of that type is sufficient to raise an exception. It proposes fewer extensions to the C++ language than this design, but in comparing the two, fewer is not always better. Because some of the mechanism can be directly affected by a programmer's use of other language constructs, a program can interfere with the correct operation of the mechanism without the knowledge of the compiler. This leads to unsafe programs in precisely the area where we want to implement safety. They have indicated that a new design is currently in the works.

Conclusion and Acknowledgements

The C++ language must support exception handling to satisfy the needs of users who wish to write robust, reliable software that can still benefit from the advantages of object oriented programming. Several people have discussed implementations of exception handling which are compatible with C++ semantics. This paper presents more the evolution of an exception handling design.

Michael Powell provided the initial exception handling model from which this paper was derived, with additional contributions coming from Jim Mitchell, Graham Hamilton, Johnathan Gibbons, Jim Kempf, and Steve Gadol. In addition to helping with the design, Graham and Jon slogged through early implementations, finding the strangest bugs...

Daniel Weise taught me about continuations, and gave me the insights I needed to understand their interactions with environments.

Doug Lea read early versions of this draft.

Bjarne Stroustrup and Andrew Koenig contributed to the discussion of these matters by providing me with a draft of their exception handling proposal. Jonathan Shopiro also provided additional comments.

References

American National Standard for Information Systems: *Programming Language C*. X3 Secretariat, 1990.

Kernighan, Brian, and Ritchie, Dennis: *The C Programming Language*. Prentice-Hall, 1978.

Koenig, Andrew, and Stroustup, Bjarne: *Exception Handling for C++*. C++ at Work Conference Proceedings, 1989.

Lamping, John: *A unified system of parameterization for programming languages*, Ph.D. Thesis, Computer Science Department, Stanford University, 1988.

Liskov, Barbara, et al.: *CLU Reference Manual*, Technical Report 225, MIT Laboratory for Computer Science, 1979.

Mitchell, James G.: *Mesa Language Manual*, CSL-78-1, Xerox PARC, 1978.

Pittman, Kent: *Exceptional Situations in Lisp*, Working Paper 268, MIT Artificial Intelligence Laboratory, 1985.

Steele, Guy L., and Sussman, Gerald J.: *LAMBDA, The Ultimate Imperative*, Memo 353, MIT Artificial Intelligence Laboratory, 1976.

Steele, Guy L.: *The Revised Report on SCHEME: A Dialect of LISP*, Memo 452, MIT Artificial Intelligence Laboratory, 1978.

Stroustrup, Bjarne: *The C++ Programming Language*. Addison-Wesley, 1986.

Tiemann, Michael: *GNU C++ User's Manual*. Free Software Foundation, 1990.

Part IV
Runtime Typing

Chapter 10

Runtime Access to Type Information in C++

John A. Interrante and Mark A. Linton

Abstract

The C++ language currently does not provide a mechanism for an object to determine its type at runtime. We propose the *Dossier* class as a standard interface for accessing type information from within a C++ program. We have implemented a tool called *mkdossier* that automatically generates type information in a form that can be compiled and linked with an application. In the prototype implementation, a class must have a virtual function to access an object's dossier given the object. We propose this access be provided implicitly by the language through a predefined member in all classes.

Introduction

Some applications need to know the names of classes, their inheritance structure, and other information at runtime. For example, the X Toolkit Intrinsics[3] define a customization mechanism based on class and instance names. With this mechanism, a user can pass a string to an application that is matched against instances of a named class. To applications, the string "*Button*font:courier14" means that the default font for all instances of Button is "courier14". InterViews[2] is a C++ toolkit that supports the X Toolkit customization mechanism. Because the C++ language currently does not support access to any type information at runtime, programmers must write code in every InterViews class that defines the class's name.

Unfortunately, every class writer who needs runtime access to type information must invent their own conventions. These conventions make the exchange of user-defined data types between programmers difficult. For instance, both OOPS[1] and ET++[5] use macros in class definitions to provide a class's name and other information about class types. Neither library can reuse a class type from the other library without modification. Even if all libraries followed a standard set of conventions, these conventions still make writing classes more tedious.

Class writers must take two steps to eliminate these problems: (1) define a standard interface for accessing type information at runtime, and (2) define a way to generate the type information automatically. In this paper, we propose the class *Dossier* as the standard interface to type information, and we describe the implementation of a tool called *mkdossier* that generates a C++ source file

From *USENIX 1990 C++ Conference Proceedings*, pp. 233-240.
Research supported by a gift from Digital Equipment Corporation, by a grant from the Charles Lee Powell Foundation, and by an equipment loan from Fujitsu America, Inc.

containing dossiers. A programmer can then compile and link this file with an application.

A type declaration might not reflect the type of an object at runtime–the object could be a subclass of the declared class. Our prototype implementation therefore requires a class to have a virtual function which simply returns the dossier for its class. Adding a virtual function presents a problem because this change requires recompilation of source code defining or using the class. We propose that the C++ language be extended to provide a predefined (not reserved) member containing a pointer to a dossier. This extension would make type information available for existing classes without requiring changes to their source code.

Dossier interface

The name "Dossier" connotes detailed information about a subject. In this case, we want a dossier to be the repository for information about a type. Although a dossier could represent information about any type, in this paper

```
class Dossier;
class DossierItr {
public:
    DossierItr();
    virtual ~DossierItr();

    boolean more();
    void next();

    // dereference through current element
    Dossier* operator ->();

    // coerce to current element
    operator Dossier*();
};
class Dossier {
public:
    Dossier(
        const char* name,
        const char* fileName,
        unsigned int lineNumber,
        Dossier** parents,
        Dossier** children
    );
    virtual ~Dossier();

    const char* name() const;
    const char* fileName() const;
    unsigned int lineNumber() const;
    DossierItr parents() const;
    DossierItr children() const;
    boolean isA(const Dossier*) const;

    // return array of dossier pointers for all classes
    static Dossier*const* classes() const;
};
```

Figure 10.1
Interface to dossiers

we will only consider class types. Accessing information for non-class types requires compiler and language support, which we did not wish to undertake before defining an interface for classes.

Figure 10.1 shows the Dossier interface. The current interface provides limited information about a class: its name, the file and line number where the class is defined, and iterators to visit parent and children classes. The "isA" function determines whether a class type is a subclass of a given class type. The "classes" function allows the application to access all defined dossiers. Figure 10.2 shows a sample function that uses an iterator to print the names of all the ancestors of a class.

We anticipate extending the interface to include size information, names of members, and member functions. We concentrated on the minimal functionality so that we could investigate the mechanism without getting bogged down in too many details. When we settle on the final details, we can extend the functionality by replacing the standard "dossier.h" header file where Dossier is defined, updating the library implementation of Dossier, and providing a version of mkdossier that generates the additional information.

Dossier implementation

The Dossier interface describes what information is available for a class type; it does not say how the type information is generated. We expect a compiler or a special tool to generate the representation of dossiers automatically so that programmers need not manually define or update dossiers. Like the virtual function table used by most C++ compilers to implement virtual function calls, only one dossier representation should exist for each class in an application. We have implemented a tool called mkdossier that we use to generate dossiers just like we use makedepend, a tool developed at MIT, to generate Makefile dependencies.

Figure 10.3 shows the role of mkdossier in building an application. The build process calls mkdossier to scan all the source files and generate "__dossier.h" and "__dossier.c". Then the build process compiles the source files, including "__dossier.c", and links them into an executable image.

Figure 10.4 shows a sample "__dossier.h", the header file that declares the generated dossiers' names. The dossiers represent information about the sample classes "App," "ArgVec," and "CPP"; mkdossier defines each dossier's name by concatenating the prefix string "__D_" and the class type's name. The application can include this header file to import dossiers into application code by name as well as use the "Dossier::classes" function to import dossiers by address.

```
void traverse(Dossier* d) {
    for (DossierItr i = d->parents(); i.more(); i.next()) {
        cout << "traversing " << i->name() << endl;
        traverse(i);
    }
    cout << "back to " << d->name() << endl;
}
```

Figure 10.2
Traversing ancestors using iterator

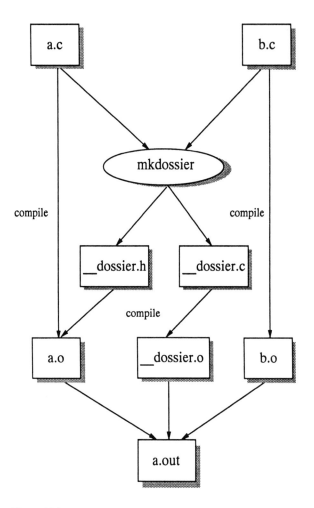

Figure 10.3
Generating dossiers with mkdossier

```
class Dossier;

extern Dossier __D_App;
extern Dossier __D_ArgVec;
extern Dossier __D_CPP;
```

Figure 10.4
Declaration of dossiers

Figure 10.5 shows a sample "__dossier.c", the source file that initializes dossiers with information about class types. Programmers can avoid having to define dossiers manually by compiling and linking this file into the application's executable image. At the end of the file, mkdossier generates a static array of pointers to all the dossiers defined in that file. The "Dossier::merge" function merges the static array into a global array containing pointers to all known dossiers so that the "Dossier::classes" function will work correctly even if the programmer compiles and links multiple "__dossier.c" files into the executable image.

Our current implementation generates the file "__dossier.h" because the compiler does not know about dossier declarations. In our proposed language extension, the compiler would automatically import dossier declarations so that the application would not have to include "__dossier.h".

```
#include "__dossier.h"
#include <dossier.h>
static Dossier* __D_App_parents[] = { 0 };
static Dossier* __D_App_children[] = { &__D_CPP, 0 };

Dossier __D_App = Dossier(
    "App",
    "/master/iv/src/bin/mkdossier/App.h", 9,
    __D_App_parents,
    __D_App_children
);
static Dossier* __D_ArgVec_parents[] = { 0 };
static Dossier* __D_ArgVec_children[] = { 0 };

Dossier __D_ArgVec = Dossier(
    "ArgVec",
    "/master/iv/src/bin/mkdossier/ArgVec.h", 4,
    __D_ArgVec_parents,
    __D_ArgVec_children
);
static Dossier* __D_CPP_parents[] = { &__D_App, 0 };
static Dossier* __D_CPP_children[] = { 0 };

Dossier __D_CPP = Dossier(
    "CPP",
    "/master/iv/src/bin/mkdossier/CPP.h", 9,
    __D_CPP_parents,
    __D_CPP_children
);
static Dossier* exportedClasses[] = {
    &__D_App,
    &__D_ArgVec,
    &__D_CPP,
    0
};
static int dummy = Dossier::merge(exportedClasses);
```

Figure 10.5
Initialization of dossiers

The current implementation of mkdossier calls the C preprocessor to put preprocessed copies of all the source files passed to mkdossier in a temporary directory. The preprocessor strips comments, includes header files, and expands macros so mkdossier can see the same code the C++ compiler sees when it compiles the source files. When mkdossier scans a preprocessed file, it conducts a regular expression search for the keyword "class" followed by text that looks like a class definition. When mkdossier finds a match, it extracts information about that class from its definition. Once mkdossier has scanned all of the preprocessed files, it writes the collected class information to the files "__dossier.h" and "__dossier.c".

Currently we explicitly tell mkdossier which dossiers it should define so we can run mkdossier on a library's source files and include the compiled dossiers in the library. We can then run mkdossier on an application's source files without mkdossier generating duplicates of the library's dossiers. Specifying which dossiers to generate is inconvenient; we are therefore modifying mkdossier to output a dossier for a class only if at least one of the source files defines a non-inlined member function of that class. AT&T cfront 2.0 uses a similar heuristic to decide when to generate a virtual function table.

Experience

We used the Unidraw library [4] as a test bed because it already defines symbolic class identifiers for most of the classes in the library. We changed the typedef ClassId from "unsigned int" to "class Dossier*" and the symbolic class identifiers from integer constants to variables. This change allowed us to use most of the library code unchanged, including all the virtual "GetClassId" member functions. We only had to replace a couple of switch statements by if statements. We replaced the virtual "IsA" member functions, which were redefined in every class, with non-virtual "IsA" member functions defined only in the base classes. The application "drawing" that uses the Unidraw library ran without error after we made these changes, thereby demonstrating that our approach is a practical way to give an application runtime access to type information. Figure 10.6 shows example code fragments from Unidraw that illustrate how we changed Unidraw classes to use dossiers.

We considered automatically generating a "GetClassId"-like function for existing class types. We could have written a tool to produce new header files with the function declaration added and modified mkdossier to produce the function definitions along with the dossiers. However, we decided that manually adding a single function definition in every class was not a significant problem. What is critical is that mkdossier automatically generate the type information so that the programmer does not have to define it.

Language extension

If a programmer wants to use class types developed externally, it is inconvenient to modify someone else's header files. A simple language extension would eliminate the need to change class definitions and also make it possible to obtain type information for typedef names in addition to class types.

We propose that a read-only member "dossier" of type Dossier* be predefined for all user-defined types. By making "dossier" predefined instead of reserved, we avoid disturbing the behavior of any existing code. The programmer would use the syntax *"typename*::dossier" to access information for a class type or typedef and the syntax *"object*.dossier" or *"object–>*dossier" to access information for a class object.

Applications need not import the Dossier interface to use a class object's "dossier" member. An application could compare the value of *"object*–>dossier" with the value of *"typename* ::dossier" to identify a class object's data type. Including "dossier.h" makes additional information about the class object's data type available.

Additionally, we propose that the compiler treat *"object–>*dossier" as equivalent to *"object*.dossier" if the class does not have a virtual table and equivalent to a virtual function call if the class has a virtual table. For such classes, *"object–>*dossier" will return the dossier associated with the class object's dynamic data type even if the compiler cannot determine the type statically. We call the "dossier" member of such classes a "virtual member variable." One possible implementation would generate a unique virtual table for every class and place the address of the class's dossier in the first slot of the virtual table.

An analysis of the Unidraw library revealed that only two out of 115 Unidraw classes would have shared their parent's virtual table if they had not defined a virtual "GetClassId" member function. We expect that requiring every class to have a unique virtual table whether or not it could have shared its parent's virtual table will cause only a small increase in the size of executables.

```
typedef class Dossier* ClassId;

extern ClassId ELLIPSE_COMP;
extern ClassId ELLIPSE_VIEW;

ClassId ELLIPSE_COMP          = &__D_EllipseComp;
ClassId ELLIPSE_VIEW          = &__D_EllipseView;

class EllipseComp : public GraphicComp {
public:
    EllipseComp(SF_Ellipse* = nil);

    virtual ClassId GetClassId();
//  boolean IsA(ClassId);    -- actually inherited from Component
};

boolean Component::IsA (ClassId id) {
    return GetClassId()->isA(id);
}

ClassId EllipseComp::GetClassId () { return ELLIPSE_COMP; }

ellipse.c:116:    if (tool->IsA(GRAPHIC_COMP_TOOL)) {
```

Figure 10.6
Examples of dossiers' use in Unidraw

Future Work

Mkdossier must rescan all the source files whenever class information changes. If mkdossier could rescan only the source files that the compiler has to recompile, mkdossier would run faster. What we need is a way for mkdossier to remember the type information it collected last time.

We can make the previously collected type information available to mkdossier by compiling and linking the file "__dossier.c" into the mkdossier executable after each run of mkdossier. To be practical, this approach requires the availability of shared libraries so that we can minimize the disk space occupied by many instances of mkdossier. Shared libraries allow us to store only the information that actually differs among all of the instances.

Alternatively, we could store the type information outside of mkdossier in an external file or in a database server. When mkdossier starts up, it reads the previous type information from the external file or the database server. When mkdossier shuts down, it writes the updated type information to the external file or database server. We plan to investigate which method would be the best method to let mkdossier scan files incrementally.

Summary

We have defined Dossier, an interface for accessing type information at runtime. We have implemented mkdossier, a tool that generates a C++ source file containing the type information. To demonstrate the practicality of our approach, we modified the Unidraw library and a Unidraw-based application to use dossier information. Finally, we proposed a simple extension to C++ that would provide a uniform method to access information for classes and typedefs.

References

[1] Keith E. Gorlen. An object-oriented class library for C++ programs. In *Proceedings of the USENIX C++ Workshop*, pages 181-207, Santa Fe, NM, November 1987.

[2] Mark A. Linton, John M. Vlissides, and Paul R. Calder. Composing user interfaces with InterViews. *Computer*, 22(2):8-22, February 1989.

[3] Joel McCormack, Paul Asente, and Ralph R. Swick. *XToolkit Intrinsics–C Language Interface*. Digital Equipment Corporation, March 1988. Part of the documentation provided with the X Window System.

[4] John M. Vlissides and Mark A. Linton. Unidraw: A framework for building domain-specific graphical editors. *ACM Transactions on Information Systems*, 8(3):237-268, July 1990.

[5] Andre Weinand, Erich Gamma, and Rudolf Marty. ET++–An object-oriented application framework in C++. In *ACM OOPSLA '88 Conference Proceedings*, pages 46-57, San Diego, CA, September 1988.

Chapter 11

Type Identification in C++

Dmitry Lenkov, Michey Mehta, and Shankar Unni

Abstract

Many applications and class libraries require a mechanism for run-time type identification and access to type information. This paper describes a general type identification mechanism consisting of language extensions and library support. We introduce the following language extensions to support type identification uniformly for all types: a new built-in type called **typeid,** and three operators **stype** (static type), **dtype** (dynamic type), and **subtype** (subtype inquiry). We also describe a library class called **TypeInfo,** which is used to access compiler generated type information. Special member functions of the **TypeInfo** class are used to extend the compiler generated type information. An implementation strategy is presented to demonstrate that the proposed extensions can be implemented efficiently. We compare our proposal with previous work on runtime type identification mechanisms.

Introduction

There have been various attempts made in C++ to implement a method of type identification for objects and a mechanism to access additional type information[3, 4, 5]. There are several reasons why such identification is needed.

- Support for accessing derived class functionality.
  Many of the commonly available C++ class libraries (such as NIH[4], InterViews[6], and ET++[5]) consist of an inheritance hierarchy with a root class (such as the Object class in NIH). When dealing with pointers to this root class, a common operation in these toolkits is to determine if a pointer points to an object of a derived class. If so, the pointer is castdown to the derived class so that a derived class member function may be invoked. Since C++ performs its type checking at compile time, type information is not available at run-time, and each toolkit uses different mechanisms for determining the actual type of the object being dereferenced. When the root class is a virtual base class (as in NIH), since the castdown is not permitted by C++, the library must invent mechanisms to circumvent this restriction. We show that our type identification scheme supports subtype queries and castdowns.

From *USENIX C++ Conference Proceedings*, 1991, pp. 103-118.

· Support for Exception Handling.

The exception handling mechanism[1][2] requires type identification at run time, in order to match the thrown object with the correct **catch** clause. The exception handling mechanism is an example of an implicit use of the type identification mechanism. Since a **catch** clause can catch a type which is a base class of the thrown object, it is necessary for the compiler to generate information about inheritance hierarchies for our proposed **subtype** operator to work.

· Support for Accessing Type Information.

There are various class-specific actions that are difficult to achieve using the normal virtual function mechanism. For example, consider the following task: count (or do some similar task) for all nodes of a particular type in a tree of polymorphic objects.

· Support for Libraries and Toolkits.

Once the type of an object has been determined at runtime, it may often be necessary to get further information about the type. For example, as described in [3], applications may need to know the names of classes and their inheritance hierarchy, if a customization mechanism uses class and instance names. Our proposal describes library support for getting additional information about a type.

In this paper, we examine the problem of type identification in C++. We propose language extensions that will support type identification, and describe methods of implementing our proposal. The goal of our scheme is to create a uniform mechanism for the creation of and access to type information.

Language Extensions for Type Identification

In this section we describe several extensions to C++ necessary to support functionality required by the applications mentioned in the introduction.

The **subtype** Operator

Applications often require the ability to determine dynamically if a pointer points to an object which is a subtype of a given type and, in certain cases, cast the pointer down to the given type. The **subtype** operator lets the programmer examine the inheritance relationship of object types at runtime. For example,

```
subtype(A, p)
```

determines if the actual type of the object pointed to by "p" is a subtype of type A.

The **subtype** operator is a predefined operator that takes a type name as the first parameter and a pointer as the second parameter. It returns a result of type int. The result is 1 if the dynamic type of the object being pointed to is a subtype of the type provided as the first parameter (otherwise 0 is returned). Note that a type is a subtype of itself. Consider three classes:

```
class List {...};

class SortedList: public List {
   ...
   Key least_key();
}
```

```
class LenSortedList: public SortedList {
   ...
   int length();
}
```

Here are some examples of how the **subtype** operator can be used. Consider Example 1:

```
List* l_p = // initialize
...
l_p = // point to some other list
...
if( subtype( SortedList, l_p)) {
   Key k = (SortedList*) l_p -> least_key();
   ...
}
...
if( subtype( LenSortedList, l_p))
   cout << ((LenSortedList*) l_p -> length());
```

Another example, Example 2, is calling a function that requires an actual parameter which is a derived class.

```
void func( LenSortedList *);
...
if( subtype( LenSortedList, l_p))
   func( (LenSortedList*) l_p);
```

In the previous two examples the castdown operation was used to allow functionality defined on subtypes to be used. However, the subtype operator also has applications that do not require a castdown operation. Consider Example 3:

```
void sort( List*);
...
List *l_p = // initialize
...
if( !subtype( SortedList, l_p))
   sort( l_p);
```

and Example 4:

```
void other_func( OtherType *);
...
OtherType p = // initialize
...
if( subtype( SortedList, l_p))
   other_func( p);
```

In Example 4, the functionality associated with the SortedList subtype is invoked as in Example 2. However actual actions take parameters of types other than SortedList. Thus the castdown operation is not needed.

C++ types fall under three different categories with regard to the subtype operator: polymorphic classes (those that have virtual functions), simple types, and non-polymorphic classes. For polymorphic classes the behavior of the **subtype** operator is illustrated above. A simple type (int, int (*)(), etc.) has no subtype (other than itself). Thus the **subtype** operator establishes equality for them with the result defined statically at compile time. Consider Example 5:

```
typedef int* int_p;
...
int_p ptr = // initialize
...
if( subtype( int, ptr))
   //action
```

The use of the **subtype** operator for non-polymorphic classes is limited because only statically defined types can participate in the operation. If the three classes defined above are non-polymorphic (no virtual functions are declared) then in Examples 1 through 4 the result of **subtype** will be 0 (and defined at compile time). Thus the **subtype** operator is not useful for simple types and non-polymorphic classes. It may be desirable to produce a warning if a **subtype** operation results in a compile time value, since the programmer may not be aware that the class is non-polymorphic.

Castdowns

In the introduction we noted that the ability to safely access type related functionality is an important requirement for application and library developers. The first two examples above show that such access in many cases requires that a pointer be cast down to a derived type. In those examples, it can be safely done at compile time. However, if virtual base classes are involved then it cannot be done statically.

Currently the C++ language does not allow a pointer to a base class to be cast down to a derived class pointer if the base class is virtual, or if there is a virtual derivation between the base class and the derived class. The reason for this is that it would require an implementation to maintain pointers from virtual base classes to derived classes. The introduction of the **subtype** operator requires us to keep information about subtype relationships, and the information for pointer conversions can be stored in these data structures. Therefore, we propose that this casting restriction be removed. Note that we cannot remove this restriction for non-polymorphic classes; however, for such classes the **subtype** operation would always fail anyway (since the static type would be used). Since cases of static casting and dynamic casting can be distinguished semantically and do not require a syntactic distinction, the introduction of an additional operator specifically for dynamic casting is not necessary.

Let us modify the classes from the previous section:

```
class List {...};

class SortedList: virtual List {
    ...
    Key least_key();
};

class LenList: virtual List {
    ...
    int length();
};

class LenSortedList: SortedList, LenList {...};
```

Now both casts in Example 1, &(SortedList*) l_p and (LenSortedList*) l_p, become illegal in the current definition of C++. We propose to extend the definition of casts and make these casts legal.

The proposed extension of the cast definition raises an additional issue. What happens if (LenSortedList*) l_p is used without doing subtype(LenSortedList, l_p), and it turns out that l_p points to an object of a class which is not a subtype of LenSortedList? Currently if one attempts:

```
B* b_p = // initialize ...
C* c_p = (C*) b_p;
```

where B and C are unrelated but have a common parent, an unchanged value of b_p is assigned to c_p. It is reasonable to do the same in the case of dynamic casting.

The Type Identification Scheme
Some of the applications described in the introduction would require a unique identifier to be associated with a type. The primary component of this type identification scheme is the predefined type called **typeid**.

The typeid Type
The **typeid** type is a simple predefined type, similar to **int** or **void***, with a few operations defined on it. Expressions evaluating to the **typeid** type can be compared for equality and inequality. Variables of the **typeid** type can be assigned or initialized with an expression of the **typeid** type. No other operations are allowed. Each unique type in an application has a unique value of the **typeid** type associated with it. We define two operators which return values of type **typeid**.

stype returns the type identifier (**typeid** value) for the static type of an expression. It can also be applied to a type name and returns the type's **typeid** value. The **dtype** operator can be applied to any expression that evaluates to a pointer to a type. If the pointer points to a polymorphic class, **dtype** returns the type identifier (**typeid** value) of the actual type of an object pointed to by this pointer. Note that this type must be determined dynamically. If the pointer does not point to a polymorphic class, **dtype** returns the **typeid** value of the static type pointed to by the pointer definition.

Consider Example 6:

```
List* l_p = new SortedList;
int num_Sorted_Lists = 0;
...
typeid t  = dtype(l_p);
if (t == stype(SortedList)) num_Sorted_Lists++;
```

The reason that **stype** and **dtype** are not predefined member functions is the same reason that **sizeof** is not a member function: both identify a fundamental property of types, as opposed to an operation on objects of those types. On the other hand, both can be applied to any types including types such as (int* (*) ()).

An alternative to the **stype** operator is to allow an explicit conversion of any type to **typeid**. However this would also require the conversion of type names to **typeid**. The above example would look like:

```
List* l_p = new SortedList;
int num_Sorted_Lists;
...
typeid t  = dtype(l_p);
if (t == typeid(SortedList)) num_Sorted_Lists++;
```

Accessing Additional Type Information
Given a **typeid**, programmers may wish to get information about the underlying type; programmers may also wish to extend the type information automatically generated by the compiler (for example, they may wish to store the name of type).

We propose a standard library function called **get_typeinfo** to convert a **typeid** into a pointer to the **TypeInfo** object. The **TypeInfo** class contains various member functions to get information about the underlying type (if it is a class). The specification of the **TypeInfo** class is shown in the next section (Library Support).

Note that the **typeid** type is really the same as a **TypeInfo***, and **TypeInfo*** could be used in its place for the extensions described above. The advantage we gain from separating these two types is that we make a clear distinction between the types recognized by the language and the types recognized by the standard library. In addition, the use of **TypeInfo*** for type identification is unsafe because a variable of this type can be assigned values unrelated to actual type identifiers.

Library Support for Type Identification

When the user calls the type inquiry function get_typeinfo(), the result is a pointer to a **TypeInfo** object. In this section we describe this class and the type inquiry function get_typeinfo(). We also describe how a class user can extend the amount of information available about this class.

The TypeInfo Class

The implementation of the language features described in the previous section will require an implementation to store some information about each class. This information can also be accessed using the **TypeInfo** class interface described below. We expect that the C++ library standardization effort will determine the minimum functionality to be provided by all implementations.

```
class TypeInfo { public:
    int sizeof();                         // size of type int
    get_num_base_classes();               // Number of base classes
                                          //      typeid
    get_base_class(int pos);              // typeid of specified base
                                          //      class int
    is_virtual_base_class(int pos);       // specified base virtual?
    visibility_of_base_class(int pos);    // public(2), protected(1),
                                          // or private(0) base class?

    // The routines are used to extend the compiler generated
    // type information
    AuxTypeInfo* get_aux_typeinfo( typeid key);
    int add_aux_typeinfo( AuxTypeInfo *info, typeid key);
private:
    // Actual implementation
};
```

The type inquiry function is specified as follows:
```
TypeInfo* get_typeinfo(typeid)
```

Extensibility

Clearly, there needs to be a way of to define and access more than just the minimal type information provided by **TypeInfo**. For example, it is possible that a developer may wish to determine the name of a class at runtime. The information stored and the association of that information with the class **TypeInfo** object needs to be examined in detail. This section describes mechanisms whereby a user may extend the type information associated with a class.

We believe that it is best to allow the class library creators and users to specify what information needs to be associated with each type.

The following mechanism is used to extend the type information associated with a type.

- We provide a member function called "add_aux_typeinfo" in the **TypeInfo** class. This member function is used to attach additional type information to the minimal type information generated for a type.
- We provide a member function called "get_aux_typeinfo" in the **TypeInfo** class. This member function is used to retrieve any additional type information that a user may have attached to a type.
- It is reasonable to expect that multiple users may wish to attach auxiliary type information to the same type. Therefore, the notion of a "key" is required. A "key" is used to distinguish between multiple auxiliary type information objects attached to the same type.

Consider an example:

```
// User wants to add a "name" field to the TypeInfo for
//    class Widget

// See the text for an explanation of the AuxTypeInfo class
class NameInfo : AuxTypeInfo {
   char *name;
public:
   NameInfo(char* n): name(n){};
};

NameInfo NameInfoObject = "Widget";
// Attach additional type information for "Widget"
get_typeinfo( stype(Widget)) ->
    add_aux_typeinfo( &NameInfoObject, stype(NameInfo));

// Assuming the user has installed name information in Widget,
// and all classes derived from it, here is how a user could
// dynamically find out the name of a class.
Widget* w = // initialized to something;
char* name = (NameInfo*) (get_typeinfo( dtype(w)) ->
                get_aux_typeinfo( stype(NameInfo))) -> name;
```

The extensibility scheme we have proposed is essentially a convenient method of adding a static member (in fact, a virtual static member) to an existing type, without having to modify the type in any way. Individual users can certainly come up with various methods of accomplishing the same result, but the goal here is to propose a *uniform* method for extending type information.

The AuxTypeInfo Class

Any additional type information should be defined as a class derived from AuxTypeInfo. Instances of this are used to link the auxiliary type information objects. The AuxTypeInfo class is defined as follows:

```
class AuxTypeInfo {
   // next auxiliary type info
   AuxTypeInfo* next;
   // The type of the class derived from this class
   typeid key;
};
```

Useful Macros

The library header file can define macros so that the additional "key" parameter can be automatically generated. For example:

```
#define ADD_TYPE_INFO( TYPENAME, INFONAME, INFO_PTR) \
    get_typeinfo(stype(TYPENAME))->add_aux_typeinfo(INFOPTR,\
    stype(INFONAME));
#define GET_TYPE_INFO( INFONAME, OBJECT_PTR) \
    (INFONAME*) (get_typeinfo(dtype(OBJECT_PTR))->\
    get_aux_typeinfo(stype(INFONAME)))
```

These macros can be used to rewrite the example described in the previous section on extensibility.

```
class NameInfo : AuxTypeInfo {
    char *name;
public:
    NameInfo(char* n): name(n){};
};

NameInfo NameInfoObject = "Widget";
// Attach additional type information for "Widget"
ADD_TYPE_INFO( Widget, NameInfo, &NameInfoObject)

// find out the name of a class.
Widget* w = // initialized to something;
char* name = GET_TYPE_INFO( NameInfo, w) -> name;
```

Implementation Strategy

In this section we describe implementation schemes where the compiler will automatically create the type identification information necessary to support the type inquiry operators. We also describe the implementation we use to allow programmers to extend the compiler generated type information with additional type information. Our goal in this section is to demonstrate that reasonable implementation schemes exist. However we assume that actual implementations will optimize these schemes for performance. Although the implementations schemes proposed in this section are geared towards AT&T C++ front end based compilers and translators, we consider them portable to other C++ implementations.

In analyzing various possible implementation schemes, we kept the following goals in mind:

- The implementation scheme should be portable to a variety of C++ implementations.
- There should be no space or execution penalty for users who do *not* use type inquiry operators.
- Reasonable space and execution performance should be expected when using type inquiry operators.
- When a program uses type inquiry operators the execution cost should be paid only when (and if) these are actually used at runtime. Any startup cost should be minimized.
- We wanted a scheme that would work with both "munch" and "patch" (see next section).

Terminology
The implementation section of this paper uses terminology that may not be familiar to everyone.

- *Munch* and *Patch*: Munch and Patch are schemes used by AT&T C++ front end based implementations to ensure that all static objects are appropriately initialized before the main program begins. After a program is linked, a "munch" implementation scans the resulting executable for special symbols and constructs additional data structures which are then relinked into the program. In a "patch" implementation, the executable resulting from a link is also scanned for these special symbols. But instead of constructing additional data structures, "patch" fixes existing data structures, for example, linking some of them together.
- *vtables*: "vtables" are tables, or data structures, which support virtual function calls. A polymorphic object will contain one or more pointers to one or more such tables.

Implementation Details
We now provide some details of a possible implementation scheme. In the second section, we described the built-in **typeid** type. Subsequently, we described a library routine **get_typeinfo** which will convert a **typeid** into a **TypeInfo***. A **typeid** is really equivalent to a **TypeInfo***, and in the rest of this section we will always use the **TypeInfo** class name.

Our overall implementation strategy is:

- One **TypeInfo** object per type:
The type inquiry operators return a pointer to a *unique* **TypeInfo** object associated with the type. The reason we need to guarantee one unique object is so that pointer comparisons can be used to determine whether two types are the same.
- **TypeInfo** objects are only allocated if necessary:
Our implementation scheme attempts to minimize the number of **TypeInfo** objects which are allocated, since we do not need to allocate one for every single type. Allocating a **TypeInfo** object for every single type we encounter in a program is not necessary, since a compiler can determine whether or not the **TypeInfo** object for a type is accessible at runtime.

Allocation of TypeInfo objects
TypeInfo objects can be referenced at runtime for any of the following reasons:

1. We must have **TypeInfo** objects for the static types of any types used in type inquiry operators. For types which are classes we must also allocate **TypeInfo** objects for each ancestor in the class hierarchy. This is needed to allow traversal of the ancestor hierarchy of a class in order to support **subtype** inquiries and the **TypeInfo** class functionality. This also supports the exception handling mechanism.
2. We must have **TypeInfo** objects for all derived classes of polymorphic base classes on which the user performs a dynamic type inquiry operation (i.e **dtype** or **subtype**). Since a derived class can be

defined in a compilation unit which is not visible to the compilation unit containing a type inquiry operator, **TypeInfo** objects have to be emitted for all polymorphic classes.

Let us now examine what rules a compiler must follow when deciding whether or not to emit type information for a given type. There is a unique **TypeInfo** object per type, and this object will contain additional information about class types. In a "munch" implementation, the mechanism for guaranteeing *unique* **TypeInfo** objects per type relies on using tentative definitions (available in both K&R C and ANSI C). This implies that the **TypeInfo** object can be initialized exactly once in one of the object files submitted to the linker, or not initialized at all (in which case the object will get a default initialization). In a "patch" implementation we may sometimes emit multiple **TypeInfo** objects for the same class, but at runtime we will always reference the same **TypeInfo** object.

Polymorphic Classes
Each polymorphic object contains a pointer to a vtable. For a polymorphic class, cfront emits one vtable for the class in the compilation unit which contains the definition of the first non-inline non-pure function; if there is no such function, then a vtable is emitted in every compilation unit in which one is required.

We will implement dynamic typing by storing a pointer in the vtable to the appropriate **TypeInfo** object. Note that every single vtable must contain this pointer, whether or not we see a **dtype** in the current compilation unit (since we do not know if a **dtype** was done in another compilation unit).

In cases where a unique vtable can be emitted for a class, we will emit a definition for the corresponding **TypeInfo** object in the same compilation unit. We expect that most classes will fall into this category.

In cases where cfront emits multiple vtables, we will have to allocate a tentative definition for the **TypeInfo** object in a munch implementation and an initialized definition for the **TypeInfo** object in a patch implementation in each such compilation unit.

Note that the use of vtables to store pointers to **TypeInfo** objects does not allow the optimization which occasionally allows derived classes to "share" vtables with their parents.

Other Types
This section describes how we handle all other types.

- Non-polymorphic classes:
  Whenever a non-polymorphic class is used in a type inquiry operation we must emit a tentative **TypeInfo** object for the class in a munch implementation, and an initialized definition for the **TypeInfo** object in a patch implementation. We must also do the same for each class in the ancestor hierarchy. See the following sections for more information on initialization of **TypeInfo** objects in munch and patch implementations.

- Non-class types:
  This includes built-in types (e.g., **int**), arrays, pointers, and references. Whenever such a type is referenced in a type inquiry operation we

allocate a tentative definition for the corresponding **TypeInfo** object. Note that such types have no additional information associated with them, and the default initialization of these objects to 0 is acceptable. The only use which can be made of these **TypeInfo** objects is address comparison, and the installation of auxiliary type information.

Patch Implementation
We have described some cases where we need to emit multiple initialized **TypeInfo** objects. This section describes how we always manage to return a pointer to the same **TypeInfo** object (Figure 11.1).

- Assume that each **TypeInfo** has a field within it called `Real-TypeInfo` of type **TypeInfo*** which is initialized to 0 at compile time for types that do not have unique TypeInfo objects. For a type which has a unique **TypeInfo** object, we will simply make its `Real-TypeInfo` field point to itself at compile time.
- Consider a class X for which we cannot find a unique place to initialize the **TypeInfo** information. Assume we allocate and initialize

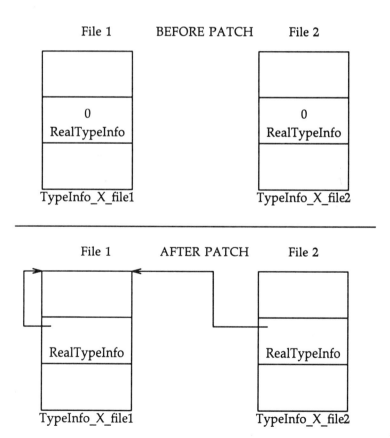

Figure 11.1
Patch Implementation

TypeInfo objects in file1 and file2 called TypeInfo_X_file1 and TypeInfo_X_file2, respectively.

- For the expression **stype(X)**, the equivalent C code we generate is:

```
C++ code     C code
stype(X)     TypeInfo_X_file1.RealTypeInfo (if in file1)
stype(X)     TypeInfo_X_file2.RealTypeInfo (if in file2)
```

- The "patch" tool will notice that there are two TypeInfo objects for X, arbitrarily pick one of them, and make the `RealTypeInfo` fields of both objects point to the chosen version. Note that since we have allocated initialized objects, patch is allowed to modify them in the object file itself.

The primary advantage of this scheme is that there is no startup cost. Note that this same scheme cannot be used by munch without incurring some runtime cost, since there is no way for munch to initialize the `RealTypeInfo` fields without generating some code to execute at runtime. The next section describes a scheme for munch which involves no runtime initializations.

Munch Implementation

We have previously described that we will emit a tentative definition for the **TypeInfo** information for certain classes if we cannot find a unique compilation unit in which to perform the initialization. At "munch" time, how do we initialize these uninitialized objects? One approach is to emit enough information in the symbol name itself, so that "munch" can allocate an initialized definition in the object file it creates. For example, the symbol used for class X could be "TypeInfo_1X4base6window" if class X had base classes "base" and "window".

Implementation of Extensibility

The third describes how the user can attach auxiliary type information to the information already stored for each type. This section provides some information on how to implement this feature.

The Role of AuxTypeInfo

The example in the third section shows the user inheriting **NameInfo** from **AuxTypeInfo**. The first parameter of the **add_aux_typeinfo** member must be an object which is derived from **AuxTypeInfo**. This section describes the reasoning behind this requirement.

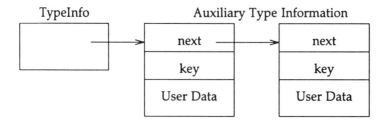

Figure 11.2
Attaching Auxiliary Information to **TypeInfo**

As shown in Figure 11.2, the implementation of auxiliary type information is essentially a chain of objects. Each entry in the chain contains two pieces of information in addition to the object supplied by the user: a "next" field, and a "key" field. We did not want the add_aux_typeinfo routine to have to allocate memory for these additional fields. By requiring the user to inherit from **Aux-TypeInfo** we guarantee that each auxiliary information object supplied by the user will contain these two fields. Note that the user may not add the same auxiliary object to two different lists, since we are chaining the actual object on the list, not a pointer to the object.

The "key" Parameter

Both the **add_aux_typeinfo** and **get_aux_typeinfo** member functions require a parameter called "key", which is of type **TypeInfo***. This section describes the rationale behind this parameter.

We would like to allow different components of a system to attach auxiliary type information for the same type. The "key" parameter is the mechanism for guaranteeing that the information added by a call of add_aux_typeinfo is the same information retrieved by a call of get_aux_typeinfo.

We considered various options for "keys" that the user may associate with the auxiliary type information object, including numbers and strings. Our proposal is to use the **typeid** of the auxiliary information structure as the key. Note that this means that two different users may not attach two auxiliary information objects of the same type to the same chain, since the keys would be the same.

Shared Library Considerations

Shared libraries are a mechanism for multiple programs to share the same copy of routines linked into a shared library; linking with shared libraries will generally result in much smaller executables files than linking with archive libraries. Shared libraries add complexity to the implementation of type identification. Although we do not go into any details of how shared libraries work (since vendors differ in their implementations), we make the following assumptions about shared libraries:

- At link time, a tool like "munch" or "patch" will not get a complete picture of all object files which belong in this executable, since shared libraries can be explicitly loaded at runtime (for example you may may load a set of graphics routines which depend on the output device you are using).
- When a shared library is created, we assume that there will be some mechanism which will allow us to run "munch" or "patch" on the shared library.
- We assume that the shared library mechanism allows us to specify a routine that will be executed when the library is first loaded.

The "patch" and "munch" schemes previously described rely on being able to process a "complete" executable; since a link involving shared libraries results in an "incomplete" executable we need to make modifications to our schemes.

The previous section describes two conditions under which we cannot initialize a unique **TypeInfo** object at compile time:

1. Polymorphic classes which do not have unique vtables

2. Non-polymorphic classes

We now describe how this would be handled in a shared library implementation. Both implementations suggested below will have some runtime initializations being performed.

Patch Implementation for Shared Libraries
The scheme of having a `RealTypeInfo` field does not work for shared libraries, because when a shared library is loaded it would be difficult (and expensive) to make each such field point to the appropriate **TypeInfo** object. The shared library patch algorithm looks like this:

1. At compile time we emit a tentative definition for a **TypeInfo** object which cannot be initialized in a unique file. We also emit an initialized definition for this **TypeInfo** object.
2. At "patch" time, we create a chain of initializations which should be performed; each entry in this chain will contain a pointer to each **TypeInfo** object which needs to be initialized, and a pointer to the corresponding initialized object. If there are be multiple initialized objects available, one is chosen arbitrarily. This algorithm applies when patching executables as well as shared libraries.
3. When _main is executed and when a shared library is loaded, all the **TypeInfo** initializations are performed before any other initialization code is executed. An initialization of a **TypeInfo** object is quick because we simply need to store a pointer to the initialized object within the **TypeInfo** object.

Patch cannot initialize **TypeInfo** objects during the patch phase itself, because of the method used by most linkers to implement tentative definitions. If a linker needs to allocate space for an uninitialized tentative definition, it will usually simply update the size of the uninitialized area, and the loader will be responsible for initializing this area to 0. Since there is no real image in the object file which contains the initialization data for uninitialized tentative definitions, there would be no way to "patch" it to a different value.

The scheme we have described does have some runtime cost, and this cost is the initialization of one word for each **TypeInfo** object allocated for non-polymorphic classes, and polymorphic classes without unique vtables. If a **TypeInfo** object is referenced in the main executable as well in shared libraries, it will be initialized multiple times.

Munch Implementation for Shared Libraries
The "munch" implementation remains similar to the non-shared library scheme. For the main executable, we create initialized definitions for all **TypeInfo** objects we find referenced. Since these are initialized definitions, there will be no runtime startup cost.

When "munching" a shared library, we cannot create initialized definitions for the **TypeInfo** objects we find referenced, since such a definition may already have been provided when munch was run on the main executable, and multiple definitions are not permitted. Instead, we generate runtime code to initialize the referenced **TypeInfo** when the shared library is loaded, and before any initialization code is executed. Note that as in the "patch" scheme, the same **TypeInfo** object may get initialized twice.

In order to minimize the runtime initialization cost, the **TypeInfo** object can contain a pointer to an initialized object created by "munch". All that needs to be done at runtime is the assignment of one pointer into the **TypeInfo** object.

Previous Work

This section describes the Dossier[3] solution to the type identification problem. Most of the commonly used C++ toolkits use some form of runtime type identification, and the Dossier scheme was developed for use in the InterViews toolkit.

Summary of Dossier Approach

In the Dossier scheme, a tool called **mkdossier** scans the source files of an application and generates a statically initialized Dossier structure for each class in the user program. This Dossier structure is accessed through a virtual *GetClassId* function which needs to be added to each class.

The paper goes on to propose some language extensions to simplify accessing the Dossier structure for a class:

- A predefined static member caller *dossier* would be added to each class.
- The syntax `typename::dossier` would be used to access the dossier of a type.
- The syntax `object.dossier` would be used to access the dossier of an object.
- The syntax `pointer->dossier` would be used to access the dossier of the class object being pointed to. If the class being pointed to was polymorphic then the dossier of the dynamic class being pointed to would be returned (i.e. *dossier* is a virtual static data member).

Comparison

The Dossier approach is similar to our approach in many respects:

- We both make available a unique value associated with a type, which allows users to perform comparisons to determine if two types are the same.
- Through this unique value, both approaches allow various kinds of functionality to be accessed by using member functions (e.g., the ability to traverse the ancestor list)

Although there are similarities in our approaches, there are some fundamental differences:

- Support for all types. We would like to support type inquiry on all types, not just classes. We consider this an important consideration in exception handling since a user may throw any type (not just classes). We also anticipate that users of parameterized types may occasionally need to perform type inquiry operations on template *type* parameters (which can be of any type).
- Language Syntax. Although both approaches implement a "virtual static data member" associated with a type, we use different syntaxes for accessing this member. The Dossier scheme uses the `::`, `.`, and

-> operators, whereas we propose introducing two new operators **stype** and **dtype**. The main reason for our choice is to provide a consistent syntax for accessing type information for all types, not just classes.

- Extensibility. Regardless of how much information is made available for a type automatically (for example, a list of ancestor classes), there will always be some applications which need additional type information. Our paper discusses a method for extending the standard type information generated by the compiler (the developer will have to take steps to ensure that this additional type information gets associated with the type).

- Implementation. The Dossier mechanism relies on a tool to process the sources for an application and generate Dossiers. Although the sources may be partitioned into multiple sets (to handle libraries), care must be taken to ensure that the same Dossier is not generated twice. Our paper describes some implementation schemes in which the compiler automatically generates the necessary information, and no additional processing is necessary.

Open Issues

The type identification mechanism presented in this paper provides a reasonably complete set of functionality for type related operations and handling type information. In developing this mechanism we discovered some issues that require further discussion.

- Non-Polymorphic Classes
  Non-polymorphic classes inherently possess a certain inconsistency with regard to type identification. Although they form a subtype hierarchy in the same way as polymorphic classes, given a pointer to a non-polymorphic base class it is difficult to determine the true type identity of the actual object being dereferenced at runtime. There are various alternatives available:

  o make all non-polymorphic classes polymorphic;
  o make all non-polymorphic classes, except for "extern C" classes, polymorphic;
  o introduce a pragma to control this;
  o introduce a compiler option;

  Each of these options has serious disadvantages.
- ptr_cast operator
  The use of casts is usually unsafe. The idea of an alternate cast operator[7] that is supposed to be applied only when a legal conversion is possible, is attractive. This operator would raise an exception if applied incorrectly.

Conclusion

We have described a general type identification mechanism consisting of language extensions and library support. The language extensions introduced support a reasonably full set of type inquiries. The library class called **TypeInfo** has been introduced to allow access to compiler generated type information. While providing access to basic information about types, it also contains member functions which can be used to extend the compiler-generated type information. An implementation strategy has been presented to demonstrate that the proposed extensions can be implemented efficiently.

The proposed type identification mechanism should satisfy the requirements of application and class library developers for type identification, access to a subtype query mechanism, and run-time access to type information.

References

[1] Margaret A. Ellis, Bjarne Stroustrup, *The Annotated C++ Reference Manual*, Addison-Wesley, 1990

[2] Andrew Koenig and Bjarne Stroustrup, Exception Handling for C++, *USENIX C++ Conference Proceedings*, 1990

[3] John A. Interrante, Mark A. Linton, Runtime Access to Type Information in C++, *USENIX C++ Conference Proceedings*, 1990

[4] Keith E. Gorlen, An Object-Oriented Class Library for C++ Programs, *Proceedings of the USENIX C++ Workshop*, 1987

[5] Andre Weinand, Erich Gamma, and Rudolf Marty, ET++ – An Object-Oriented Application Framework in C++, *ACM OOPSLA '88 Conference Proceedings*, 1988

[6] Mark A. Linton, John M. Vlissides, and Paul R. Calder, Composing user interfaces with Inter-Views, *Computer*, 22(2):8-22, February 1989

[7] Bjarne Stroustrup, Personal communication

Part V
Distributed Computing

Chapter 12

Solving the RPC Problem in GNU C++

Michael D. Tiemann

Abstract

The C++ programming language is being used in a number of projects which implement some form of distributed execution model. While each of these projects differ in their goals and implementations, all of them ultimately depend on some kind of remote procedure call (RPC), a facility which is not easily supported by C++. For this reason, many different extensions to C++ have been implemented, each one coping with this problem in its own, unique way. This paper presents a new construct called a "wrapper", which provides a more general solution to the problem than previous work, and in some cases, provides greater efficiency as well.

Wrappers are a highly experimental feature, implemented in the GNU C++ compiler; this paper represents the start of their evolution. GNU C++ is a highly optimizing native code C++ compiler for the Sun3 and the VAX running BSD 4.[23]. The compiler, as well as a C++ source level debugger, GDB+, a linker, documentation, and library support, is available as free software, under the terms of the GNU General Public License.

Introduction

The Experimental Systems (ES-Kit) research at the Microelectronics and Computer Technology Corporation (MCC) is focused on development of rapid implementation technologies applicable to low cost prototyping of parallel computing systems. The architecture of these systems will be based on hardware modules, linked together via bus and/or message communication channels. These modules will provide system-level functionality such as disk, memory, processor, etc., allowing a variety of architectural configurations to be assembled and measured without great expense. The operating system for a machine comprised of these modules must support parallel applications, and it must provide a convenient interface to UNIX. The software language platform must support rapid reconfigurability to match the hardware, software module reusability, and great enough efficiency that high-performance designs can be reasonably proven against more traditional systems.

Such requirements immediately qualified the C++ programming language. Using the object oriented programming model to separate program functionality into logical blocks (of both code and data, generic operations can implemented and interfaced in a number of different ways, all in a consistent

From *USENIX 1988 C++ Conference Proceedings*, pp. 343-361, 1988.

manner. Reusability is one of the keys to rapid prototyping. By allowing the user to define the semantics relating to such operations as type conversion and even the operators in expressions, code can be written that looks natural, while in fact its operations may be quite complex. The abstract data typing facilities of C++ make it possible to design from a very high level, and then refine the implementation by substituting functionality and/or behavior where desired. Yet C++ can still be compiled into very efficient code, usually as efficient as normal C code would be.

For all of its strengths, C++ has some notable shortcomings as well. Just as a user on a single processor system would like control over the type abstractions of their application, users of parallel systems need to gain control over the programming languages semantics as control and data moves across logical and physical machine boundaries. C++ fails to provide any mechanism for this requirement, and few general purpose languages do. The absence of a good way to specify RPCs in C++ has led some groups away from the language[Cap87], and others to extend it in differing, incompatible ways[Gri87, Cal87, Gau87, Lin87].

The ES-Kit project, too, has developed some extensions to the C++ programming language which give programmers control at these boundary conditions, and preserve, in a very substantial way, all the efficiency one could expect using a language like C. The baseline compiler for these extensions is the GNU C++ compiler, a highly optimizing, native code C++ compiler, largely compatible with C++ V1.2 from AT&T.[1] The compiler also has a C++ source level debugger, GDB+, and a linker which supports incremental linking with correct C++ semantics.

This paper will begin with a presentation of the ES-Kit software environment, as a motivation for the implementation goals which resulted. A section on related work gives this work context, and suggests that the approach, while well suited to C++, is relatively language-independent. The implementation of wrappers is then presented, along with their semantics and a suggested syntax. The implications (and limitations) of wrappers are then discussed, and future areas of research are outlined. The paper finishes with a discussion of other uses to which wrappers can be put.

Requirements and Goals

Remote procedure calls form the basis of the ES-Kit parallel execution model. Unlike the serial environment, where procedure calls are mainly used to enhance maintainability of software through modularity, the ES-Kit programming model uses them to create parallelism. When a (remote) procedure call is made, control forks, with one thread acting on the procedure call, while the other returns to the caller. It is at the option of the caller whether to block the caller thread until the call has completed, or to continue. It is absolutely essential that the programming language provide the user with a convenient way to manage this execution model, or better yet, forgetting about it, just as a procedure-call oriented environment makes the use of its call stack simple and painless, and something which can almost always be ignored.

---

[1] All C++ 2.0 features are implemented except for multiple inheritance.

The basic problem in implementing a system which abstracts procedure calls in C++ is that, like C, C++ does not provide any operations on function calls except to execute them. It is possible to say `sizeof (int)`, and the C++ compiler will return the system's integer size in bytes, but one cannot ask for the length of an argument list, or reliably get the number of arguments passed, their types, their positions and dispositions on the stack, etc. Thus, it is extremely difficult for the systems programmer to extend an abstraction when one hardly exists.

For reasons that were not immediately obvious, it was decided that the compiler would handle this problem in as general a fashion as possible, subject to the following constraints:

1. any C++ member function call can be an RPC,
2. the client source code should not reflect whether the member function call is local or remote,
3. the solution must be portable (preferably implementable within the limitations of a C virtual machine),
4. there should be minimal (if any) change to the GNU C++ compiler,
5. it easily supports existing RPC environments (such as Sun RPC),
6. it is easy to implement blocking vs. non-blocking semantics,
7. it is easy to describe how objects should be passed (migrated) for the call.

Related Work

The parallel execution model of the ES-Kit environment is derived from Halstead's work on *futures*[Hal85]. One of the main differences between the ES-Kit environment[Led88] and Halstead's Multilisp environment is that C++ is statically typed, hence futures can have specific future types, leading to somewhat improved efficiency and safety. This realization was also made by Liskov in her presentation of *promises*[Lis88]. The ES-Kit future is like Liskov's *promise*, though we have not implemented other features of her work, such as *call-streams*.

The CLAM system[Mi186] provides an RPC facility which relies on a *bundler*. Bundlers are attached to parameters when passing explicit pointers does not have the desired semantics. For example, if a routine wanted to send a string as an argument to a remote procedure, passing the address of the string on the local machine does little good. A bundler can format the string into a parameter that is suitable for interhostal transit. Bundlers must be explicitly placed with each parameter in need of bundling.

The Sun RPC library[Sun88] is a collection of procedures which provide remote argument passing for certain builtin types, and a stub generator (rpcgen) which builds the RPC interface. `rpcgen` accepts a language that looks like restricted C declarator syntax, with a dash of Pascal-style variant records. If the user wishes to pass structures or other types which are not among the builtin types, which are not among the builtin types, s/he can declare these types in the XDR language, and argument passing functions will be automatically generated. The user must change the program interface to use rpcgen by only passing references (pointers in C) as arguments to possibly remote functions. Sun's RPC protocol also requires that the procedure call complete before control is returned to the user.

On the SmallTalk front, Paul McCullough[McC87] has implemented something he calls "Transparent Forwarding." There is a striking similarity between the structure of his work and the work being presented here. In fact, there is almost a direct correspondence between the three classes he needed to add to SmallTalk and the three pieces which I will present as being necessary components of an interesting wrapper design. Perhaps this similarity is a direct result of the similarity of the initial goals, and specifically, the transparency requirement.

A GNU C++ wrapper should not be confused with Zeta-Lisp wrappers. Zeta-Lisp wrappers were a more primitive idea which evolved into *whoppers*, a mechanism very similar to GNU C++ wrappers. It is hoped that the reader will excuse the author from not adopting the *whopper* nomenclature.[Gum88]

An alternative which was not investigated was extending C++ to incorporate *reflection*. Reflection is a very powerful technique which, in essence, allows the system to encapsulate itself and then perform computation on that encapsulation. The inverse operation, reification, allows the system to then "become" that system which the reflection captured. Reflection and reification are mentioned here because they are interesting concepts, and because the wrapping of a function call is, in a very limited way, a reflective operation.

More detailed comparisons with related work will be expanded inline.

Implementation of Wrappers

In the ES-Kit kernel, parallelism is achieved by using "futures." When an application makes a RPC, the ES-Kit kernel intercepts the call, creates a new process which will carry out the computation, and returns to the caller a "future" (typically a more refined type, such as a `future_int`, a `future_char_star`, etc.). A future is essentially a reference to the result of the function call which will be available "some time in the future." As long as the caller does not attempt to evaluate the future, it will not block. When the caller does try to evaluate it, if the future has not yet completed, the kernel puts the caller to sleep, and wakes it up when the future is ready. If the future had completed by the time the caller attempted to evaluate it, the caller gets the value of the future, and proceeds normally. This model of parallelism is natural, largely transparent, and centers around being able to translate what look like normal function calls into requests for computation to be scheduled by the kernel.

As soon as a preliminary version of the GNU C++ compiler was available, it became evident that in order to make life bearable for application programmers, these requests for computation must be as easy to write as a normal function call. To make it easier to port "normal" C++ programs into the ES-Kit environment, the more these requests could resemble normal function calls, the better.

Introduction to Wrappers

The problem of implementing a transparent, user-definable RPC mechanism is handled by adding a construct called a *wrapper* to the compiler. A wrapper is a new syntactic construct that allows the programmer to specify an alternate implementation of member function calls. An RPC handler can then just be seen as a special case of this. The basis idea behind a wrapper is the notion that in order to execute a member function call, it is necessary only to know the object for that call (which will become the this pointer), the member function for that object being called, and the arguments to that function. A wrapper abstracts procedure calls by having the compiler translate member function calls into encapsulations of member function calls, and passing these encapsulations to the wrapper.

First, an example of their syntax will be presented, followed by a description of their semantics:

```
struct foo
{
    foo ();         // foo constructor
    ~foo ();        // foo destructor

    virtual ()foo (int (foo::*)(...). ...);
                    // a virtual wrapper

    int g (int);    // foo member function g
    virtual int h (int, int); // foo member function h
};
```

A wrapper has a very distinct syntactic form from operators, member functions, constructors and destructors. Initially, the idea was to pun wrappers with an overloaded operator (actually the combination of two overloaded operators, yielding operator->()()). Bjarne Stroustrup suggested starting from a clean syntactic point, to avoid the kinds of ambiguity problems that such punning can pose. He proposed the syntactic form seen here, of placing empty parenthesis just in front of the declarator. This syntactic form permits one to specify many different ways of encapsulating (or executing) member function calls.

As can be seen from the declaration of the wrapper (which in this case happens to be virtual), the wrapper has, as its arguments, all the information it needs in order to wrap calls for either foo::g or foo::h. Wrappers are member functions, and hence calls to the wrapper have a this pointer. They take a pointer to member function argument which is initialized by the compiler to the value of the (possibly virtual) member function being wrapped. The rest of its argument list, which is left untyped for now, serves as the destination for the arguments of wrapped function.

In these examples of syntax, the wrapper "wraps" all function calls, but the user can specify whether to wrap the virtual or non-virtual function, and whether to wrap using a virtual or non-virtual wrapper:

```
main ()
{
    foo *a;

    a->g (100);             // wrap 'foo::g' with virtual wr.
    a->h (101, 102);        // wrap 'virtual 'h' with virtual wr.

    a->foo::h (103, 104);   // wrap 'foo::h' with virtual wr.

    a->foo::() g (200);     // wrap 'foo::g' with foo's wr.
    a->foo::() h (201, 202);   // wrap virtual 'h' with foo's wr.
    a->foo::() foo::h (203, 204); // wrap 'foo::h' with foo's wr.
}
```

Now that ideas behind wrappers have been sketched, it is time to look at them a little more deeply.

Wrappers are intended to encapsulate, and not necessarily substitute for, calls to member functions. As a result, when a member function call is being compiled, the compiler performs all conversions necessary on the arguments to that member function. Once this has been done, but before the code for the call is emitted, the compiler then computes the address of the member function that is to be wrapped, and makes that address an additional argument at the head of the argument list. The wrapper is then called with the resulting argument list, again converting any arguments from this list to match the types specified by the wrapper.

Wrapper Issues

If all member functions of a class have the same type signature (numbers and types of arguments, and return values), then writing wrappers for them is a very simple task. Problems arise when one wishes to write a single wrapper to handle member functions with distinct type signatures. In such a situation, the different argument lists can be matched by using the C++ '...' notation, leaving the types and number arguments to the wrapper unchecked. This makes putting function calls into wrappers very easy, but makes getting them back out rather difficult.

If wrappers were added to the language without any additional support, it might leave more loose ends dangling than it tied up:

1. How does one keep a specific function call from being wrapped?
2. How does one keep a particular member function from being wrapped?
3. What happens when passing a derived member function to a base wrapper?
4. How does one handle type conversion in an argument list full of '...'?
5. Should constructors be wrapped?
6. Should wrappers be recursive? (can a call to a wrapper be wrapped?)
7. Should function calls within wrappers be wrapped? (where is the bottom?)
8. How does one wrap a function call via a pointer-to-function (which may be missing type information?)
9. How should return values be handled? (overload based on return types?)

Such a list looks long, but when looking at recent work on this problem (in LISP and SmallTalk, not just C++!), one sees that it looks familiar. After presenting our solutions to these problems for C++, a comparison will be made with McCullough's work on SmallTalk. The two are strikingly similar, both yielding extensions which are easily implemented, have low impact of the efficiency of the system as a whole, and provide great expressive power.

Not Wrapping

The first two issues bring up the question of escape hatches. No matter how wonderful a particular language feature is, there always appears to be some case where it is more desirable to get around it. Sometimes one wishes to defeat the feature at compile-time (such as calling a virtual function directly, rather than by the virtual function table), other times one wishes to defeat the feature at run-time (which is usually done with if-then-else control logic).

Distributed programs tend to have run-time behavior which is hard to predict at compile time. In the context of RPC, the main reason not to go through an RPC wrapper is because it is known (somehow ahead of time) that the call will be local, and should therefore not go through the extra levels type conversions. Because this locality information may be available at compile time or only at run time, the means of getting the information to the compiler should be general enough to produce an efficient solution in either case.

An attractive solution is to provide a *wrapper predicate*.

A wrapper predicate is a binary operator, which takes an object and a member function pointer, and returns zero if the function should not be wrapped, and non-zero otherwise. An example of the syntax is given in the "Generic Wrappers"; the syntax is defined subsequently.

A default wrapper predicate always returns the value 1 (indicating that the function should be wrapped). Wrapper predicates are inherited, and may therefore be required to handle member functions which are not members of the class that the wrapper predicate belongs to. In that case, the wrapper predicate should provide a "default" case (which normally would return a non-zero result).

Wrapper predicates, when they are necessary, can be defined to be inline, and using standard constant-folding techniques, compile-time decisions can be made based on their otherwise run-time semantics. This is not an unreasonable expectation of a C++ compiler, since such constant folding is already implemented in the C++ compilers from AT&T and GNU.

Wrapper predicates provide both run-time and compile-time escape hatches for wrapper users. They also seriously affect encapsulation (in the same way that declaring a private function public in a derived class definition does), and should probably be used only when necessary.

Making Wrappers Generic

Typically, the user would like all RPCs to be handled in a uniform fashion (much as normal procedure calls are now). To that end, it is desirable to specify one wrapper which will uniformly handle all procedure calls. In a strongly-typed world, this is not always possible. The implicit conversion of a pointer to an object to a pointer to a base class of that object is anti-symmetric with respect to "pointers to member functions." That is to say, we can only reliably convert "pointers to member functions" from a "pointer to base class member function" to a "pointer to derived class member function." It is therefore not type-safe to pass a pointer to a derived member function to a wrapper in a base class, as can be seen in the following example:

```
struct B { virtual f (); ... };
struct D : public B { virtual f (); virtual g (); ... };
int foo (B*, int (B::*)());
int bar (D*, int (D::*)());
int surprise ()
{
    B bb; D dd;
    foo (&bb, &B::f);      // ok
    bar (&bb, &B::f);      // error: B* does not convert to D*
    // ok! f is in base class
    foo (&dd, &D::f);
    // error! int (D::*)() does not convert to int (B::*)()
    foo (&dd, &D::g);
}
```

The real problem with passing a pointer to a derived member function to a wrapper expecting a pointer to a base member function is that type information is lost. Fortunately, this problem can be solved with minimal overhead. If this and the pointer to member function argument (call it pmf) are composed within a wrapper, the compiler can know that combination to be type-correct. This is a direct result of how the wrapper is called. An assignment to this and/or pmf, or an implicit conversion of pmf (including the implicit conversion that occurs when pmf is composed with another object, or further passed as an argument) means that typewise, all bets are off. The compiler could insert code to test whether the composition is indeed valid, relying on a runtime encoding scheme based on information held in the virtual function table, or it could just simply disallow such things from happening. It can also prevent assignments to this and the pointer to member function argument within wrappers.

Passing pointers to member functions against the inheritance hierarchy grain is the first (and by far the easiest) problem to handle. The second problem to handle is making a single wrapper wrap all member functions, regardless of their argument lists. Wrappers are supposed to encapsulate a very simple, very powerful idea, and it would be nice to specify the implementation of that idea as concisely as possible. If a different wrapper must be declared for every different function, the whole purpose of wrappers is defeated.

All argument lists can be matched by declaring a wrapper with an untyped argument list, i.e., '...'. However, this argument list may need to maintain type information until the arguments can get to the ultimate target of the procedure call. To accomplish this, we allow wrappers to specify a *typing function*.

Types are not values in C++, so it is not possible to specify the typing function directly. However, the compiler can generate such a function which is generally useful in the two most important cases. The default typing function is the mapping of types according to standard C promotion rules. All C and C++ compilers have such a function built into them. A user-defined typing function can be synthesized by specifying the result type that all arguments should be converted if the value appears within the untyped part of a function's argument list. Such a result type is called a *synthetic type*.

A synthetic type should be designed in such a way that it can ravel and unravel any kind of type that may be passed as an argument to (or from) a wrapper. The compiler enforces such rules in a lazy fashion, i.e., when a type conversion is impossible, the user will get an error message. It does not tell the user whether his synthetic type is a priori complete.

Because C++ is primarily a statically typed language, there is not a great deal of support for encapsulating type information in a representation that can be stored, retrieved, and used to reconstruct a well-typed value at runtime. This restriction also currently applied to types which appear to be run-time dependent, but can actually be computed statically from the program's control graph. Although not well supported by C++, most distributed systems implemented in C++ (at least all that this author has seen) implement some kind of type which performs this magic by hand, usually with some extension to the compiler. Fortunately, one such group taking a look at such extensions is Dr. Stroustrup's. His work on parametric types will be very influential on (and will hopefully obviate the need for) synthetic types. In the mean time, here is an example of a synthetic type:

```
struct DT                  // a synthetic type
{
    DT (int);              // encode an int
    operator int ();       // decode an int

    DT (double);           // encode a double
    operator double ();    // decode a double

    DT (void);             // encode a void type!
};
struct Base
{
    // wrapper predicate (from section 4.3):
    int ()?Base (int (Base::*)(...));

    // wrapper w/synthetic type:
    DT (DT...)Base (int (Base::*)(...), ...);
}
```

It is important to note the distinction between wrappers and stub generation. Wrappers (and wrapper predicates and synthetic types) do not themselves comprise a stub generator. However, they can be used to greatly simplify the interface to one.

What Should be Wrapped?
Until one has implemented a C++ compiler, it is difficult to appreciate what a typed value is in C++. Object construction is a process of type elevation. Starting with an untyped chunk of memory, a base constructor renders it typed with a base type. Such an instantiation may involve the initialization an object's virtual function table pointer, and initialization of some of its members. After the objects base types have been initialized, each type in the lattice between the base types and the final type of the object will be initialized. It is not until this process of initialization has been completed that the object can say "I am." Because of this, it makes no sense to have a wrapper wrap calls to constructors, since the object has not been completed, just as it makes no sense to stop initializing once an object has an `operator=` in its scope, and starts using assignment semantics for the rest of the operation.

Suppose a user wished to define her/his own wrapper for purposes of either augmenting and/or reimplementing wrappers derived from base classes. Should that wrapper be wrapped by those from the base class, or should the wrapping stop at the first wrapper? This is indeed a very hard question, since it essentially forces the distinction between wrappers as an initialization of function-call objects, in which case a recursive interpretation might be nice, and wrappers as an alternate function-call implementation (or operator), in which case the first applicable wrapper applies, and nothing more.

The wrapper extension is a large one, and one which should be evaluated carefully. To keep things manageable, the latter interpretation is the one which has been implemented. If justifiable needs for the former develop, it would not be hard to handle them with a new, appropriate syntactic form.

Dealing With Return Values
Return values are a necessary evil in C++. Every machine (and almost every compiler) handles return values in its own way. To make matters worse, return values may come back in a register, or a set of registers, or sit atop the

stack, or not be returned at all, but may "fill in" and address handed to them by the caller; these variations may all exist within the same compiler!

The C++ programming language does not allow overloading based upon return type, and furthermore does not allow typeless return values (as it does allow for its argument types). While these restrictions may seem unnecessary (and even an annoying obstacle) for the task at hand, it is well to adhere to them nonetheless. Portability reasons alone make it impossible to do otherwise: because a compiler is required to do nothing more than create a coherent call/return interface, it is not possible to predict ahead of time how many kinds of return values a wrapper will need to implement.

A wrapper, therefore, is limited to accepting member functions which return a certain type, requiring that new wrappers be written for functions that return new types. Because of this, recursive wrappers are not necessarily desirable, since wrappers of base types cannot wrap functions which return objects of derived types. There is, however, no restriction that a wrapper must return the same type as that of the function it is wrapping. Note that a wrapper need not return the same type as the function that it wraps. Also note that the following two wrappers are distinguishable as having different argument lists, and does not constitute (to first approximation) overloading based on return type:

```
int X::()X(int        (X::*)(...), ...);
double X::()X(double (X::*)(...), ...);
```

Syntax and Semantics of Wrappers

Syntax
The syntax of wrappers is somewhat baroque, in keeping with C's (and consequently C++'s) notorious declarator syntax. A wrapper for class T has declarator name ()T. Its return value, argument list, virtual attributes, etc., are declared just as for normal member functions. The first argument in the wrapper must be of type pointer to member function type, or type void *.

A wrapper predicate for type T has the declarator name ()T. It takes only one argument, which must be of type pointer to member function type. Its return type is integer.

A synthetic type T2 is associated with a wrapper for type T by placing it in its wrapper parenthesis followed by '...', i.e., (T2...)T. The type T2 must be a user-defined type, and it must be declared before use. Naturally, for this type to be of any use, it must have at least one constructor.

Semantics
A wrapper is applied as follows: Given a class B with a wrapper W, a class D with a member function F, and given that D derives from B, P is a pointer to type D, and F is not a constructor or a wrapper, then W may wrap the call to P->F(...) under the following conditions:

1. there is no wrapper predicate P in any class between B and D in the type lattice, or
2. the wrapper predicate P returns a non-zero result given arguments O and F.

Under no other conditions would an attempt be made to wrap the call to F.

Wrapping takes place as follows: all arguments to the original function are converted according to the argument list of **F** (as per normal C++ (and ANSI C) semantics). If the wrapper or the wrapper predicate do not satisfy normal C++ visibility rules, it is an error. If **D** derives from multiple base classes **B1** and **B2**, and both provide a wrapper, an ambiguity error is reported; similarly for wrapper predicates. If there are no visibility or ambiguity problems, a function call is wrapped by prepending a pointer to the member function being wrapped to the argument list of the function, and passing the resulting argument string to the wrapper. The wrapper treats the argument list as a normal function call would, with the exception of its treatment of arguments which the wrapper converts to a synthetic type.

If a synthetic type is specified for a wrapper, then:

1. it must be unique, and
2. it must convert any argument passed to it, and
3. all conversions must satisfy normal C++ visibility rules, and
4. all parameters which are not explicitly typed by the wrapper are converted to the type of the synthetic type, and
5. argument lists which contain synthetic types as a result of converting arguments are terminated with a synthetic type encoding the void type.

It should be stressed again that synthetic types are a provisional measure until a determination can be made as to how to (better) use parametric types, if they are added to C++.

Implementation Notes

The representation of pointers to member functions must be done in a host-independent manner. By filling the virtual function table with all member functions available to a given class, and distributing a class's virtual function table to each node which could host an instance of that class, a member function's address can be represented by its index in the (extended) virtual function table. This index is, of course, host-independent.

Computing virtual function tables which permit explicit non-virtual function calls is somewhat tricky. This is because an object of derived type must be able to make explicit calls to member functions from either the derived or base classes. Phillipe Gautron solved this problem with a simple algorithm [Gau87], and this algorithm is incorporated in the GNU C++ compiler.

It is possible for a function to be called with a variable number of arguments. Unfortunately, it is not also possible to build an argument list of variable size. That is, one can make two calls to the same function, one call with five arguments and another call with seven arguments, but each of the calls has a fixed number of arguments (five and seven, respectively). For this reason, if a wrapper is to call a function with the arguments it receives, and if it does not know (at compile time) how many arguments with which to call this function, it is constrained to build an argument buffer, and let the receiver of that buffer format a proper call stack.

A solution to this problem which would be the extension of `varargs`. The `varargs` construct provides C programmers with the ability to process arguments from an argument list, where the arguments have unknown size and type. These arguments are accessed by a pseudo-function `va_arg` which takes a pointer to the variable argument declaration and the type of the argument to get. Functions which use `varargs` usually have some means of detecting when all arguments have been processed. If one had pseudo-functions `va_push` and `va_call`, then one could use the normal call stack (or register window parameter convention, or whatever) to pass a variable number of arguments. This would be most useful when passing an unknown number of arguments, all of the same type. Such an extension is probably better left to the compiler. No extension of this kind has been implemented in GNU C++ as of this time.

The GNU C++ compiler, for historical reasons, also prepends the length of the argument list to the parameter list, so that pure value-passed argument lists can be copied into message buffers efficiently. This argument is treated as a visible "invisible argument," hence a wrapper specified in GNU C++ look like:

```
class X {
    protected: int ()X (int arglen, int (X::*)(...), ...);
    ...
};
```

When this hack is no longer needed, it will be removed.

Comparison With a SmallTalk Model
The solution to the RPC problem using wrappers bears a striking resemblance to work done by Paul McCullough at Xerox PARC to add similar (transparent) features to SmallTalk.

His model starts out with a proxy class which implements only one method, the universal method doesNotUnderstand:. This would correspond to the ES-Kit approach of implementing a future which provides a wrapper. Transparency is achieved because in both cases, all messages that involve the proxy (future) object are trapped by that object.

To provide better performance (and provide greater flexibility) McCullough has something called a **PolicyMaker**, which decides whether and what should be sent where. A wrapper predicate provides almost the same functionality.

Finally, when a RPC is to be made in McCullough's extended SmallTalk, objects are sent via a **TransporterRoom** object, which takes care of communication protocols between machines, as well as the linearization of messages and object. This is clearly analogous to the possible behavior of synthetic types.

Other changes he needed to make, for example, to have his proxy objects respond to some messages (like a **PrintYou!** method from a debugger), or to have them interact with SmallTalk's == operator, are language dependent implementation details. In fact, he had to reimplement the primitive == operator (which was hard-coded for efficiency reasons) so that == could be used to test for equality of remote objects via proxy. Because C++ is a compiled language, overloading `operator==` has no impact on efficiency, and consequently no extensions for this need to be made.

Other Uses for Wrappers

It was claimed at the outset of the paper that wrappers were a general extension to the C++ programming language. Besides RPC, to what other use, then, can they be put? This question is answered by looking at other systems which make the function-call abstraction a first-class item, and then making the obvious connections.

before: *and* after: *Methods*

It is occasionally desirable to specify function prologue code, or function epilogue code, or both, for a class of functions. For example, a program profiler might start each function being profiled with code to call a profiling routine, and code at the end of the function to report that function has finished.

Instrumentation and debugging information is very often specified as things which must be done before and/or after a function is executed. The Zeta-Lisp system (and other Common Lisp systems, no doubt), provide before: and after: hooks.[2] Wrappers provide the programmer with a means of executing hooks without changing the code of the function being executed. For example, here is a wrapper which profiles how often certain functions are executed:

```
inline void ()X(void (X::*pmf)(int, int), int i, int j)
{
    start_call (pmf);     // ::start_call or (*this->start_call)
    (*pmf)(i, j);
    finish_call (pmf);    // ::finish_call or (*this->finish_call)
}
```

This example shows that wrappers can handle cases as general as any handled by before: and after: methods, since the wrapper can execute its own, class-specific, or instance-specific before: and after: methods.

One advantage of having before: and after: methods is that they are distinct from the function call, so that the problems of building the called functions argument list within the wrapper need not be faced.

One could use a wrapper predicate as a before: hook, and always return O, causing the wrapper predicate's code to be executed without going through a wrapper.

Memoization

Memoization is a technique which can save computation. For example, if one knows that a particular function is functional (it contains and modifies no state), then one can be assured that repeated calls to that function with the same parameters will yield the same results. This can be very useful when a particular task must be performed at some unknown point in a program, and its result used subsequently.

Memoization is implemented in the GNU C++ compiler. The instruction recognizer assigns an integer instruction code value to an instruction based on the (tree) pattern of that instruction. The instruction code is needed in several different places within the compiler, but none of those places can be sure that the results have yet been computed. If the compiler were to eagerly compute these codes (as soon as the instruction was generated), its work might be wasted, since the instruction may later be optimized: a three-address add instruction may become a two-address add instruction, and later even just a move, or be optimized away completely! It is therefore undesirable to try to recognize an instruction until its code value is needed. A function called

---

[2] A *hook* is a slot in a program where one can deposit a function to be executed.

recog_memoized recognizes the instruction, and memoizes the result. The result remains valid unless the instruction is changed (i.e., by the optimizer). Given this implementation, an instruction is recognized only as many times as it needs to be. The small overhead of memoization is more than offset by the savings of not having to recognize the same instruction more than once.

Simulators are also a good example of an application which can benefit from memoization. Simulators tend to have large "functional" units; computing the value for one such unit may be expensive, but that value may not change if the stimuli for that unit does not change (or vary more than a certain amount).

Wrappers provide a natural means to memoize functions. When a user has isolated a function (or set of functions) which appear to be good candidates for memoization, s/he can define a wrapper, and have the wrapper implement the lookup/execute machinery of memoization. The memoization can be enabled or disabled without interfering with the original function (being memoized) in the least. An example of a memoized factorial function is distributed with the GNU C++ library.

Wrappers can also be used to look for such functions: a memoization table can be constructed, and at the end of the run, statistics on how stimuli variation affected the "memoized" functions can be printed. C++ is already used in many simulation systems; adding memoizing wrappers to these existing platforms will preserve encapsulation, while possibly improving performance.

Synchronization

Remote procedure calls are useful for implementing formalisms in distributed systems other than merely making procedure calls. For example, in Grass [Gra86], a synchronization mechanism called *mediators* is presented. In the section of the paper describing possible implementations, RPCs are used so that multiple clients can exchange messages with a single mediator. As the paper states "in the perception of the client process, a remote procedure call appears to be no different than a simple local procedure call."

A provider of resources can implement a synchronization mechanism inside of a wrapper, and have all calls which depend on these resources go through this wrapper. All such resources can then be managed in a consistent manner by a single wrapper, simplifying maintenance. When a new resource allocation procedure is added, the provider need only concern herself/himself with the interface to the resource, and not with the interface to the synchronization mechanism. The wrapper automatically takes care of that.

Possibilities for Future Work

Handling Return Types

The handling of return types is currently very unclean. While a well-designed synthetic type can allow wrappers to handle any argument type which may appear in the argument list of a wrapper, a single wrapper cannot handle a task as simple as wrapping both a function which return an int and a function which returns a double.

This problem can be solved by making a reference to the return value available as one of the parameters of the wrapper. The compiler could choose whether to pass the wrapper a reference to the object being initialized by the function call, or a reference to a temporary, which could then be copied to presumably register-resident object. Such a choice would make initialization by wrappers essentially as efficient as returns from normal functions. This has the benefit of allowing the implementor of the synthetic type to take advantage of building the return value where it will ultimately end up, rather than in a temporary buffer which will have to be copied. C++ is good about letting class designers be smart about initializing arguments, but not about coordinating return values.

Types as Values
When a call to a function f gets wrapped, arguments are first converted to the types which f expects, then to the types that the wrapper expects. The wrapper may cause f to be executed, in which case the arguments that came into the wrapper must eventually be re-converted to what f expects. All this converting can be inefficient, especially if it is not desirable.

An *inline wrapper* may convert arguments directly to the type the wrapper expects (bypassing f's conversions completely). These arguments can then be passed the function being wrapper (or any other function) using the type information of the function being called. An inline wrapper permits parameters of a wrapped call to undergo only two conversions instead of three.

John Rose presents a similar idea [Ros88], in a much more general framework. The greatest problem with wrappers is the amount of type information one must give up in order to encapsulate, within the language, something as general as user-defined function calls. If there were some reasonable way for the user to compute more directly with types, a lot of the complexity of designing a wrapper, a wrapper predicate, and synthetic types would go away.

It also appears that Bjarne Stroustrup's work on an implementation of parametric types for C++ may help accomplish the same goal. Any extensions made with respect to wrappers must be especially careful with regard to possible implementations of parametric types. For example, it is even possible that if parametric types are expressive enough, wrappers could become an operator like '&', a purely polymorphic operator which is applied by the compiler in certain cases. Rules for expressions of this type (type wrapper-of-function?) can then be implemented by parametric type rules.

Wrappers for Constructors
The SOS project [Sha87] provides an execution environment with dynamic linking. The dynamic linking extensions which they have added to C++ make it possible to migrate objects from one machine to another and/or from one address space to another. It is implemented by having all member function calls (including calls to constructors!) go through an extended virtual function table. When a new object instance is created, a call is made to find (dynamically loading if necessary) the extended virtual function table the object will need. The object is allocated, and the constructor is called with the object, the virtual function table (as an extra hidden parameter), and whatever other arguments the call to that constructor specifies.

Since the call to the constructor is made via the virtual function table, and the virtual function table is not a priori linked with the application, the code for the constructor does not need to be linked until an object of that type is actually allocated. At that time, all member functions that object needs are linked in.

If it were possible to wrap calls to constructors, then the special function calls needed to find the virtual function table, pass the virtual function table pointer to the constructor, and the other vagaries of the system could be handled without the need to make more specific compiler hacks.

Conclusion

Wrappers are an attempt to add flexibility to C++ where it is desperately needed, while incurring minimal (possibly zero) runtime overhead. Wrappers provide a very nice encapsulation of procedure-oriented computation, making it easier to write self-scheduling parallel programs, given the right environment. They can also be used to profile functions in a user-definable way, which can be useful for finding optimization opportunities, such as memoization.

The current implementation of wrappers suffers from the lack of certain primitives within the C++ language, notably the lack of an ability to construct and manipulate parameter lists as first-class objects. It is hoped that the extensions presented in this paper will help to further clarify more precisely what primitives are lacking, and provide a context in which to implement them usefully.

This paper has presented a number of possible extensions to the C++ programming language. While some of these extensions are implemented in the GNU C++ compiler, many are not, and some perhaps should not be. A language which changes every day is no more useful than a language which never changes – a sensible compromise must be sought which allows the language to evolve while remaining stable enough to be usable.

Wrappers are not a new idea, at least not any more so than object-oriented programming is new. Both have been around for a while, in various guises. A comparison between a C++ implementation and a SmallTalk implementation of transparent RPC showed the ideas underlying wrappers useful in both cases, and even showed that their solutions were structurally very similar.

This paper presents implementation issues and strategies which make wrappers a reasonable extension to the C++ programming language, and other issues which show that there is still work to be done. Wrappers have been implemented in GNU C++; however, their implementation should be expected to change if related language features, such as parametric types, simplify or generalize their use.

Acknowledgments

This work was funded in part by MCC, the MCC Experimental Systems Project, DARPA (contract number MDA972-88-C-0013). The Institut National de Recherche en Informatique et en Automatique (INRIA) also hosted me during the time much of this paper was being written. This paper reflects the opinions of the author, and does not necessarily represent the views of the US Government, MCC, or the staff of the ES-Kit project.

Bill Leddy was the principle designer of the ES-Kit kernel; his needs precipitated most of these ideas. Wayne Allen, Gumby Wallace, and Jon Shopiro listened well to early ideas concerning wrappers, and offered many useful suggestions. Bjarne Stroustrup coined the term "wrapper," and provided me with a syntax, and suggested that wrappers might be worthwhile. Doug Lea and John Rose contributed ideas and inspirations which have been woven into this paper. Phillipe Gautron pointed out the need to encode non-virtual functions in special ways in virtual function tables, and also showed me his algorithm for doing that. Marc Shapiro got out the red pencil when I needed a reviewer. Most of all, I would like to thank Richard Stallman and contributors to the GNU project, for sharing their software with me.

Bibliography

[Cal87] Call, Lisa A., Cohrs, David L., and Miller, Barton P. "CLAM: an Open System for Graphical User Interfaces." OOPSLA 87 Proceedings. October, 1987.

[Cap87] Caplinger, Michael. "An Information System Based on Distributed Objects." OOPSLA 87 Proceedings. October, 1987.

[Gau87] Gautron, P., and Shapiro, M. "Two extensions to C++: A Dynamic Link Editor and Inner Data." Proceedings and Additional Papers from the First USENIX C++ Workshop. Santa Fe, New Mexico, November 9-10, 1987.

[Gra86] Grass, J.E., and Campbell, R.H. "Mediators: A Synchronization Mechanism." Proceedings from the 6th International Conference on Distributed Computing Systems. May, 1986.

[Gri87] Grimshaw, Andrew S., and Liu, Jane W.S. "Mentant: An Object-Oriented Macro Data Flow System." OOPSLA 87 Proceedings. October, 1987.

[Gum88] Gumby Wallace, Private communication.

[Hal85] Halstead, R. "Multilisp: A language for concurrent symbolic computation." ACM Transactions on Programming Languages and Systems 4. October, 1985.

[Led88] Leddy, B. "ES-Kit Kernel Release 1 Design Notes." MCC Technical Report number ACA-ESP-141-88.

[Lin87] Linton, Mark. "The Design of the Allegro Programming Environment." Proceedings and Additional Papers from the First USENIX C++ Workshop. Santa Fe, New Mexico, November 9-10, 1987.

[Lis88] Liskov, B., and Shrira, L. "Promises: Linguistic Support for Efficient Asynchronous Procedure Calls in Distributed Systems." Proceedings of the SIGPLAN '88 Conference on Programming Language Design and Implementation. June, 1988.

[Mae87] Maes, P. "Concepts and Experiments in Computational Reflection." OOPSLA 87 Proceedings. October, 1987.

[McC87] McCullough, P. "Transparent Forwarding: First Steps." OOPSLA 87 Proceedings. October, 1987.

[Ros88] Rose, J. "Refined Types: Highly Differentiated Type Systems and Their Use in the Design of Intermediate Languages." Proceedings of the SIGPLAN '88 Conference on Programming Language Design and Implementation. June, 1988.

[Smi88] Smith, Robert J. II. "Experimental System Building Blocks." MCC Technical Report number ACA-ESP-102-88.

[Sta88] Stallman, R. "Internals of GNU CC." (Last updated version 1.25). Free Software Foundation. Cambridge, Massachusetts, 1988.

[Sun88] Sun Microsystems, "Network Programming." Part Number 800-1779-10. Revision A, May 9, 1988.

[Tie88] Tiemann, M. "User's Guide to GNU C++." MCC Technical Report number ACA-ESP-099-88.

Chapter 13

Reliable Distributed Programming in C++:
The Arjuna Approach

Graham D. Parrington

Abstract

Programming in a distributed system is fraught with potential difficulties caused, in part, by the physical distribution of the system itself. By making the distribution of the system *transparent* it is hoped that the task becomes comparable with that of programming a more traditional centralised system. Object-oriented programming systems are natural starting points for such an attempt due to the inherent modularisation and encapsulation properties they possess. *Arjuna* is one such system, programmed in C++, which permits the construction of reliable distributed applications in a relatively transparent manner.

Objects in *Arjuna* can be located anywhere in the distributed system and are accessed as if they were purely local to the application. The use of remote procedure calls to perform the actual accesses is hidden by the use of stub generation techniques which operate on the original C++ class descriptions thus furthering the illusion of transparency. Reliability is achieved through the provision of traditional atomic transaction mechanisms implemented using only standard language features.

Introduction

Although the physical construction of a distributed system is relatively easy today, the programming of such a system remains a complicated task even for the most accomplished of programmers. In addition to the many additional ways in which distributed systems can fail when compared to their more traditional centralised brethren, the complexity of the communications protocols required to make use of remote resources is often daunting. Consequently many researchers have attempted to overcome these burdens either by providing the illusion that programs are still executing in a centralised environment by making the distribution of the system *transparent* to the programmer, or alternatively by adapting familiar programming techniques and metaphors to the distributed environment (for example, extending the procedure call notion to that of remote procedure call).

Designing and building large complex applications is itself extremely difficult requiring discipline on the part of both designer and programmer. Since such systems are usually too large to be understood in their entirety by a single person, they must be designed and implemented as a set of smaller

From *USENIX 1990 C++ Conference Proceedings*, pp. 37-50.

pieces, each of which is itself sufficiently small to be comprehensible. Many disciplines, some with formal underpinnings, are available to aid this process of decomposition. One such technique that has gained substantial popularity is the object-oriented programming technique whereby the system is partitioned into a set of logical objects that interact with each other to achieve the required system functionality. Each such logical object is self-contained and provides a well-defined interface that permits the orderly interaction between the object and any other objects in the system. Using this paradigm results in systems that are inherently modular, and since each object is self-contained the object-oriented programming paradigm supports the notions of data abstraction and information hiding directly. It is these properties that make object-oriented systems a natural choice for exploitation in programming distributed systems. To the programmer it should not matter where in the distributed system the actual objects are located, all that is required is a means by which operation invocations can be sent to the correct objects wherever they reside. Thus programming a distributed application should be no more complex than programming a centralised application providing that object location and access can be made transparent.

This paper describes the *Arjuna* [1] programming system currently under development at the University of Newcastle upon Tyne. Implemented in C++ [2] *Arjuna* provides a number of flexible and integrated mechanisms for naming, invoking operations on (local or remote) objects, concurrency control, recovery control, object state management, etc. This flexibility is achieved by exploiting the inheritance capabilities of the implementation language.

Arjuna

While having similar aims to many other research projects (for example, *Emerald* [3], *Clouds* [4], *Avalon* [5], *Argus* [6], and *Camelot* [7]), *Arjuna* started with one major premise that differentiates it from them all in that the entire system had to be implementable using only standard compilers and systems. Thus it was decided at the outset that modifying a language or its compiler was not permissible. Since object-oriented languages seemed a natural starting point, the ready availability and portability of C++ was immediately appealing. The system that resulted comprises a stub generation and RPC system for distribution purposes, an object store for the storage of persistent objects, and a hierarchy of classes each of which contributes parts of the functionality required by the system as a whole.

Since the original design was conceived under version 1.1 of C++ the design was based upon the use of single inheritance only. Whether multiple inheritance would be an advantage or not remains open at this time. The decision to restrict the implementation of the system to standard compilers only, however, had a major impact in that it required that the programmer make explicit use of the inherited facilities.

The inheritance capabilities of the language provided a basis for the provision of basic capabilities to handle recovery, persistence and concurrency control to the programmer, while at the same time giving flexibility to the system by allowing those capabilities to be refined as required by the demands of the application. Thus the core class hierarchy of *Arjuna* appears to the programmer as the following:

```
StateManager
    LockManager
        User-Defined Classes
    Lock
        User-Defined Lock Classes
    AtomicAction
    AbstractRecord
        RecoveryRecord
        LockRecord
        and other management record types
```
etc.

The following sections describe parts of the *Arjuna* system in more detail.

Stub Generation

Stub generation in *Arjuna* is different to that employed in other systems [8, 9, 10, 11, 12] in that it does not require the use of a separate Interface Description Language (IDL). Instead the *Arjuna* stub generator [13] is based upon the philosophy that the interface to an object has already been precisely specified (in C++) when the object was originally designed with a non-distributed implementation in mind. To this end the *Arjuna* stub generator accepts as input the standard C++ header files that would normally be input to the C++ compiler. This naturally enhances the transparency of the system in that the programmer need only produce a single object description as if the system was not distributed and rely on the stub generator to produce the distributed version automatically. Similarly, the programmer need not be concerned about mapping the C++ types used to the types supported by the IDL – in *Arjuna* they are the same.

Stub generation is not without its problems which principally stem from the lack of a shared address space between the caller and the actual object. Potential problems include those of:

- *Machine Heterogeneity.* Different machines may have different representations of various primitive data types. For example, byte ordering, arithmetic precision, etc.
- *Parameter Semantics and Types.* Stub generation usually utilises a copy-in, copy-out style of parameter passing which does not necessarily match the semantics of the local parameter passing semantics. Furthermore, certain types of arguments may be disallowed, for example, procedures.
- *Self-Referential Structures.* Linked data structures (which may even be circular) are an obvious source of potential errors
- *Failures.* Failure of an RPC is far more problematical to handle than failure of a local procedure call since the latter typically only occurs when the entire program fails or the error is expected. A procedure executed remotely can fail completely independently of the caller in unexpected ways.

The *Arjuna* stub generator attempts to compensate for these problems are far as it can automatically but there are cases where assistance from the programmer is required. For example, heterogeneity is handled by converting all primitive types to a standard format understood by both caller and receiver.

RPC System Interface

The RPC mechanism used in *Arjuna* (a multicasting version of *Rajdoot* [14]) is designed for general purpose use, and is thus not language specific. As a consequence it requires the programmer to convert and pack all arguments and results for a call explicitly into the buffers used by the RPC mechanism. Furthermore it requires clients to provide binding information which details the location of the remote service. Its primary primitives are:

- *Initiate*. This establishes a binding between the client and the server through the use of a manager process listening on a well-known port at the server's site. This manager process handles binding requests by forking an appropriate process and passing it the communication port to allow it to reply to the client. The server process then creates a new port and returns it to the client establishing a direct client-server connection. The manager process is not involved beyond the creation of the server.
- *Terminate*. This primitive terminates the binding between a client and a server and kills the server process.
- *Call*. This primitive performs the actual RPC. Its main parameters are an opcode indicating which procedure to invoke in the server and a buffer for the call arguments.

The actual interface to the underlying RPC mechanism is provided in *Arjuna* via the classes `Client_rpc`, `Server_rpc` and `rpc` which are C++ interfaces to the underlying RPC mechanism. The precise implementation details of these classes are irrelevant to this paper and so will not be presented here. What is important, however, is the interface they provide to the client and server stubs. The class rpc shown below

```
class RPC
{
    ...      // RPC opcode, buffers, etc.
};

class rpc : public RPC
{
public:
    rpc(long = 0);
    rpc(long, Buffer*);
    ~rpc();

    ...      // several useful operations
};
```

is the primary interface to the underlying RPC mechanism. Instances of this class are created and manipulated by both client and server stubs and are passed through the C++ interface to the RPC mechanism. In fact, the stub generator actually interfaces to the system via the classes `ClientAction_rpc` and `ServerAction_rpc`. These classes are derived from `Client_rpc` and `Server_rpc` and provide identical interfaces to those classes. They exist to ensure that any atomic action management information is correctly propagated between client and server.

This separation of the details of the actual RPC from the interface seen by the generated stub code is important and has many advantages. In particular, stubs can be generated without regard for the actual RPC mechanism used providing that the RPC mechanism complies with the required interface specification. In fact, as a simple experiment the underlying RPC system was replaced by the SUN RPC [15, 16] mechanism without requiring any change to the stub generator or its output.

Remote server creation

The RPC mechanism requires an explicit call on its *Initiate* and *Terminate* primitives to create and destroy a remote object server and bind it to the client. The problem is when to perform these operations. Fortunately C++ provides a neat solution through the provision of constructor and destructor operations which are normally used for object initialisation and destruction. For remote objects the stub generator creates constructor and destructor operations that call the underlying RPC primitives. The resulting sequence of events then becomes:

- The (stub) object comes into scope in the application program and automatically invokes the object constructor.
- The stub generated constructor binds client to server using *Initiate*.
- A normal RPC is then made to invoke the real constructor for the object in the server passing any arguments supplied to the stub object constructor. This ensures that the remote object has been constructed at the same point in the application as the stub object and utilising the same arguments.
- All further operations are made as RPCs as operations are invoked in the client.
- When the stub object goes out of scope in the application, the generated destructor operation invokes the real destructor in the server via RPC before cleaning up the RPC connection using *Terminate*. This ensures that the real object is destroyed when the stub object is destroyed.

Parameter Marshalling

Implementing remote procedure calls inevitably requires a mechanism by which arguments and results can be transferred between the client and the server. This typically involves packing the arguments into a buffer used by the underlying RPC transport mechanism for transmission and then unpacking them again at the receiving machine. These operations are frequently referred to as marshalling and unmarshalling.

Since the input to the stub generator is C++, there are several distinct kinds of parameters that may need marshalling:

- *Basic Types.* These are the standard built in types such as *char, int, float, unsigned,* etc.
- *Aggregate Types.* Arrays of other types.
- *Classes.* These are the fundamental units of abstraction and encapsulation in C++ and are the primary types for which stub generation is required.

In *Arjuna*, the C++ interface to the RPC mechanism uses an instance of the class Buffer (shown below)

```
class  Buffer
{
    char *buffer_start;
    ...
public:
    Buffer (long);
    ...
    boolean pack (char);
    boolean pack (int);
    boolean pack (double);
    boolean pack (char*);
    ...
};
```

for parameter and result transmission purposes. This class provides overloaded pack and unpack operations that allow simple types to be marshalled and unmarshalled to and from the buffer with ease. Using this class an individual variable of basic type (say *int*) can be marshalled via the simple statement:

```
BufferInstance.pack(variable);
```

Similar statements can be generated to marshall arrays, etc., however, complications arise in marshalling and unmarshalling instances of classes. Recall that class instances are assumed to be encapsulated entities, thus only member or friend functions can access the internal state variables. The stub generator, therefore, augments the operations of any class with the two additional public member functions:

```
virtual void marshall (Buffer&);
virtual void unmarshall (Buffer&);
```

In order to avoid having to generate different code to marshall variables of different types the stub generator exploits the operator overloading capabilities of the language. Traditionally in C++, the operators '<<' and '>>' are overloaded to allow input and output of variables, including instances of classes (given suitable definitions of these operations by the programmer). The stub generator makes use of precisely the same technique, but defines the same operators to be the equivalent of marshall (<<) and unmarshall (>>) when applied to RPC buffers. The net result of this is that variables of any type can always be marshalled using a statement of the form:

```
BufferInstance <<  variable
```

As an example consider the following simple class definition:

```
class Date
{
    // TRANSMISSIBLE

    int day, month, year;
public:
    Date (int, int, int);
    void set (int, int, int);
};
```

This class represents an object which will not be accessed via RPCs but may be sent as a parameter to some other remote object. When processed by the stub generator the resulting output header and the code generated for the marshall operation and redefinition of the operator << are shown below.

```
class Date
{
    int day, month, year;
public:
    Date (int, int, int);
    void set (int, int, int);
    virtual void marshall (Buffer&);
    virtual void unmarshall (Buffer&);
};
inline  Buffer& operator<<  ( Buffer& rpcbuff, Date& topack )
{
    topack.marshall(rpcbuff);
    return rpcbuff;
}
void Date::marshall ( Buffer& rpc_buff )
{
    rpc_buff << day;
    rpc_buff << month;
    rpc_buff << year;
}
```

As can be seen, the public interface to the class is unchanged beyond the addition of the marshalling operations and instances of this class behave as they would have if the stub generator had not been used.

Remote Objects
The stub generator currently distinguishes between objects designed to be accessed remotely and those that are merely transmitted as arguments. Only in the former case is full stub code generation required (the latter only needs marshalling code generation as shown in the previous section).

For remotely accessible objects code must be generated for all of the public operations supported by the object together with an appropriate server capable of decoding the incoming RPCs and dispatching them to the correct operation in the real object. Thus the stub generator produces two distinct code fragments – one for the client, the other for the server.

For example, consider the simple class definition given below:

```
#include "Date.h"

class Calendar
{
    Date today
    ...
public:
    Calendar ();
    ~Calendar ();
    void setdate (Date);
    void getdate (Date&);
    ...
};
```

This class allows the user to create and manipulate remote calendar instances (for the purpose of arranging a meeting perhaps). Running this class definition through the stub generator yields the following two class definitions

```
class  CalendarClient
{
    ClientAction_rpc *clientclass_rpc;
    Group *clientclass_server;
public:
    CalendarClient (ClientAction_rpc * = 0);
    void setdate (class Date);
    void getdate (class Date &);
    ...
};
class CalendarServer
{
    Calendar *therealclass;
    rpc *Calendar_1002 (Calendar *, rpc *);
    rpc *Calendar_1003 (Calendar *, rpc *);
    rpc *setdate_1004 (Calendar *, rpc *);
    rpc *getdate_1005 (Calendar *, rpc *);
public:
    CalendarServer ();
    void Server (int, char **);
    rpc *Dispatch (Calendar *, rpc *);
};
```

As can be seen, the client class (CalendarClient) provides the same public
interface as the original class but its instance variables and the implementation
of all of the operations have changed. Suitable name mapping tricks played
with the standard preprocessor ensure that the programmer can still use this
class under its original name maintaining transparency.

The generated server class (CalendarServer) contains a pointer to the real
object which is only assigned when the object is actually created and initialised
when an RPC for the constructor arrives. Similarly the object is destroyed
when the RPC for the destructor arrives. Sample code generated for the
getdate routine is as follows:

```
void CalendarClient::getdate (class Date& Par_0)
{
    rpc *callrpc = 0;
    rpc *result = 0;
    int validresult = 0;

    Buffer& rpc_callbuff = * new Buffer();
    rpc_callbuff << Par_0;

    callrpc = new rpc(1005, &rpc_callbuff);
    result =  clientclass_rpc→Call(clientclass_server, callrpc);

    if ((result != 0) && (result→get_opcode() == S_DONE))
    {
        Buffer& rpc_retbuff = *result!get_buffer();
        rpc_retbuffer >> Par_0;
    }

    if (callrpc != 0)
        delete callrpc;
    if (result != 0)
        delete result;
}
```

Failure handling

The handling of RPC failures is the major problem in stub generation. This problem is actually exacerbated by the use of C++ since return values may be arbitrary complex objects. Unfortunately, there is no automatic solution to this problem. The stub generator only knows that operations pass and return instances of particular types when invoked and relies on being able to initialise a return value by unmarshalling it from the RPC reply. If the RPC fails the stub generator has no way of automatically producing code to return an error instance of the return type since it has no knowledge of how to construct such an instance. Handling such failures then becomes the task of the programmer. One possible approach, however, is to extend the current mechanism utilised to control the actual stub generation process (via special comments in the class definition) to include details of special error versions of objects which can be returned if an RPC fails. The current implementation takes the cavalier attitude that doing nothing is the safest approach, thus if the RPC call fails output parameters remain unset and nothing is returned.

Reliability

Arjuna application reliability is based upon the use of the well known atomic action (atomic transaction) concept [17]. Atomic actions have the properties of

- *Failure Atomicity*. All of the operations that comprise the action complete successfully or none of them do.
- *Serialisability*. The concurrent execution of actions is equivalent to some serial order of execution
- *Permanence of Effect*. Once completed new system states produced by actions are not lost.

Actions are implemented in *Arjuna* by the class AtomicAction which provides operations that correspond to those that would be familiar to any database programmer – Begin, End, and Abort.

Instances of AtomicAction must be explicitly declared and used by the programmer as appropriate to the application. Instances of AtomicAction only control when certain events happen on objects, that is, if an atomic action aborts any objects manipulated within it must have their prior state restored and concurrency control information updated. In order to accomplish this AtomicAction instances maintain a list of instances of classes derived from AbstractRecord. Each of these classes manages a certain property, thus RecoveryRecords manage object recovery, LockRecords manage concurrency control information etc. It is thus sufficient for the operations of AtomicAction to run down this list at runtime invoking the appropriate operation (for example, top_level_commit) on each record instance. This record based approach provides complete flexibility in that new record types can be created as required (other record types currently handle persistence, distribution and object scope).

Recovery and Persistence

The failure atomicity and permanence of effect properties of atomic actions require that objects be both recoverable and persistent. These capabilities are provided by the classes StateManager and ObjectState. StateManager is the root base class of the entire *Arjuna* class hierarchy. As such it provides naming capabilities (in the form of unique identifiers), operations for the activation and deactivation of persistent objects along with state-based recovery. Since recovery and persistence have complimentary requirements (the only difference being where information is stored and for what purpose) the system uses instances of `ObjectState` for both purposes. When not in use persistent objects are stored in a passive form in an object store as instances of the class `ObjectState`. When first used they are automatically activated by the system which results in the conversion of the object into its standard run-time form. Deactivation occurs when the top-level action commits at which time the object is again converted back into an `ObjectState` for storage in an object store. Instances of `ObjectState` maintained for recovery purposes are held entirely in memory. More precise implementation details can be found in reference (18).

Conversion of objects between their passive and active forms is controlled by the system but uses operations supplied by the programmer. These operations, `save_state` and `restore_state`, must be provided (this is enforced by the compiler in R2.0 by making them pure virtual functions) otherwise neither the recovery system nor the persistence mechanisms will function properly.

Concurrency Control

Concurrency control in *Arjuna* is the heavyweight control required for the serialisability property of atomic transactions [19, 20], not the lightweight control supplied by semaphores or monitors. Concurrency control is provided by the system in the form of strict two-phase locking which, by default, supports a traditional multiple reader, single writer policy. It is implemented by a class derived from `StateManager` (the class `LockManager`) in conjunction with the class `Lock`. User defined objects are derived from `LockManager` and thus inherit concurrency control capabilities from it, and recovery, naming and persistence capabilities through it from `StateManager`.

`LockManager` is solely responsible for managing requests to set a lock on an object or release a lock as appropriate. It deliberately has no knowledge of the semantics of the actual policy by which the lock requests are granted. Such information is maintained by the `Lock` class instances which provide operations by which `LockManager` can determine if two locks conflict or not. This separation is important in that it allows the programmer to derive new lock types from the basic `Lock` class and by providing appropriate definitions of the conflict operations enhanced levels of concurrency are possible.

Exploiting C++ Syntax

One criticism that could be leveled at the original *Arjuna* system is that it required explicit usage by the programmer to be effective. That is, the programmer must declare and use atomic actions appropriately, and make correct calls to the concurrency controller at the appropriate points in the code for an operation. Neglecting to do so was likely to lead to some potentially highly undesirable results. Thus, while the system provided great flexibility it also required careful use to avoid potential problems.

This criticism stemmed from the original design decision to use standard 'off-the-shelf' components in building the system. From the outset there was never any intention to either modify the C++ language itself or add features into any particular compiler. *Arjuna* was designed to be portable to any system that had a C++ compiler (regardless of origin) and ran Unix. Thus it was impossible to determine whether any operation modified a particular object without help from the programmer, since determining this fact would require semantic analysis of the particular operation.

However, with the release of R2.0 of the C++ language this criticism need no longer apply since it is possible to generate appropriate calls to the *Arjuna* system automatically as part of the stub generation process using only syntactic analysis of the signature of any particular operation. The key to this feature is the exploitation of the fact that operations can now be marked as *const* which implies that they do not modify the object to which they are applied. Utilising this syntactic marker allows the stub generator to insert calls to the concurrency controller to create read locks automatically when *const* operations are invoked, and to create write locks when non-*const* operations are invoked. In addition operations can have code generated that automatically creates and starts an atomic action when the operation is invoked, and commits or aborts it depending upon the result of the operation.

Retrospective

In retrospect C++ has proved to be an adequate language for programming a reliable distributed system like *Arjuna*. Where it has failed it has done so in part because of the actual implementation of the language by the currently available compilers and due to lack of certain facilities at the language level. In the following sub-sections these failures are examined in more detail.

Distribution and Stub Generation

The ultimate aim of the stub generation system is to take a standard C++ header file defining some class and produce from it an equivalent header containing a replacement stub-class definitions together with the code that implements the client and server operations of the stub classes.

This approach has several potential problems that arise due to a variety of causes. Firstly, typical C++ header files contain not only class definitions but also inline function definitions, macros, manifest constants, various preprocessor directives etc. Secondly, type information about parameters, etc. may be incomplete. For example, declaring a variable to be a pointer to some type does not imply that the variable points to a single instance of that type – it might actually point to an array (particularly if the type is *char* * – that is, a pointer to character which by convention is used to represent a string), or a list, etc. For this reason, the stub generator imposes certain semantics upon pointers such that a pointer to a type always points to only one instance of that type – even for the *char* type. While this may seem to impose restrictions, classes can be written for strings etc. which make this restriction an inconvenience at worst.

Other problems arise due to the fact that, as was noted earlier, remote procedure calls typically provide a restricted set of capabilities over traditional calls. Thus the stub generator imposes the following restrictions upon the form of the class and the operations its supports:

- No public variables. The existence of public variables in a class definition breaks the fundamental encapsulation property assumed by the stub generator, so any such variables are removed automatically (with warnings) as the class definition is processed.

- Variable length argument lists to operations are disallowed since the stub code needs to know exactly the type and number of arguments to each operation for marshalling purposes. This restriction could be removed by allowing the programmer to specify a marshalling routine for such operations explicitly.
- Inline operation definitions are currently discarded as they make no sense to the stub generated version of the class at the client. Future versions of the stub generator will ensure that such inlines are made available in the server.
- Classes cannot contain static members since the stub generator cannot enforce the semantics of such variables correctly.
- Lack of support for operator overloading.

Some of these restrictions are due to weaknesses in the stub generator (for example, inlines and operator overloading) and will be removed in future versions. Others are fundamental to the technique of stub generation (static member variables) and will remain compromising the level of transparency achievable.

Using C++ as both the input and output language of the stub generator has had both benefits and problems. On the benefit side, application level location and access transparency is achieved due to the complete lack of a separate interface definition language. Similarly, exploitation of the operator overloading capabilities of the language in the output code has reduced the complexity of parameter marshalling considerably.

Reliability

Since atomic actions are not part of the actual implementation language there is a problem related to the scope of objects. Ideally the scope of an atomic action and of any objects it controls should be the same. However, it is easily possible to create programs where this is not true. For example by creating an action in an outer block, and an object in some inner block. In this case the object is automatically destroyed as the inner block is exited despite the fact that its ultimate fate has not yet been decided since the atomic action under whose control its operations have executed is still active. The *Arjuna* system attempts to compensate for this as much as possible by retaining object states until the outcome of the controlling action is known if the object is destroyed prematurely. Similar problems arise if objects are created and deleted on the heap while an atomic action is active. The problem then is how can the deletion of a heap object (and the associated freeing of memory) be undone if the action that did the delete aborts.

The lack of automatic garbage collection of objects is also problematical, since in a distributed system it is very easy to lose track of who is responsible for finally deleting a particular object, the net result of which is objects are active longer than necessary tieing up potentially valuable system resources.

Finally the lack of an exception handling mechanism remains a current problem (which may be eventually solved if the proposed exception handling mechanism is ever added to the language) which makes the transparent handling of RPC failures difficult if not impossible to implement.

Recovery and Persistence

The implementation of recovery and persistence is currently based upon the use of programmer supplied `save_state` and `restore_state` routines. Although the system uses R2.0 language features to force definition of these operations (pure virtual functions) errors in coding these routines can bring chaos. Such explicitly provided routines are needed because current compilers do not carry over type information about class member variables to execution time. If such information was available standard versions of `save_state` and `restore_state` could process it and obviate the usual need for the programmer to provide such routines. However, even then, there would still arise occasions where programmer assistance is required – particularly in the case where objects contain pointers to other objects, in order to determine precisely what constituted the state of any object. Similar techniques to those employed by the stub generator for producing the marshalling operations could be employed (that is `save_state` is almost equivalent to `marshall`) but that approach will never be completely automatic and will continue to require programmer assistance in several cases.

Conclusions

Object-oriented programming languages and systems still provide an ideal starting point for programming distributed applications and operating systems (for example, *Choices* [21]) due to their inherent modularity and encapsulation properties. However, using standardly available implementations of such systems may not provide sufficient support upon which to build distributed applications. It is in this area that C++ fails principally – current implementations are too biased towards a shared memory model of execution. Instead what may be required is a new implementation of the language such that the compiler can provide extra information not normally provided by the standard implementations – for example additional information about types and how they are laid out in memory, etc. If such a compiler existed and the proposed language extensions for exception handling, etc., were implemented within it, then C++ would be a far more realistic vehicle for implementing a reliable distributed system than it currently is.

Acknowledgments

The work reported here has been supported in part by grants from the UK Science and Engineering research Council and ESPRIT project No. 2267 (Integrated Systems Architecture).

References

1. S. K. Shrivastava, G. N. Dixon, and G. D. Parrington, "An Overview of Arjuna: A Programming System for Reliable Distributed Computing," *IEEE Software*, Vol. 8, No. 1, pp. 63-73, January 1991..

2. B. Stroustrup, *The C++ Programming Language*, Addison-Wesley, 1986.

3. A. Black, N. Hutchinson, E. Jul, H. Levy, and L. Carter, "Distribution and Abstract Types in Emerald," *IEEE Transactions on Software Engineering*, vol. SE-13, no. 1, pp. 65-76, January 1987.

4. P. Dasgupta, R.J. LeBlanc, and E. Spafford, "The Clouds Project: Designing and Implementing a Fault Tolerant Distributed Operating System," Technical Report GIT-ICS-85/29, Georgia Institute of Technology, 1985.

5. D. Detlefs, M.P. Herlihy, and J.M. Wing, "Inheritance of Synchronization and Recovery Properties in Avalon/C++," *IEEE Computer*, vol. 21, no. 12, pp. 57-69, December 1988.

6. B. Liskov, "Distributed Programming in Argus," *Communications of the ACM*, vol. 31, no. 3, pp. 300-312, March 1988.

7. A. Z. Spector, R. Pausch, and G. Bruell, "Camelot: A Flexible, Distributed Transaction Processing System," *Proceedings of CompCon 88*, pp. 432-439, February 1988.

8. B. N. Bershad, D. T. Ching, E. D. Lazowska, J. Sanislo, and M. Schwartz, "A Remote Procedure Call Facility for Interconnecting Heterogenous Computer Systems," *IEEE Transactions on Software Engineering*, vol. SE-13, no. 8, pp. 880-894, August 1987.

9. A. D. Birrell and B. J. Nelson, "Implementing Remote Procedure Calls," *ACM Transactions on Computer Systems*, vol. 2, no. 1, pp. 39-59, January 1984.

10. P. B. Gibbons, "A Stub Generator for Multilanguage RPC in Heterogeneous Environments," *IEEE Transactions on Software Engineering*, vol. SE-13, no. 1, pp. 77-87, January 1987.

11. M. B. Jones, R. F. Rashid, and M. R. Thompson, "Matchmaker: An Interface Specification Language for Distributed Processing," *Proceedings of the 12th Annual ACM Symposium on Principles of Programming Languages*, pp. 225-235, January 1985.

12. Sun Microsystems Inc., "Rpcgen Programming Guide," in *Network Programming Manual*, 1988.

13. G. D. Parrington, "Distributed Programming in C++ via Stub Generation," Technical Report, Computing Laboratory, University of Newcastle upon Tyne, January 1990.

14. F. Panzieri and S. K. Shrivastava, "Rajdoot: A Remote Procedure Call Mechanism Supporting Orphan Detection and Killing," *IEEE Transactions on Software Engineering*, vol. SE-14, no. 1, pp. 30-37, January 1988.

15. Sun Microsystems Inc., "External Data Representation Standard Protocol Specification," in *Network Programming Manual*, 1988.

16. Sun Microsystems Inc., "Remote Procedure Call Protocol Specification," in *Network Programming Manual*, 1988.

17. J. N. Gray, "Notes on Data Base Operating Systems," in *Operating Systems: An Advanced Course*, ed. R. Bayer, R. M. Graham and G. Seegmueller, pp. 393-481, Springer, 1978.

18. G. N. Dixon, G. D. Parrington, S. K. Shrivastava, and S. M. Wheater, "The Treatment of Persistent Objects in Arjuna," *The Computer Journal*, vol. 32, no. 4, pp. 323-332, August 1989. (also in Proceedings of the Third European Conference on Object-Oriented Programming ECOOP89, ed. S. Cook, pp. 169-189)

19. P. A. Bernstein, V. Hadzilacos, and N. Goodman, *Concurrency Control and Recovery in Database Systems*, Addison-Wesley, 1987.

20. G. D. Parrington and S.K. Shrivastava, "Implementing Concurrency Control for Robust Object-Oriented Systems," *Proceedings of the Second European Conference on Object-Oriented Programming, ECOOP88*, pp. 233-249, Oslo, Norway, August 1988.

21. R. H. Campbell, V. Russo, and G. Johnston, "Choices: The Design of a Multiprocessor Operating System," *Proceedings of the USENIX C++ Workshop*, Santa Fe, November 1987.

Chapter 14

The Separation of Interface and Implementation in C++

Bruce Martin

Abstract

A C++ *class* declaration combines the external interface of an object with the implementation of that interface. It is desirable to be able to write *client* code that depends only on the external interface of a C++ object and not on its implementation. Although C++ encapsulation can hide the implementation details of a class from client code, the client must refer to the class name and thus depends on the implied implementation as well as its interface.

In this paper, we review why separating an object's interface from its implementation is desirable and present a C++ programming style supporting a separate interface lattice and multiple implementation lattices. We describe minor language extensions that make the distinction between the interface lattice and implementation lattice apparent to the C++ programmer. Implementations are combined using standard C++ multiple inheritance. The operations of an interface are given by the union of operations of its contained interfaces. Variables and parameters are typed by interfaces. We describe how a separate interface lattice and multiple implementation lattices are realized in standard C++ code.

Introduction

The class construct of the C++ language[10] mixes the notion of an interface to an object with the implementation of it. This paper demonstrates how to separate interface from implementation in C++.

An *interface* declares a set of operations. An object typed by that interface guarantees to support those operations. An *implementation*, on the other hand, defines *how* the object supports those operations, that is an implementation defines the representation of the object and a set of algorithms implementing the operations declared in the interface.

An interface may contain other interfaces and add new operations. An object whose type is given by the expanded interface supports the *union* of the operations of the contained interfaces and the new operations. An object supporting the expanded interface may be accessed by code expecting an object supporting one of the contained interfaces. If an interface is defined by combining multiple interfaces, an interface lattice results.

Similarly, an implementation may be provided in terms of other existing implementations. That is, rather than providing implementations for all of the

From *USENIX 1991 C++ Conference Proceedings*, pp. 51-63.

```
class stack {
    int elements[MAX];
    int top_of_stack;
  public:
    void push(int);
    int pop();
};
```

Figure 14.1
A C++ Class, stack

operations of an interface, an implementation may *inherit* some code and representation from other implementations. In the presence of multiple inheritance of implementations, an implementation lattice results.

If interface is separated from implementation, the interface lattice of an object need not be the same as the implementation lattice of the object. That is, the structure of the interface lattice need not be equivalent to the implementation lattice. Furthermore, there may be several different implementation lattices supporting the same interface.

Why Separate Interface From Implementation?

Separating interface from implementation is desirable for achieving flexible, extensible, portable and modular software. If client code[1] depends only on the interface to an object and not on the object's implementation, a different implementation can be substituted and the client code continues to work, without change or recompilation. Furthermore, the client code continues to work on objects supporting an expanded interface.

Snyder describes in [9] how combining interface and implementation in a single class construct violates encapsulation. Snyder demonstrates that changing an object's implementation affects clients of that object when inheritance is used both for reusing code and for subtyping.

Our primary motivation for separating interface and implementation in C++ is to cleanly map C++ on to a system of distributed objects. In a distributed environment, allowing multiple implementation lattices for an interface is essential. Interfaces are *global* to the distributed environment, while implementations are *local*. For a distributed program that crosses process, machine and administrative boundaries, maintaining a single implementation of an interface is difficult, if not impossible. However, as described in [6], it is feasible in an RPC based system to maintain a global space of interfaces.

C++ Classes

A C++ *class* combines the interface of an object with the implementation of that interface. Although C++ encapsulation can hide the implementation details of a class from client code, the client code must refer to the class name and thus depends on the implied implementation.

Consider the C++ class, stack, in Figure 14.1. The stack abstraction is implemented by an array, elements, and an integer, top_of_stack. Both

---

[1]We refer to code invoking an operation on some object as *client code*. The term *client* does not necessarily denote distributed computing.

the abstraction and the implementation are named, `stack`. Client code that declares variables and parameters of class stack identifies both the abstraction and the implementation.

A C++ *derived class* may add both to the interface of an object and to its implementation. That is, the derived class may add new public member functions and private members. The single class construct implies a single combined interface and implementation lattice.

Consider the derived class, `counted_stack` of Figure 14.2. It expands the public interface by adding a member function, `size()` and it inherits the private members, `elements` and `top_of_stack`. It is impossible to be a `counted_stack` without also containing the array, `elements`.

C++ 2.0 has added *pure virtual functions, multiple inheritance* and *virtual base classes* to the language. This paper shows how those constructs can be used to support a separate interface lattice and multiple implementation lattices.

Related Work

Languages such as Ada and Modula 2 explicitly separate the interface to a program module from the implementation of it. These languages do not have mechanisms for inheriting implementations.

The Abel project[1] at Hewlett-Packard Laboratories has explored the role of interfaces in statically typed object-oriented programming languages. Abel interfaces are more flexible than those described here for C++. In particular, the return type of an operation may be specialized and parameters generalized in an extended interface. C++ requires them to be the same.

Several object-based distributed systems ([7, 2, 3, 8]) use or extend C++ as the programmer's interface to the distributed objects. In such systems, interfaces are not explicit but rather considered to be the public member function declarations of a C++ class. As such, interface and implementation lattices must have the exact structure at all nodes in the distributed system. This paper demonstrates how such C++ distributed systems can have an explicit, global interface lattice and multiple, local implementation lattices.

Separation Model

This paper presents a model for C++ programs in which an interface lattice can be supported by different multiple implementation lattices. We describe the model in terms of some minor language extensions that have been implemented in a preprocessor producing standard C++ 2.0 code. The language extensions make the separation between interface lattice and implementation lattice apparent to the C++ programmer; they also make our

```
class counted_stack:
  public stack {
    int no_items;
  public:
    int size();
    void push(int);
    int pop();
};
```

Figure 14.2
A Derived Class, `counted_stack`.

description clearer. However, the model could be viewed as a C++ programming style and programmers could write the C++ we describe in the third section directly. The language extensions enforce the style.

Throughout the paper, we use an example of a *bus stop*. The interface *BusStop* is given by combining the interface *PeopleQueue* with the interface *Port*.

Interfaces

Figure 14.3 gives the interface to a queue of people. The interface declares three operations: enq adds a person to the queue, deq removes and returns a person from the queue and size returns the number of people in the queue.

The interface represents a contract between client code invoking an operation on an object meeting the PeopleQueue interface and code implementing the interface. The contract states that the object will support the three operations specified in the contract. It says nothing, however, about the implementation of those three operations.

Similarly, Figure 14.4 gives the interface to a Port. A Port represents a place where a vehicle departs at some time for some destination. The dest operation returns a reference to an object meeting the city interface and the departs operation returns a reference to an object meeting the time interface.

An operation declaration gives a name and the types of parameters and return values. Parameters and return values are either C++ primitive and aggregation types or they are references to objects supporting an interface. They are *not* typed by a C++ implementation class. For example, in the PeopleQueue interface of Figure 14.3, the enq operation takes as a parameter a reference to an object supporting the person interface, the deq operation

```
interface PeopleQueue {
    enq(person *);
    person *deq();
    int size();
};
```

Figure 14.3
The Interface to a Queue of People

```
interface Port{
    city *dest();
    time *departs();
};
```

Figure 14.4
The Interface to a Port

```
interface BusStop :
    PeopleQueue, Port {
    boolean covered();
};
```

Figure 14.5
The Interface to a Bus Stop

returns an object supporting the person interface and the size operation returns an integer value.

An interface declares the *public* interface to an object; there are no public, protected or private labels, as there are in C++ classes.

Interfaces can be combined and expanded. Figure 14.5 defines a BusStop interface in terms of a PeopleQueue and a Port. The declaration states that a BusStop is a PeopleQueue and it is a Port. An object meeting the BusStop interface supports all of the operations defined by the PeopleQueue and by the Port; it can be used in any context expecting either an object meeting the PeopleQueue interface or one meeting the Port interface. In addition, a BusStop supports the covered operation. (The covered operation is true if the bus stop is covered.)

Figure 14.6 presents a graphical representation of the interface lattice for a BusStop.

The containment of interfaces is not as flexible as discussed in [1]. Operations are simply the declarations of member functions in the C++ sense. Refinement of parameter or result types is not supported. As in C++, an operation whose name matches another operation but whose parameters differ is considered to be overloaded.

Ambiguities cannot result when combining multiple interfaces; the operations of an interface are declarations, not definitions.

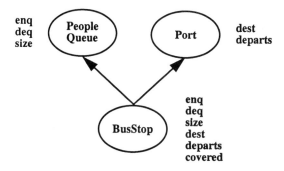

Figure 14.6
Interface Lattice for a Bus Stop

```
class linked_people
  implements PeopleQueue {
    recptr *head, *tail;
  public:
    linked_people() { head=tail=NULL; }
    enq(person *p);
    person *deq();
    int size();
};
```

Figure 14.7
A Linked List Implementation of a Queue of People

Implementations

Interfaces alone do not result in executing programs. Programmers must also provide *implementations* of an interface. Figure 14.7 gives an implementation, named linked_people, of PeopleQueue. It uses a linked list to represent the queue. Figure 14.8 gives an implementation, named people_buffer, of PeopleQueue. It uses an array to represent the queue.

Notice in Figures 14.7 and 14.8 that a class is declared to be an implementation of an interface using the implements keyword. Multiple implementations of the same interface can exist in a single C++ program; people_buffer and linked_people both implement the PeopleQueue interface.

Classes provide algorithms implementing the operations declared in the interface and may declare state and local member functions. Local member functions are called in implementation code. Implementations may also define constructors and destructors for the implementation. A constructor is inherently implementation dependent. For example, the constructor for the people_buffer in Figure 14.8 takes an integer argument indicating the upper

```
class people_buffer
  implements PeopleQueue {
    person **buf;
    int last;
  public:
    people_buffer(int sz) {
        last=0;
        buf = new person *[sz];
    }
    enq(person *p);
    person *deq();
    int size() {return last;}
};
```

Figure 14.8
An Array Implementation of a Queue of People.

```
class muni_stop
  implements BusStop
  reuses public: linked_people {
    boolean shelter;
  public:
    muni_stop(boolean cov){
        shelter=cov;
    }
    city *dest();
    time *departs();
    boolean covered() {
        return shelter;
    }
};
```

Figure 14.9
Municipal Bus Stop Implementation of the Bus Stop

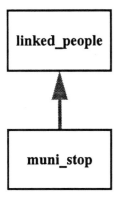

Figure 14.10
Graphical Representation of the muni_stop Implementation

```
class inter_city
  implements BusStop
  reuses public: pair,
    public: people_buffer {
  public:
    inter_city();
    boolean covered() {
        return true;
    }
};
```

Figure 14.11
Intercity Implementation of the Bus Stop

bound on the size of the buffer, while the constructor for the linked_people takes no arguments.

Notice that the parameter types of operations are given as other interfaces, not implementations. Thus, it would be impossible to define an operation that took a linked_people as a parameter. Similarly, local and member variables are typed by interface, not implementation. By doing so, client code is independent of a particular implementation.

Implementations may *reuse* other implementations. For example, Figure 14.9 gives an implementation of BusStop, named muni_stop, suitable to represent municipal bus stops. It reuses the implementation of linked_people.

Figure 14.10 gives a graphical representation of the muni_stop implementation.[2] Figure 14.11 gives a different implementation of BusStop, named inter_city. It reuses both the people_buffer and the pair[3] implementations. Figure 14.12 gives a graphical representation of the inter_city implementation.

Notice that Figures 14.10 and 14.12 contain multiple implementation lattices, that they have different structures, and that the *implementation* lattice of Figure

[2]We use ovals to represent interfaces and rectangles to represent implementations in all graphics.
[3]The pair implementation of the Port interface is left to the reader as an exercise.

14.10 is not structurally the same as Figure 14.12's *interface* lattice. Without separating interface and implementation, this would not be possible.

Implementations reuse other implementations according to C++ inheritance semantics. A class declares the operations it will implement and inherits the ones it does not. Thus, for example, the muni_stop implementation of the BusStop interface given in Figure 14.9 declares and implements the dest, departs and covered operations but reuses the enq, deq and size functions from the linked_people class. On the other hand, the inter_city implementation declares and implements only the covered operation and reuses the others from people_buffer and pair.

Ambiguities are resolved in the C++ way, by the programmer. If a class inherits ambiguous member functions from multiple classes, the class must also declare the member function and provide an implementation of it. There is, of course, no ambiguity caused by interfaces – the interface lattice is separate.

Programmers control the visibility of the declarations in the implementation lattice using public, private and protected. However, member functions that implement operations declared in the interface lattice are, by definition, public.

Object Instantiation
Implementations are named when an object is instantiated by the new operator or allocated on the run time stack. However, to promote modularity and flexibility, this code should be isolated. Client code that refers to an object via variables typed by the object's implementation, rather than by one of its supported interfaces, creates unnecessary dependencies on implementation; the client code can only be used with objects of that implementation.

Most code should refer to an object using variables typed by interface. For example, if an instance of the muni_stop implementation is created like this:

```
BusStop *bs = new muni_stop(false)
```

all further references to it will be typed by its interface, BusStop, not by its implementation.

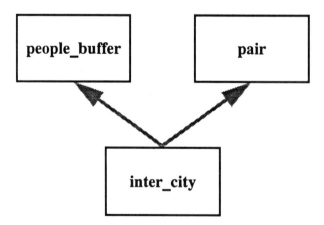

Figure 14.12
Graphical Representation of the inter_city Implementation

Similarly, when an object is allocated on the run time stack, it should be referred to by an interface it supports. A muni_stop implementation and a inter_city implementation are created on the run time stack in Figure 14.13. The identification of the implementation should be isolated to these declarations. The simulate function is defined to operate on two objects supporting the BusStop interface, independent of implementation. The simulate function is a client of the objects. It cannot see anything about the implementations; the types of the parameters do not name implementations.

Design Goals

The design of the separation model was constrained by three practical requirements.

First, the separation model needed to be easily realized in C++. This meant that at some level, the separation model had to be a programming style. This constrained the model. For example, the model allows an object of an extended interface to be accessed by code expecting an object of a contained interface but as shown in [1], the notion of a contained interface is stronger than it need be.

Next, the design of the separation model was also constrained by a desire to preserve the C++ inheritance model for reusing implementations. The rules for when to declare a member function in a class, the C++ approach towards ambiguities and the definitions of virtual and non-virtual base classes were preserved for implementations.

Finally, what the separation model adds should be simple. To use the separation model, the C++ programmer must learn

- that an extended interface supports the union of the operations of its contained interfaces,
- that variables and parameters should be typed by interfaces not by implementations,
- that code instantiating an object names an implementation and should be isolated
- and that all class member functions implementing operations declared in interfaces are public.

Realization in C++

We now discuss how to realize the separation model in C++ and some of the problems we encountered in realizing it. Although we describe this in terms of

```
muni_stop ms(false);
inter_city ic;
simulate(BusStop*,BusStop *);
    :
    :
simulate(&ms, &ic);
    :
    :
```

Figure 14.13
Naming Implementations When Allocated on Run Time Stack

the behavior of our preprocessor for the language extensions given in the second section, it could be viewed as a programming style and the C++ programmer could write this code directly.

The presentation assumes some understanding of C++ implementation strategy, particularly for multiple inheritance. It is too detailed to repeat here; we refer the reader to [11].

Interfaces

An interface is translated to a C++ class of the same name containing only pure virtual functions. Pure virtual functions, those defined with the odd =0, indicate the C++ class will *not* provide an implementation of the function. A C++ class with a pure virtual function cannot be instantiated via the new operator or on the stack. These are the desired semantics for interfaces. Figure 14.14 gives the Port interface of Figure 14.4 translated to standard C++.

Interfaces contain *only* pure virtual functions; C++ allows pure virtual functions to be declared in a class that also contains implementation. Doing so breaks the strict separation of interface and implementation.

Combining Interfaces

The separation model defined the operations of an extended interface to be the union of the operations in its contained interfaces and the added operations. Furthermore, the separation model allows an object supporting an interface to be accessed in a context expecting an object of one of the contained interfaces.

Combining interfaces by inheriting the C++ abstract classes representing the interfaces almost works. The *isa* relationship is provided by inheriting C++ abstract classes. However, C++ 2.0 does not allow pure virtual functions to be inherited and requires them to be redeclared in derived classes. When translating an interface declaration, the preprocessor generates the union of the pure virtual functions in the derived abstract classes. Figure 14.15 gives the

```
class Port {
  public:
    virtual city *dest()=0;
    virtual time *departs()=0;
};
```

Figure 14.14
C++ Representation of the port Interface

```
class BusStop :
    public virtual PeopleQueue,
    public virtual Port {
  public:
    virtual boolean covered()=0;
    virtual int enq(person *)=0;
    virtual person *deq()=0;
    virtual int size()=0;
    virtual city *dest()=0;
    virtual time *departs()=0;
};
```

Figure 14.15
C++ Representation of the BusStop Interface

BusStop interface of Figure 14.5 translated to standard C++. Notice that the BusStop is declared to be a derived class of both PeopleQueue and Port but redeclares the pure virtual functions from both.

The C++ abstract classes representing interfaces are inherited as virtual base classes.

As discussed in [11], using non-virtual base classes may make sense for some implementations. It does not for interfaces. Virtual base classes are semantically closer to the separation model's notion of interface combination.

Using virtual base classes to represent interfaces results in an "inconvenience" for the programmer. Without virtual base classes, type casting is implemented as pointer arithmetic. Programmers are allowed to do unsafe type casting from a reference to a base class to a reference to a derived class because it requires a simple address calculation. However, C++ represents virtual base classes as a pointer in the derived class to the virtual base class. Casting from a derived class to a virtual base class is not a simple address calculation but instead follows the pointer to the virtual base class. Casting from a virtual base class to a derived class is not supported.

Some might consider the restriction on type-unsafe casting to be a benefit of representing interfaces as virtual base classes! However, C++ programs often do need to cast from a base class to a derived class. Achieving this in a type-safe fashion requires associating type information at run time with objects such as proposed in [4]. Basically, implementations can return the addresses of the "interface part" being requested. One possible result, of course, is that the implementation does not support the requested interface and the cast fails.

Implementations
An implementation is represented as a C++ derived class of the interface it implements. An implementation is also a C++ derived class of the C++ classes representing the reused implementations.

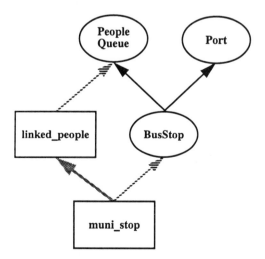

Figure 14.16
Resulting C++ Class Lattice for muni_stop

Figure 14.16 graphically represents the resulting C++ class lattice for the muni_stop implementation. Similarly, Figure 14.17 graphically represents the resulting class lattice for the inter_city implementation. The ovals denote interfaces, the rectangles denote implementations, the solid arrows represent the *isa* relation, the dashed arrows represent the *implements* relation and the grey arrows represent the *reuses* relation. From a C++ point of view, these distinctions are irrelevant; the ovals and rectangles are all classes and the structure represents a multiple inheritance class lattice.

Binding Implementations To Interfaces
If a class provides an implementation of an operation, the programmer declares and defines the member function for that class. The translation described above works.

On the other hand, if the implementation reuses other implementations, the obvious translation does not quite work. Consider the C++ representation of the inter_city implementation of Figure 14.11 to be the C++ code of Figure 14.18.

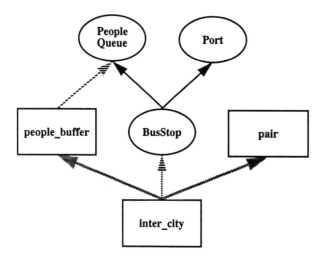

Figure 14.17
Resulting C++ Class Lattice for inter_city

```
class inter_city :
    public virtual BusStop,
    public: pair,
    public: people_buffer {
  public:
    inter_city();
    virtual boolean covered() {
        return true;
    }
};
```

Figure 14.18
Incorrect C++ For The inter_city Implementation

C++ inheritance does not work directly; the class in Figure 14.18 inherits pure virtual functions and implemented functions. In C++ 2.0 inheriting a pure virtual function is not allowed. In C++ 2.1 it is allowed but the resulting class is still viewed as ambiguous[5].

To overcome these problems, the preprocessor for the separation model generates explicit calls to the inherited functions. For example, the inter_city implementation given in Figure 14.11 reuses the enq member function from people_buffer. In the generated C++ code of Figure 14.19, an explicit call is generated to people_buffer::enq.

Of course, in order to preserve C++ inheritance for implementations, calls are not generated when the multiple inheritance of implementations is ambiguous. In that case, the programmer must declare and define a member function to resolve the ambiguity.

We note that the above binding discussion does not pertain to state or local member functions since they are not part of the abstract classes representing interfaces. C++ inheritance applies directly.

Finally, to tie all of this together, we present the generated C++ class lattice in Appendix A for the muni_stop implementation. Without the language extensions, appendix A represents what the programmer would write instead of the interfaces in Figures 14.3 through 14.5 and the implementations in Figures 14.7 and 14.9.

```
class inter_city :
    public virtual BusStop,
    public: pair,
    public: people_buffer {
  public:
    inter_city();
    virtual boolean covered() {
        return true;
    }
    virtual int enq(person *p0 ){
        return people_buffer::enq(p0);
    }
    virtual person *deq() {
        return people_buffer::deq();
    }
    virtual int size() {
        return people_buffer::size();
    }
    virtual city *dest (); {
        return pair::dest();
    }
    virtual time *departs () {
        return pair::departs();
    }
};
```

Figure 14.19
Correct C++ Code for the inter_city Implementation

Object Layout

When an object is defined by separate interface and implementation lattices, the C++ layout of the object in memory is analogous to the logical separation model described in this paper. The layout of an object contains an implementation part and an interface part. The implementation part of an object is *physically separate* from the interface part. Furthermore, for all objects meeting the same interface, the interface part is structurally identical; the differences in representation are found only in the implementation part of the object. This is as it must be for a compiler to generate client code without knowing anything about the implementation of an object.

Figure 14.20 graphically depicts the layout of an object implemented by muni_stop. The implementation part is above the thick line and the interface part is below it. As a result of using virtual base classes to represent interfaces, the addresses of the various interfaces supported by the object are also stored as pointers in the implementation part. Type casting from the implementation to one of the supported interfaces by the object simply follows the pointer. The addresses of the contained interfaces are stored as pointers in the interface part. Type casting from an interface to one of its contained interfaces simply follows the pointer. An BusStop object implemented by inter_city differs from Figure 14.20 in the implementation part only. The structure of the interface part is identical.

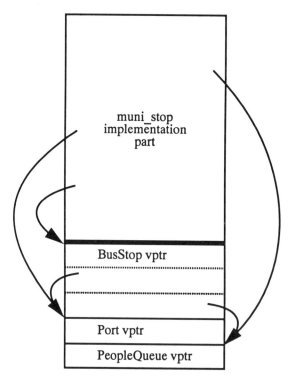

Figure 14.20
Physical Layout of an object Implemented by muni_stop

Performance
Characterizing the execution and storage cost of using a *programming style* is tricky. What do we compare a program written according to the style to? The use of the programming style may have influenced the programmer to define and implement a completely different set of abstractions to achieve the same task.

We can, however, characterize the performance of a specific transformation. Assume we mechanically transform an existing C++ class lattice into a separate interface lattice and a single implementation lattice such that the transformed code has the same behavior as the original code. The original class lattice, the interface lattice and the implementation lattice all have the same structure.

The interface lattice contains operations defined by the public member functions of the original class lattice. For non-function public members, we introduce operations of the same name.

The implementation lattice adds the non-public members of the original C++ class lattice. The non-function public members are implemented as simple inline functions that return their values.

We compare the differences in execution time and storage use.

Execution Cost
The original and transformed code have the same execution cost. All virtual functions in the original class lattice remain virtual in the transformed code. Since the separation model requires that all operations are virtual functions, non-virtual member functions become virtual functions in the transformed code. However, to maintain the same behavior, all calls to non-virtual functions in the original code must be transformed to class qualified calls. Because of these transformations of function calls, the original calls to non-virtual functions remain direct function calls. Similarly, inline functions are still expanded at the point of the call.

Storage Cost
Instances in the transformed code require more space than instances in the original C++ code.

The implementation part of an instance of a transformed class is increased by a pointer to each virtual base class representing the supported interfaces. (See the arrows from the implementation part of Figure 14.20.)

The instance also includes storage for the interface part. Each interface in the interface part stores a pointer to its virtual function table, a pointer for each of its contained interfaces and replicates its immediate contained interfaces.

Conclusions

In this paper we have reviewed the motivation for separating the interface to an object from the implementation of it. We have described how a separate interface lattice and multiple implementation lattices can be achieved in a C++ program. We have described some minor language extensions that make the separation model apparent to the C++ programmer. We have implemented a preprocessor for the language extensions.

We have described how the separation model is realized in C++. As such, the separation model could be viewed as a C++ programming style. However,

C++ could support this style, without imposing it, more directly. In order to eliminate the awkward binding of implementations, described in the section called "Binding Implementations to Interfaces", pure virtual functions should be distinguished in C++ inheritance semantics. In particular, a derived class should be able to inherit a pure virtual function. Furthermore, no ambiguity should result if a pure virtual function and an implemented function of the same name are inherited; the implemented function should be inherited in favor of the pure virtual function declaration. These changes would make this a more palatable C++ programming style.

The separation model forces a programmer to create at least two names – one for the interface and one for each implementation. The use of pure virtual functions in C++ does not. Requiring a separate name for the interface is what results in modular, flexible, distributed code.

Acknowledgments

I would like to thank Peter Canning, Mike Cannon, William Cook, Warren Harris, Walt Hill, Jussi Ketonen, Bob Shaw and Alan Snyder for commenting on the C++ separation model.

References

[1] Peter Canning, William Cook, Walt Hill and Walter Olthoff. "Interfaces for Strongly-typed Object-oriented Programming", In *Proceedings of the Conference on Object-Oriented Programming Systems*, Languages and Applications, pages 457-467, 1989. Also Technical Report STL-89-6, Hewlett-Packard Labs.

[2] David Detlefs, Maurice Herlihy, Karen Kietzke and Jeannette Wing. "Avalon/C++: C++ Extensions for Transaction-based Programming", In *USENIX C++ Workshop, 1987.*

[3] Yvon Gourhant and Marc Shapiro. "FOG/C++: A Fragmented Object Generator", In *Proceedings of the 1990 Usenix C++ Conference*, April 1990.

[4] John Interrante and Mark Linton. "Runtime Access to Type Information in C++", In *Proceedings of the 1990 Usenix C++ Conference*, April 1990.

[5] Stan Lipman.Electronic mail from Stan Lipman, ATT Bell Laboratories, April 1990.

[6] Bruce Martin, Charles Bergan, Walter Burkhard and J.F. Paris. "Experience with PARPC", In *Proceedings of the 1989 Winter USENIX Technical Conference. Usenix Association,* 1989.

[7] S. K. Shrivastava, G. N. Dixon, F. Hedayati, G. D. Parrington and S. M. Wheater. "A Technical Overview of Arjuna: a System for Reliable Distributed Computing", Technical Report 262, University of Newcastle upon Tyne, July 1988.

[8] Robert Seliger. "Extended C++", In *Proceedings of the 1990 Usenix C++ Conference,* April 1990.

[9] Alan Snyder. "Encapsulation and Inheritance in Object-oriented Programming Languages", In *Proceedings of the Conference on Object-Oriented Programming Systems, Languages and Applications.* Association of Computing Machinery, 1986.

[10] Bjarne Stroustrup. The C++ Programming Language. Addison-Wesley Publishing Company, 1986.

[11] Bjarne Stroustrup. "Multiple inheritance for C++", In *Proceedings of the EUUG Spring 1987 Conference,* May 1987.

Appendix A: Generated C++ Code For `muni_stop`

```
// Interfaces:
class PeopleQueue {
  public:
    virtual int enq(person *)=0;
    virtual person *deq()=0;
    virtual int size()=0;
};
class Port {
  public:
    virtual city *dest()=0;
    virtual time *departs()=0;
};
class BusStop : public virtual PeopleQueue, public virtual Port {
  public:
    virtual boolean covered()=0;
    virtual int enq(person *)=0;
    virtual person *deq()=0;
    virtual int size()=0;
    virtual city *dest()=0;
    virtual time *departs()=0;
};

// Implementations:
class linked_people : public virtual PeopleQueue {
    class recptr *head ,*tail;
  public:
    linked_people () { head =tail =NULL ; }
    virtual int enq (person *);
    virtual person *deq ();
    virtual int size ();
};
class muni_stop : public virtual BusStop, public linked_people {
    boolean shelter ;
  public:
    muni_stop (boolean cover ) { shelter =cover;}
    virtual int enq(person *p0) {
        return linked_people::enq(p0);
    }
    virtual person *deq() { return linked_people::deq(); }
    virtual int size() { return linked_people::size(); }
    virtual city *dest();
    virtual time *departs();
    virtual boolean covered() { return shelter; }
};
```

Postscript

The original design center of C++ was most clearly articulated by Bjarne Stroustrup in his two papers included in the first section of this volume, "The Evolution of C++, 1985 to 1987" and "Possible Directions for C++". In looking at these articles with an eye for the underlying principles that were being used to determine the shape of the language, three requirements arise as the unifying base of the language.

The first of these requirements is support for an object model based around the notions of data abstraction, encapsulation, and polymorphism. This was the essence of the object model for the early language, and was the central notion behind the abstraction of a class.

A class defined both data and the operations on that data. But the data definition could be hidden (as could much of the operations) either from the rest of the world (if the data or operations were private) or from all the world other than a select few (if the data or operations were protected). Access to the data that was the state of an object could be hidden behind a set of operations. The way these operations were implemented, and in fact the very data to which those operations gave access, were hidden.

Thus the data that was the state of an object was both abstracted from the user of the object, and encapsulated behind a set of operations that acted as a firewall between the implementor of a class and the user of instances of that class.

The final part of the object model was the notion of inheritance and polymorphism that were part of the legacy of the Simula language. Classes could be built by extending other classes; the new class would be all of the old and a little bit more. So objects of the new class would also be objects of the old class (plus a little bit more), and could be treated as such by code that only knew that old class, not the new.

The second requirement that helped form the early design center of the C++ language is that code written in the language must be efficient. This was a major criteria for the language, so much so that features that were in other object oriented languages but that could not be implemented efficiently on the machine architectures of the time were rejected, not because they were at odds with the object model or were not useful, but because they would slow programs written in the language.

From the first, C++ was designed as a language for systems programmers, and as such it had to be used to write programs that ran quickly and took up a minimum amount of space. This latter requirement argued against any attempt to add garbage collection into the language, as such an addition would take control of memory usage away from the programmer. The need for speed meant that type checking was moved, whenever possible, to compilation time and out of the time taken to run the program. While there are other reasons to have strongly typed languages or to require hand allocation and reclamation of storage, the reasons for keeping these features out of the system were for the sake of efficiency.

The third of the early requirements is that the language stay as close to the C language as possible. This requirement was more important to the development of the language than most realize.

Keeping C++ close to C made the language seem to be easier to learn. Indeed, an experienced C programmer could begin writing programs that compiled under the C++ preprocessor within hours of picking up the C++ language manual. That those programs tended to be C programs that used a little C++ syntax was generally not recognized until months later, when the programmer had actually made the switch from the procedural to the object-oriented paradigm of programming. By then, of course, it was unlikely that the programmer would go back to the old language.

But this ability to draw programmers into using the language was not the only advantage of keeping C++ close to C. By keeping this requirement as part of the design center of the language, early users of C++ were able to call the vast amounts of C-based libraries that were available. The similarities in the languages made it easy (at that point) to allow programs written in one language to call programs written in the other. Thus C++ was able to communicate with the existing, non-object-oriented world.

This ability to call and be called by C (and languages that could call or be called by C) allowed C++ to avoid the "autistic child" syndrome that had plagued other object-oriented languages. These earlier languages, by not supporting an easy way to call and be called by other, non-object-oriented languages, required that the programmer renounce all that had gone before and enter into a world that was purely object-oriented. While such an approach had many advantages with respect to the purity of the object model that could be supported, it also required that the universe be re-invented when the change in language was made. By avoiding that requirement, C++ made migration to the language possible at far lower cost than offered by other object-oriented alternatives.

Having this as the design center, the language was good at certain things and not so good at others. Unlike most widely available object oriented languages available at the time, C++ allowed the writing of programs that were efficient enough to run very well on general purpose hardware.

C++ did allow hiding the details of the implementation of a class, allowing new implementations to be written and included into libraries without affecting the users of the code. This allowed bugs to be fixed more easily, even when fixing those bugs meant changing some of the underlying data structures. Since those data structures were hidden (and we soon learned that data should almost always be protected) the changes couldn't alter the behavior of existing code.

C++ didn't have much of a model of inheritance, but the model that it did have allowed a considerable amount of code reuse (generally confined to the person or group who had written the code that was being reused). But this simple notion of inheritance, combined with the notion of polymorphism, did give developers perhaps their most powerful tool: the ability to extend a class library to do new things using the language. If you had developed code that used a class, you could add new sub-classes of that class to the library and the old code would simply work, treating the new class as it did the old. With the use of virtual functions, you could even change the behavior elicited by the old code when it called what it thought was the old class but what was in fact the new class. Thus new features could be added without the old code having to be changed.

These were major advantages for those of us doing software development and who were willing to try the object-oriented approach. However, there were a number of things that object-oriented languages had up until then been good at doing that C++ was unable to do. For example, C++ was not the sort of language that lent itself to the style of interactive program development that many who had used earlier object-oriented languages expected. C++ placed considerable weight on the work done by the compiler. This was in keeping with the principle of efficiency, which allowed giving up rapid compilation if the result was compiled code that was more efficient. C++, as a result, seemed stuck in the edit/compile/test loop familiar to C programmers. This environment was seen as a great leap backward to those familiar with the environments provided by SmallTalk and the object-oriented variants of Lisp.

While C++ was designed to allow hiding of the construction of individual classes of objects and to allow the extending of such classes with new specializations of old classes, it did not offer any way of changing a class hierarchy in a way that was invisible to clients of that group of classes. This meant that bugs in individual classes could be fixed without affecting the client of the class, and that class hierarchies could be extended and used by clients of the old classes. But a mistake in the initial design of a class structure would have to be lived with for the life of the library unless one could get the clients of that library to agree that fixing the mistake was important enough that the clients of the hierarchy should change as well.

A third example of the limitations of the early versions of C++ concerned the way in which code could be reused. The notion that a subclass inherited all of the code from its ancestors (with the possible exception of virtual functions) allowed the reuse of large amounts of code during the process of specializing the behavior of a class hierarchy. However, this reuse, which many saw as the main reason for using an object-oriented language, was limited to a particular class hierarchy. There was no way of selectively sharing, or of sharing some of the code from one class with a totally unrelated class.

This often led to difficult design decisions. Programmers were often confronted with a class that would have much in common with two other classes, neither of which were related. A choice would have to be made as to which of the unrelated class was to be the parent of the new class. Once that choice was made, the code that was common between the new class and the class that was not related had to be included in the new class, and any fixes to the code in one place had to be remembered to be made in the other.

Thus while C++ was a good language that offered many advantages (especially to its target audience of C programmers) it was lacking in many respects. Unlike many software entities, these drawbacks were not addressed by a single design and implementation group, but were debated by a wider community of users. The articles in this volume show some of the debate.

There are a number of aspects to this debate that I find interesting when viewed from the historical perspective. I can't remember any other language that evolved in this fashion from such an early stage. The debate was open, informal, and the group at Bell Laboratories that was the original owner of the language was immensely open and responsive to the community. Certainly the influence of Bjarne Stroustrup and, to a lesser extent, Andrew Koenig were greater than that of other individuals. But the evolution of the language did come close to taking place in an open marketplace of ideas.

This open marketplace tended to be populated by programmers, many of whom were on the leading edge of software development. This had a number of side effects, not the least of which was to make the debate more spirited than it would have been if a group of less forceful personalities had taken part in the discussions. Another side effect was that proposals for additions to the language rarely took the form of suggestions for adding some kind of functionality that would meet a particular need. Instead, those who had encountered a limitation in the language would point out the limitation and then show what could be done to get past that limitation.

An example of this is the early group of authors calling for multiple inheritance to be added to the language. Some called for the feature to allow them to distinguish between inheriting the interface to a class and the implementation of that class (for example, Andrew Schulert and Kate Erf, "Open Dialogue: Using an Extensible Retained Object Workspace to Support a UIMS", Proceedings of the 1989 USENIX C++ Conference). Others called for it so that code from unrelated classes could be reused in a new class; indeed, many of the first examples Cargill has shown can be done without multiple inheritance were attempts to get this kind of code sharing.

Separating interface inheritance from implementation inheritance is very different from allowing code reuse from multiple unrelated classes. However, this distinction was at least blurred if not lost since those wishing either called for the addition of multiple inheritance to the language.

The effect of all this was that features were added to the language without a clear understanding of what function those features were to add. In the case of the addition of multiple inheritance, for example, the attempt to add a feature that addressed all of the needs of those calling for multiple inheritance resulted in an inheritance scheme that is so complex that there is a real question as to whether the added functionality is worth the price in complexity.

In fact, what many thought would be added by allowing multiple inheritance was gained through the addition of templates. Templates allow the programmer to produce code that can be shared by multiple inheritance hierarchies allowing common code to be shared between those hierarchies. Indeed, the first published attempt at showing the use of multiple inheritance (R. S. Weiner and L. J. Pinson, "A Practical Example of Multiple Inheritance in C++", Sigplan Notices, 24(9) September 1989) attempts to construct an array of integer class from an array class and an integer class. This is a classic attempt to get code sharing across unrelated inheritance hierarchies, and is just the sort of thing that templates were added to the language to support.

If the community had realized that templates (or something like them) were the way of sharing common code between unrelated classes, would there have been as much call for multiple inheritance? Perhaps not. Further, if the real need for multiple inheritance was to separate interface inheritance from other forms of inheritance, could multiple inheritance have been made less complex?

I see the same sort of pattern emerging in the debate about adding access to runtime type information to the language. When this feature was originally proposed by Interrante and Linton, the main reason for needing information about the actual type of an object at runtime was to allow the object to be reconstructed from a persistent form. Lenkov, et.al., also want to have access to runtime type information, but they need the information to allow the catching of objects by exception handlers.

While both articles call for access to type information at runtime, in fact the purpose of that access is very different in the two cases. The difference is large enough, in fact, that an addition to the language that will satisfy the needs of Lenkov will not satisfy the needs of Interrante and Linton. Lenkov only needs to be able to find out from an object what the type of that object is. Interrante and Linton need to be able to find out from something that was once an object but is now a stream of data what sort of object it was so that they can reconstruct that object.

Which of these bits of functionality is needed most in the language is not the subject of debate. Instead, the debate has centered around how to add access to type information.

If anything has characterized the debate over the evolutionary path of the C++ language, it has been this concentration on what feature to add to the language rather than what functionality is needed. Perhaps this is because of the makeup of the community--being software developers, we have been trained to propose solutions rather than ask for solutions from someone else.

The end result has been the addition of features to the language with little or no thought to how the addition of those features affects the design center of the language. Yet each addition to the language extends the set of problems the language is meant to address. Thus each addition changes, to a greater or lesser extent, the design center.

At this point, it is unclear just what the design center of the language is. Certainly all of the original principles that formed the early design center of the language have been violated to a greater or lesser extent. While the language still supports an object model based on data abstraction, encapsulation, and polymorphism, the object model has been extended to one far more complex than that of the early language. Multiple inheritance makes the notion of polymorphism far less simple than the early one of specialization. Templates extend the notion of an object to include what are essentially functions from types of objects to new types of objects. If runtime access to type information is added to the language (and it currently looks as though it will be added) then the notion of polymorphism has been extended to include movement down the inheritance hierarchy as well as up.

The second principle of the early design center, that the language should be as efficient as possible, is still adhered to, but in a subtly different form. As was noted in the discussion of the debate around exception handling, the design center no longer calls for all parts of the language to be efficient. Instead, the principle now appears to be that those parts of the language that are commonly used must be efficient, and those parts of the language that are not efficient must not make programs that do not use those parts of the language any less efficient. Put somewhat differently, the design principle now allows some features to be expensive, as long as programs that do not use that feature are not required to pay any part of the expense. This requires programmers to know what features are efficient and which are inefficient. The old design center allowed programmers to simply assume that all of the features in the language were efficient.

The third of the original design principles, that the language be as much as possible like C, is now nearly moot. One can still write code in C++ that looks like C, but not if one wishes to use any of the features of C++. Multiple inheritance, templates, exception handling, and other additions to the language have incrementally added syntax and semantics to C++ that distinguish it from C. The two languages are still recognizably offshoots from the same base. But it is increasingly difficult to maintain that C++ is a simple extension to C.

That the design center has changed over the years is not surprising. Indeed, the original design center was based on the belief that the benefits of object-oriented programming could be added to the C language with a minimal set of changes. The task has proven to be far more complex than any of us thought it would be, and so a change in the direction can be viewed as simply the recognition of the difficulty of the task. If nothing else, the evolution of C++ has shown that support for a different kind of programming requires more than a small set of incremental changes to a language.

What seems to have been lost over the years since the Santa Fe conference is the common understanding of what the design center of the language is. While it is clear that the original design center, enunciated by Stroustrup, is no longer sufficient to guide the development of the language, there has been no discussion of a replacement for that design center. Indeed, it is not at all clear that the current community of users is even in agreement about what the language ought to be capable of doing and, perhaps more important, what it should not attempt to do.

The lack of a clearly articulated, generally accepted design center for the language has resulted in a lack of a set of principles that can be used to judge the direction of language change. The danger is that the language will attempt to become something that does everything, with the result that it will do nothing well.

In his book "Wonderful Life", Stephen Gould argues that one should not confuse biological evolution with progress. The forces that shape the survival of one species over another, Gould points out, are far more random than what is required to allow one to claim that species more recently evolved are in any way more advanced or superior to those from which they evolved.

Without a clear design center that can be used to determine a notion of progress in the evolution of the language, the changes that have been made to C++ over the period covered by the articles in this book take on many of the aspects of biological evolution. The language has been able to adapt itself to the changing environment of the increasing number of users. But with no clear goal for the language, the evolution of the language can only be seen as change, not progress towards that goal.

Index